PABLO ESCOBAR'S STORY PART 3
NARCOS FALL

SHAUN ATTWOOD

ACKNOWLEDGEMENTS

A big thank you to Mark Swift (editing) and
Jane Dixon-Smith (typesetting and book-jacket design)

SPELLING DIFFERENCES: UK V USA

This book was written in British English, hence USA readers
may notice some spelling differences with American English:
e.g. color = colour, meter = metre and = jewelry = jewellery

SHAUN'S BOOKS

English Shaun Trilogy
Party Time
Hard Time
Prison Time

War on Drugs Series
Pablo Escobar: Beyond Narcos
American Made: Who Killed Barry Seal? Pablo Escobar or George HW Bush
The Cali Cartel: Beyond Narcos
Clinton Bush and CIA Conspiracies: From The Boys on the Tracks to Jeffrey Epstein

Un-Making a Murderer: The Framing of Steven Avery and Brendan Dassey
The Mafia Philosopher: Two Tonys
Life Lessons

Pablo Escobar's Story (4-book series)

SOCIAL-MEDIA LINKS

Email: attwood.shaun@hotmail.co.uk
YouTube: Shaun Attwood
Blog: Jon's Jail Journal
Website: shaunattwood.com
Instagram: @shaunattwood
Twitter: @shaunattwood
LinkedIn: Shaun Attwood
Goodreads: Shaun Attwood
Facebook: Shaun Attwood, Jon's Jail Journal,
T-Bone Appreciation Society

Shaun welcomes feedback on any of his books.
Thank you for the Amazon and Goodreads reviews!

CONTENTS

INTRO

Many authors have tried to dissect Pablo's character, with each only providing a few pieces of the puzzle. The first Escobar book I wrote was part of a series exposing the War on Drugs. Since its publication, I've received requests to write his biography in more detail and without the War on Drugs politics. This new series of books containing approximately 1,000 pages is my response.

After doing a talk about Pablo in London, I was approached by a Colombian. She said that there was far more information available about him in the Spanish-speaking world. On a mission, I ended up getting hundreds of thousands of words translated, which transformed my understanding of his story. Previously, I had viewed him through the filters of the English-speaking world – and many of those authors had an agenda such as portraying certain people or government agencies in particular ways.

This book also includes everything I have learned about El Patrón while researching information for my books on the Cali Cartel and Barry Seal. Since the explosion of interest in Pablo, far more up-to-date information has become available thanks to those closest to him who later became authors, including his wife, Victoria Eugenia Henao (*Mrs Escobar: My Life with Pablo*); his ex-lover and TV celebrity, Virginia Vallejo (*Loving Pablo, Hating Escobar*); his son, Juan Pablo (*Pablo Escobar: My Father*); and his former hit man, Popeye (*The True Life of Pablo Escobar* and *Surviving Pablo Escobar*) – who was released after serving 23 years, started a popular YouTube channel, but was arrested for extortion and died from oesophageal cancer on February 6, 2020 in Bogotá, aged 57. Two of the men chiefly responsible for Pablo's demise, Don Berna (*Killing the Boss*) and Carlos Castaño (*My Confession*), also published books about their roles, which contradicted the

CHAPTER 1
FINAL ELITE KIDNAPPINGS

Diana Turbay – the daughter of ex-president Julio César Turbay Ayala – was a brunette with kind eyes and a magnetic personality. In August 1990, she was invited to interview a priest who was part of a guerrilla group called the National Liberation Army. Due to the risks, her friends and family warned her not to go, but she was not the type to shrink from danger if good could be achieved. She had once travelled into guerrilla territory on a mule, hoping to gain an understanding of their motivations. To help the peace process along, she had visited a camp to meet an M-19 leader who had once attempted to kill her father by firing a rocket at his room. If interviewing the priest would make things safer for Colombia, she would gladly risk her life.

On August 30, a beat-up van arrived in Bogotá to take Diana and her crew to the priest. Two young men and a woman emerged, claiming they were part of the guerrilla leadership. West of Bogotá, they switched from the van to two other vehicles. After eating at a tavern, they took a dangerous road in heavy rain, and had to stop at dawn until a landslide was cleared.

After a sleepless night, they met a patrol with five horses at 11 AM. For four hours, Diana rode on a horse, while most of the group trekked through mountain forest and a valley with houses nestled into coffee groves. Recognising Diana from the TV, some of the locals yelled greetings. In the evening, they arrived at a deserted ranch near a highway, with a view of Medellín. A young man said he was with the guerrillas but offered no more information. Perplexed as to why they weren't in guerrilla territory yet, they consoled themselves with the likelihood that the priest wanted to meet them in the least obvious place as a precaution.

After two hours, they stopped in Copacabana, at a small house with white walls, its roof tiles green from moss. Diana and a female companion were given the best room at the back; as its windows were boarded over, a light was kept on. The guards didn't have the usual weapons used by the guerrillas. One was even wearing a Rolex.

Three hours later, a masked man greeted them on behalf of the priest. He said that for security, the women should travel to the priest first. Getting split from her male colleagues troubled Diana. One of them whispered that she shouldn't go anywhere without them. With alarm in her eyes, she gave him her ID.

Before sunrise, the women were moved to a bigger house. Her male companions arrived on September 10, 1990. Diana confided that she was depressed over having led them into what she suspected was a trap. She said that she didn't fear for herself, but if anything happened to her colleagues, she wouldn't find any peace. Throughout the night, she was kept awake by thoughts of what her husband, children and parents were going through. The next night, she and two female colleagues were forced to trudge along a path in the rain.

Her distressed parents asked the government to locate her through their channels of communication with the guerrillas, but their groups denied any knowledge of her in a joint statement. Unknown to Diana and her family, the pretend meeting with the priest had been organised by Ricardo Prisco of the Prisco gang.

Finally, a guard announced: "You're being held by the Extraditables. But don't worry, because you're going to see something you won't forget."

After learning that his daughter was with the Extraditables, ex-president Turbay chose not to acknowledge anything publicly until he knew the kidnappers' demands. Questioned by the media, he said, "My heart tells me that Diana and her colleagues have been delayed because of their work as reporters, but that it isn't a question of their being detained."

Pablo ordered a second kidnapping of Diego, the son of the previous president's secretary Germán Montoya, who had double-crossed El Patrón. Told to rent an apartment in the building where Montoya lived, hit men were instructed to kill his bodyguards in the basement and take him out to the trunk of a car. Unable to rent the apartment, they learned that two of Germán Montoya's sisters had a restaurant and they went around unprotected.

Nineteen days after Diana's disappearance, on September 19, 1990, Marina Montoya was closing her restaurant in northern Bogotá. With her foot in a cast due to a sprained ankle, her sister was absent that day. After she had locked the doors, three men arrived, two of whom had recently visited the restaurant, left generous tips and had amused the staff with their humour and good nature. Recognising the two knocking on her window, Marina allowed them inside. After putting her in an armlock, they dragged her outside, where she grabbed a lamp post and screamed for help. A knee slammed into her spine, rendering her barely able to breathe. They dumped her unconscious body into the trunk of a blue Mercedes 190.

Four hours later, Francisco Santos, *The Time's* editor-in-chief, was on a busy side street in an armoured jeep, when a car pulled up in front and another behind. Four armed men emerged, one carrying a mallet for breaking bulletproof glass. Rather than resist, Francisco opened his door to talk to the kidnappers and found himself with a gun pointed at his forehead.

"Get out of the jeep with your head lowered."

After opening the driver's door, a kidnapper shot the 38-year-old chauffeur in the skull, the bullets firing with low thuds due to a silencer. Within minutes, the kidnappers and hostage were gone. After the police discovered the jeep with the dead driver, the news announced unconfirmed reports of his kidnapping.

Having meticulously planned the crime for almost four months, the kidnappers used sidewalks to avoid traffic, with Francisco sat between two of them, wearing glasses painted with nail polish to block his view. Sat silently, he registered every turn the car made on its journey to a garage and estimated roughly where his destination was. A kidnapper grabbed his arm, escorted him down a hall and up to a cold second floor. With his glasses removed, he examined the tidy bedroom, the boarded-up windows, the solitary light ball, a double bed with old sheets, a TV and a table with a radio. After giving him a bottle of strong alcohol, his kidnappers rushed downstairs to watch a soccer game. Hoping to steady his nerves, he drank half of the bottle, but felt nothing other than a desire to turn on the radio and listen to the game, the result of which was a disappointing draw: 2-2. At 9:30 PM, he appeared on the news in a dinner jacket accompanied by beauty queens. The kidnapping had happened so fast, he had only just learned that his driver had died.

Wearing a flannel mask, a kidnapper brought him a grey sweatsuit, which he was required to change into. From Francisco's jacket pocket, the kidnapper confiscated his inhaler.

"You can't take that. I have asthma. If I have an asthma attack, I could die without that."

The kidnapper returned it. "You can use the bathroom in the hall. You can listen to the radio and watch TV with no restrictions other than keeping them at the normal volume. Now, I need you to lie down." A thick rope attached to the bed was tied around his ankle. On a mattress next to the bed, the kidnapper was soon snoring.

Hearing a rooster crowing at night, Francisco was surprised and assumed it was crazy. In the darkness, his reality began to sink in. He thought about his wife, his new-born girl, his almost 2-year-old son and his sister's husband, who had died on Avianca Flight 203, bombed by Pablo. During the crisis, Francisco had warned his family that one of them would be dead by the end of the year. Trying to shake off the shock, he attempted to build confidence in his own survival. Hearing the kidnapper's breathing change, he assumed that the man was awake, and asked, "Who is holding me?"

"Who would you prefer to be held by, guerrillas or traffickers?"

"I think it's Pablo Escobar."

"That's right. Actually, it's the Extraditables."

President Gaviria was reviewing TV ads when an adviser whispered that Francisco had been kidnapped. After removing the glasses he had used to watch TV, he said, "Keep me informed." As the ads played, each adviser whispered the news to the next in row. When the ads ended, he gave the order for his security adviser to immediately arrange a Council on Security meeting. After discussing the ads, he attended the meeting, which was quickly interrupted by the announcement of Marina Montoya's kidnapping, which had happened before Francisco's at four o'clock.

"I think this is just the beginning," Juan Vitta – one of Diana's crew – told another captive. "With Francisco Santos, they now have two aces in their hands. The thing against Marina Montoya is pure and physical revenge against her brother Germán. This poor lady is going to pay for the mess that her brother caused to the traffickers."

In a hotel in Florence, Italy, Hernando Santos, Francisco's father, 78, was convalescing after five bypass surgeries. Calling from Bogotá, his nephew announced he had bad news.

"What's happened?" he asked, assuming his son had been assassinated.

"Francisco's been kidnapped."

"Thank God," he said, relieved his son was alive. "OK. Don't worry. We'll see what we have to do." All the family members at the hotel in Italy arranged to return to Colombia.

At night, Diana kept a secret diary of whatever was on her mind, which ranged from thoughts on politics to things happening around her. Her first entry was dated September 27, 1990: "Since Wednesday the 19th, when the man in charge of this operation came here, so many things have happened that I can hardly catch my breath." During the early weeks of her captivity, no one had publicly claimed responsibility, which, according to her diary, was to enable the kidnappers to kill her quietly when she was redundant to them. "That's my understanding of it and it fills me with horror." As usual, she was more concerned with the safety of her colleagues than herself.

"For the past two weeks," said the hostage Azucena, who worked on Diana's newscast, "I've been afraid that I am pregnant. I've missed my last two periods."

"That's great news," Diana said. Having been told that they would be released on the first Thursday of October, their spirits had been raised, boosted even further when their conditions improved, including better food and an increase in their permitted range of movement.

In October, the kidnappers instructed Francisco to create proof that he was not dead. Aided by two packets of cigarettes and a black coffee, he wrote a letter to his family, and slowly dictated the heartfelt words to a mini-cassette recorder. "Everyone who knows me knows how hard this message is for me." Not wanting to alarm anyone, he maintained a calm voice. Reading the newspaper headlines proved that he was still alive on the present date. After his letter was published, he reread it, and became concerned about the part where he had asked the president to do everything possible to free the hostages, while not ignoring the laws and precepts of the constitution because they are good not only for the nation but also for the freedom of the press, which was being held hostage as well. Regretting his words, he felt doomed. Convinced that he would be killed, he started to obsess over an escape plan.

Diana's father was doing everything in his power to try to get the government to negotiate a peaceful settlement with Pablo, which public opinion now favoured. After the first round of bombings and assassinations, the outraged public demanded retribution and imprisonment. During the next round, the public still supported extradition. But now the bombings had gone on for so long that the public wanted peace.

Cabinet member and presidential adviser, Rafael Pardo, offered an idea to the exasperated president: if a trafficker surrendered and confessed to a crime, he would not be extradited and would earn a sentence reduction, with a further reduction available if property was given to the state. President Gaviria added modifications. As it was unacceptable that they could not be prosecuted for lack of evidence, he proposed that, in addition to the surrender, in order not to be extradited, they must confess to a crime that would allow a judge to indict them. For the surrender and confession, there would be a reduction of one third of the sentence. With the help of the justice minister, a draft was made: "Capitulation to the Law."

The Council of Ministers accepted the proposal with two restrictions. Firstly, it would only be applicable for crimes committed prior to the effective date of the decree. Secondly, only extradition for the crimes confessed would be prevented. They feared that the traffickers would try to avoid extradition by confessing to misdemeanours. The president made the proposal public and the US accepted it with slight reservations.

As the decree didn't absolutely guarantee non-extradition, Pablo was unhappy: "Because it must be in writing, in a decree, that under no circumstances will we be extradited, not for any crime, not to any country." He wanted traffickers to be pardoned in the same way as the M-19, which had been allowed to become a political party. He also demanded safety guarantees for his family and friends, and a prison impregnable to his enemies.

Publicly, Diana's father denied getting any messages from the Extraditables, even though he had received a three-page handwritten letter, "A respectful greeting from the Extraditables," which he believed was Pablo's pseudonym. The hostages were "in good health and in good conditions of captivity that can be considered normal in such cases." The letter railed against police brutality. It included three conditions for Diana's release. Firstly, the suspension of military operations against the traffickers in Medellín and Bogotá. Secondly, the withdrawal of the Elite Corps, the special police unit fighting the traffickers. Thirdly, the dismissal of its commander and twenty officers accused of torturing and murdering 400 young men from the Medellín slums. Failing these conditions, the Extraditables would engage in a war of extermination by bombing the big cities and assassinating judges, politicians and journalists. "If there is a coup, then welcome to it. We don't have much to lose." The Extraditables wanted a response within three days delivered to a room at the Hotel Continental in Medellín.

A notary took the response to the hotel. As soon as he entered the designated room, the phone rang. "Did you bring the package?"

"Yes." Two young, well-dressed men entered the room to get the response.

Within a week, Pablo dispatched Guido Parra to negotiate with the parents of some of the hostages. The 48-year-old had practiced law for decades and was considered an expert. Wearing a light suit, with a bright shirt and tie, he said he was Pablo Escobar's attorney.

"Then the letter you've brought is from him?"

"No," Guido Parra said, realising his mistake. "It's from the Extraditables, but you should direct your response to Escobar because he'll be able to influence the negotiation."

Julio César Turbay and Francisco's father took the response from the Extraditables to the president, who met them in a small room adjacent to his private library. The president said that Guido Parra was a bad emissary. "Very smart, a good lawyer, but extremely dangerous. Of course, he does have Escobar's complete backing." After studying the letter, the president cast doubt on its authenticity. Maybe it was somebody playing a trick by impersonating Pablo. He said that the intelligence agencies had been unable to ascertain the locations of the hostages. The two parents left the meeting disheartened.

An announcement from the boss of the house raised the hostages' hopes: "You'll be released on December 9 to celebrate the election of the Constituent Assembly."

"I would like to interview Pablo Escobar," Diana said. Towards the end of October, she was told that her request had been approved.

For weeks, Diana's parents had requested evidence from the kidnappers to show that she was alive. In October 1990, a cassette tape arrived. "Daddy, it's difficult to send you a message under these conditions, but after our many requests, they've allowed us to do it. We watch and listen to the news constantly."

Hoping for a progress report, Julio César Turbay took the recording to Francisco's father and they visited the president in his library. Over whiskey, the president blamed the lack of progress on the Extraditables for demanding a more specific decree. Having worked on the decree all afternoon, he believed that tomorrow would bring better news.

The next day, the two parents found the president in a grim mood. "This is a very difficult moment. I've wanted to help you, and I have been helping within the limits of the possible, but pretty soon I won't be able to do anything at all."

Dismayed, Turbay stood. "Mr President, you are proceeding as you must, and we must act as the fathers of our children. I understand and ask you not to do anything that may create a problem for you as the head of state." Pointing at the president's chair, he said, "If I were sitting there, I'd do the same."

Afterwards, Turbay said to Francisco's father, "We shouldn't expect anything else from him. Something happened between last night and today and he can't say what it is."

On October 30, sixty-one days after Diana's kidnapping, the Extraditables announced: "We acknowledge publicly that we are holding the missing journalists."

The radio stated: "When the Extraditables demanded that the government give them political status and thus have their crimes condoned, President Gaviria restated that this was not possible and had the full support of former President Turbay, father of Diana Turbay, the journalist kidnapped by the Extraditables. Mr Turbay restated that constitutional principles are untouchable. President Gaviria also insisted on inviting the cartels' members to accept the decree that was issued."

The commando of the Extraditables had been assigned to kidnap Maruja Pachón, a journalist from an elite family. On November 7, 1990, driving near the national park to the east of Bogotá, a military truck approached a vehicle parked suspiciously. One of Pablo's men, Pájaro, displayed a DAS bracelet and the truck went away. Years later, Pájaro stated, "This is how Bogotá works – a city flooded with a racket of armed bureaucrats and retinues: a bracelet is taken from an official entity and everyone opens the way."

At 7:05 PM, Maruja scanned the area by the national park for threats, before getting in the back of a plush Renault 21 on the driver's side. After opening the opposite door, her sister-in-law and assistant, Beatriz, sat next to her. Having only slept for three hours due to a party on the previous night, Maruja shut her eyes and said, "Please take us home." Used to varying the routes, the driver headed north through three green lights in moderate traffic. Dressed in a dark suit and black tie, he had been on the job for three days, replacing the lucky soul who had occupied the position for ten years.

Maruja's inability to detect any threats was a credit to the men following her: one in a Mercedes, another in a yellow cab, four on foot in jeans and sneakers, one dressed as a businessman complete with a briefcase and one at a cafe who was coordinating the operation. When she had entered her car, the men on foot had taken the cab and the Mercedes, and prepared their guns. Aware of the routes her chauffeur selected, the drivers of the Mercedes and the yellow cab followed the Renault 21.

After twenty minutes, Maruja was almost at her home, where she lived with her children and husband, the politician Alberto Villamizar, who had survived a previous assassination attempt by Pablo's hit men, and had endured the death of Lara Bonilla, his colleague in New Liberalism. Ascending the street, the driver noticed the yellow cab accelerate. It screeched ahead and obstructed his path. He hit the brakes. With the force of a battering ram, the Mercedes sandwiched the Renault from behind.

The cab's doors opened. Three armed men marched towards the Renault. Another three jumped from the Mercedes.

Maruja yelled at the driver to flee by taking the vehicle across the footpath. With no room to manoeuvre, he froze. Bracing for gunfire, and holding onto her handbag, Maruja yelled at Beatriz, "Get down on the floor!"

"The hell with that. On the floor they'll kill us." Assuming it was a robbery, Beatriz removed two rings from her hand and threw them out of the window.

The doors opened from outside. A bullet from a gun with a silencer tore through glass and penetrated the driver's skull. He was dragged out and shot three times in the head. The kidnappers hoped that witnessing the murder would stun the women into not screaming for help.

"You're the one we want, Señora. Get out!" An arm with gorilla-like strength yanked Maruja from the car. Two men carried her to the Mercedes, still holding her handbag. Their car sped off with Maruja on the back seat, sat between two kidnappers, her head pressed against one of their knees, her body twisted and compressed so that breathing was awkward.

"Take it easy," said the kidnapper on the passenger seat. "We only need you to deliver a message. We'll have you home in a couple of hours. Just don't move or else there'll be trouble."

A teenager attempted to extract Beatriz, who yelled, "Don't touch me!" which startled him. "I'll get out by myself. Just tell me what to do."

"Into that car and down onto the floor," he said, pointing at the cab. "Move!"

On the back seat, Beatriz lay down and the teenager covered her with his black leather jacket, which stunk like ammonia. Two more kidnappers got in. Doors slammed and the car roared away. Communicating by radio, a kidnapper with Beatriz yelled orders at the other car, which was stuck in traffic due to an accident. Unsettled, the driver of the Mercedes bumped into a taxi. Commanded to keep moving, he drove over sidewalks.

In possession of cardamom seeds with tranquillising effects, Maruja asked her captors for permission to retrieve some from her jacket. While allowing her to chew them, they confiscated her handbag. "Who are you people?" she asked.

"We're from the M-19."

"Seriously," Maruja said sceptically, "are you traffickers or guerrillas?"

"Guerrillas. There is no need to worry. We want you to deliver a message. Seriously. Shove her down to the floor because we are approaching a police checkpoint. Now, don't move or say anything, or else we'll kill you."

"That's a gun pointing at you," a man said, jabbing it into her ribs.

At the checkpoint, Maruja continued to chew the seeds and tried not to imagine her fate. As the car progressed past the checkpoint, she stayed on the floor rather than suffer the discomfort of her skull getting pushed against knees.

"This is it," a kidnapper said, after five minutes on a dirt road.

With a jacket wrapped around her head, which was bent forward, Maruja got out. All she could see was her feet, which shuffled across a courtyard and then a tile floor. The jacket was removed to reveal a small room containing a mattress, lit by a red-light bulb dangling from the ceiling.

In dirty clothes, two short teenagers entered, with sections of sweatpants wrapped around their heads with holes for the eyes and mouth. "Hand over your jewellery for security purposes. We'll keep it safe here." She surrendered a diamond and emerald ring, but not her earrings.

On the floor of the cab, Beatriz was oblivious to the journey, while aware of the stress of the men whose progress had been hindered by traffic delays. Her bent leg had turned numb, and the inescapable stink of the jacket was rendering her dizzy.

A kidnapper noticed her attempting to rearrange her body. "Take it easy, sweetheart. Nothing bad will happen to you. We just need you to deliver a message." Realising she had an issue with her leg, he helped her to move it. Offended by the term sweet-heart, she feared that she would be killed. At the destination, she emerged with the jacket around her head.

"Don't look anywhere other than down."

She found herself in a room with Maruja.

"Beatriz! You are here, too," Maruja said, revising her assumption that they had freed her sister-in-law. She was glad of the company, while sad her friend was there. They hugged.

In charge of the house, a masked man appeared. He took the rings from Beatriz, but not her gold chain. "It's a military operation. Nothing will happen to you. We brought you here so you can deliver a communique to the government."

"Who is holding us?"

"That doesn't matter," he said, displaying a machine gun. "I need to tell you one thing: the machine gun has a silencer. Nobody knows where you are or who you are with. If you scream or try anything else, nobody will ever see you again. Now we must separate you. We're going to let you go. We took you by mistake."

"Oh, no," Beatriz said. "I'm staying with Maruja."

"What a loyal friend you have!"

"I agree. Thank you, Beatriz."

"Do you want anything to eat?"

"No. Just water. My mouth is bone dry. Can I get a cigarette from my bag?" From his own stash, he gave one to Maruja.

At the Clinic for Psychotherapy and Human Sexuality, Dr Guerrero received a call. "Are you acquainted with Beatriz Villamizar?"

"Yes, of course. She's my wife."

The policeman paused. "OK. Try to stay calm."

"What has happened?"

"On the corner of Carrera Quinta and Calle 85, a driver was murdered in a light grey Renault 21 with a Bogotá licence plate, PS-2034. Do you know the number?"

"I've no idea. Just let me know what's happened to Beatriz."

"All we can tell you presently is that she's missing. On the seat, we found her handbag and a notebook in which it said to call you if there is an emergency."

Having advised Beatriz to include his contact details, there was no doubt that his wife had been abducted nearby to Maruja's house. After cancelling a lecture on the evolution of animal species, he asked a urologist to take him to the crime scene.

Working on a campaign for the Constituent Assembly, Alberto Villamizar had spent the afternoon at *The Time's* offices. Having not slept much the previous night due to a party, he had come home and collapsed on his bed fully dressed, only to be awakened by his son shortly before 7 PM. His stern intellectual face was showing bags under hazel eyes framed by short brown parted hair and a slight beard turning grey. He noticed that Maruja was not home. As she usually called if she were running late, he grew concerned and called her office. "When did Maruja leave work today?"

"Maruja and Beatriz left a little later than usual, so they should be there at any minute."

Relieved, Alberto entered the kitchen for water, when the phone rang, which his son answered. The change in his son's voice alarmed him. "Something's happened outside!" They raced out of the building, followed by Beatriz's son. Rather than wait for the elevator, they rushed down the stairs. The doorman shouted at them that somebody had been killed.

Alberto arrived at the kidnapper's car, abandoned on a street corner, while the police were trying to keep onlookers away. On closer examination, he noticed blood on the street and on the driver's seat, and plenty of broken glass. Whose was the blood?

In shock, Dr Guerrero told Alberto that Maruja probably wasn't even in the car, because her bag was absent. Having identified Beatriz's belongings, he had convinced himself that only his wife had been kidnapped.

Back at his house, Alberto answered routine police questions and called President Gaviria. "My wife and sister have been abducted. I'm holding you responsible for their lives."

"You listen to me, Alberto. Everything will be done that can be done. I'll immediately instruct my security adviser to take charge of the matter. He'll keep me updated on the situation. I'm going to send you two men for you to choose. If you want to try a rescue by force, you'll have to go face General Maza, and if you want to find another way out, you'll have to talk to Rafael Pardo."

"Let's discard military options. I'm going to look for contacts to mediate between the government and Pablo."

With members of his family having held prominent positions in the military over the years, Alberto had inherited a warlike spirit, which he could draw on when needed. On this occasion, he had decided that tact and patience would be crucial in any negotiations with Pablo. Anything else would be as useless as the government's heavy-handed response to the Palace of Justice occupation by the M-19. With his wife's life on the line, he softened his tone against the traffickers, which upset General Maza and the DEA, who had viewed him as an anti-trafficker crusader. Just like he had done with Galán, General Maza schemed to reduce Alberto's security.

"Can we use the bathroom?" Maruja asked.

With filthy cloths wrapped around their heads, both were allowed to the bathroom provided they kept their eyes on the floor. Going first, Beatriz was repulsed by the dirty toilet in a miniscule room with a tiny window. After closing the door which didn't lock, she stepped on the toilet and gazed out of the window at an adobe house with a red roof.

While she was in the bathroom, the radio announced her identity. After she re-emerged, the leader of the kidnappers said, "We know who you are now. We can use you, too. You're staying with us."

The broadcast continued: "The kidnappers bumped into a taxi, whose driver remembered two numbers from their licence plate. He also described their car. The police have determined their escape route."

Panicking, the kidnappers decided to evacuate the house immediately. The women would be transported in the trunk of a new car.

"Can we have a little rubbing alcohol?" Maruja asked, afraid of suffocating on the journey.

"We don't have any. You'll go in the trunk and that's that. Now remove your shoes and hurry up!"

With their heads covered, they ended up in a garage. After their head covers were removed, the women were placed into the trunk. In the foetal position, they were surprised that they had enough space. Air was available because the car had been modified for kidnapping, including the removal of its rubber seals.

"We're carrying ten kilos of dynamite," the leader said. "If anyone shouts, coughs, cries or whatever, we will leave and blow up the car." He shut the trunk.

On the journey, cool fresh air entered from the sides of the trunk, refreshing the women. While Maruja contemplated the uncertainty, Beatriz peeped through an opening at the kidnappers: two men on the back seat and a female passenger holding a baby. Passing a shopping centre, she determined they were heading north. The car took a dark unpaved road and stopped at a checkpoint. Unable to see, she heard music and other cars. The possibility of a trunk inspection resurrected their hopes of getting rescued. But after five minutes, the car proceeded through the checkpoint. Ten minutes later, it parked and the trunk was opened. With their heads covered, they walked, gazing down, and passed through a living room with people whispering.

"You're about to see a friend of yours," the leader said.

Entering a tiny, dimly lit room, their eyes discerned two hooded men on a small mattress, watching TV. The back windows had been painted to simulate that a light was on. On a small bed with iron posts was an elderly female resembling a ghost, all skin and bones and flat white hair, her eyes frozen as if she were on the verge of death.

"Marina," Maruja whispered, shocked.

Missing for half a year, Marina Montoya was the 64-year-old sister of the previous president's secretary, Germán, whose son had been kidnapped to pressure the government. The secretary general had urged the president to broker a secret deal with Pablo, but after the release of his son, the government had reneged on its commitment. The kidnapping of his sister had been retaliation by Pablo, who had felt betrayed by the previous administration. As Pablo always punished those who double-crossed him, many assumed that she had been killed.

Once a stately figure, Marina had withered from illness and worry. She had charmed some of the guards, who treated her as a grandmother. She had raised seven children and was also a second mother to family members in Antioquia. Strong and independent, she had worked selling life insurance and cars. Despite her talents and good nature, many of her closest family members had suffered disasters and untimely deaths. Her chiropractor husband had been seriously mentally ill for twenty years. Four of her brothers had died: one from a heart attack, one crushed by a traffic light, and two in a car crash. A brother who enjoyed travelling had disappeared. Resigned to die, she believed that her death at the hands of the kidnappers was an inevitable extension of the cruel fate that had struck her family.

Believing that Marina was scheduled to be executed, the women assumed that they had been brought to Pablo's death row, and that they would be killed. Terrified, they attempted to get Marina to acknowledge them.

The 9:30 PM news on November 7, 1990 drew their attention: "The director of FOCINE, Maruja ... wife of the well-known politician Alberto Villamizar, and his sister Beatriz ... were kidnapped at 7:30 PM." The news cited one of the reasons for the kidnapping: Maruja was the sister of Galán's widow.

From the news, Pablo learned that by taking Maruja, he had accidentally kidnapped the wife of his old enemy, the politician Alberto Villamizar, who had been railing against the traffickers. The kidnappers had assumed that Beatriz was just a simple secretary, and as a witness to the crime, they had intended to execute her. Holding her hostage would increase Pablo's bargaining power. He knew that the Villamizar and Pachón families – of which the widow of Galán, Gloria Pachón, was part – were close to the president and provided an excellent means of pressure.

In the house holding Diana and the other hostages, urgent news interrupted a soccer broadcast: Maruja and Beatriz had been kidnapped. The news reduced Diana's expectations of being released. Her colleague, Hero Buss, concluded that he was a disposable pawn in Pablo's horror movie. His companion in captivity, Juan Vitta, grew so depressed that he stopped eating and started to waste away, as if he had chosen to die to escape from the situation. Hallucinating his dead relatives, he chatted with them. Hero Buss warned the guards that they would be held responsible if Juan died.

One of the Prisco brothers, Conrado, arrived to treat Juan. Without wearing any disguise, he spoke to Hero Buss in German. "You are suffering from extreme stress," Conrado told Juan. "You need something decent to read to take your mind off your situation and away from the ups and downs caused by the political news. The poison caused by stress is capable of killing a healthy person."

The kidnappers kept telling Maruja and Beatriz that they were part of a military operation. They explained the rules to the women: "You can only speak if the matter is urgent. Never speak above a whisper. Never get off your mattress. If you need to sit, stretch your legs, talk to each other or smoke, then you need to ask us for permission. If you are going to cough, you need to put a pillow over your mouth to reduce the sound." The women received bags for their belongings and two sets of clothes each: pink and grey sweatsuits, thick men's socks and knickers that they washed in the shower.

Exhausted and shivering from the cold, Maruja eventually dozed off, only to be occasionally roused by her smoker's cough or the heel of one of her captors kicking her in the head for snoring.

"They'll gag you to stop you snoring," Marina said. "They'll tie you to the mattress so you can't move around as much."

While the women slept, the kidnappers, mostly poor young men, watched rented action movies. Juan Vitta later stated that their favourite was *The Godfather*, which they repeated so many times that he was forced to memorise its dialogue. He said: "They found in it a connection with a kind of underworld to which they belonged and a sublimation, if not a justification, of the way of life they had chosen."

Mobbed by the media, Alberto prepared a message in the belief that the hostages would hear it on radio or TV. "I demand that Maruja and Beatriz be treated with the respect they deserve as honourable women who have nothing to do with the war. From this moment on, I'm going to devote all of my time and energy to obtaining their release."

General Maza arrived at Alberto's house, which was full of concerned family members and colleagues from politics. "I want you to know that I'm opposed to an armed rescue," Alberto said, concerned that Maza might violate President Gaviria's policy of having no rescue attempts without the consent of the victims' family members. "I'd like to be sure that it won't happen, and that I will be consulted before any decision is reached." After agreeing and discussing the kidnapping, Maza suggested getting a wiretap on Alberto's phone in case the kidnappers rang.

The government's security adviser called. "The president has appointed me the mediator between the government and the family. I'm the only one authorised to make official statements about the case. I believe that the kidnapping is a strategy by the traffickers to put pressure on the government regarding extradition."

Alberto called Maruja's sister, Gloria. "I've got something awful to tell you …"

Dr Guerrero and his son visited the president of the Patriotic Union, who was a member of the Notables, a group of elite family members formed in December 1989, to mediate between the government and the kidnappers.

"Will you act as a mediator with Pablo Escobar and persuade him to hold me hostage in exchange for Beatriz?"

"Don't be an ass. In this country, there's nothing you can do."

At dawn, Dr Guerrero arrived home, dejected. His anxiety prevented sleep. On a radio interview at 7 AM, having lost his mind, he challenged the kidnappers to stop hiding and behave like men by showing their faces. Hearing the broadcast, his wife feared the hostages would pay the price for his remarks. He closed his psychiatric office because he felt that his mental health was worse than that of his patients. With his insomnia and anxiety attacks increasing, he drank excessive amounts of whiskey.

Unable to eat or sleep, Alberto spent the remainder of the night studying the latest developments in drug trafficking and extradition, before heading out to meet the justice minister. He also met the president of the Patriotic Union, who told him, "Don't forget that this is for the long haul, at least until next June after the Constituent Assembly, because Maruja and Beatriz will be Escobar's defence against extradition. Anyway, I am resigning from this bullshit," he said, referring to the Notables. "We don't do anything but stand around like assholes."

Back home, Alberto slammed two whiskeys, which left him even more tired. At 6 PM, his son convinced him to eat. The phone rang. Gaviria wanted him to come to the presidential palace to talk in the library, where he held informal meetings.

At 7 PM, the president arrived in the library. With the initial shock subsiding, Alberto was coming to terms with the reality that the president couldn't do much for him. They both agreed that Pablo was responsible, and that the hostages were bargaining chips in government negotiations.

"The essential thing isn't knowing it," Gaviria said, "but getting Escobar to acknowledge it. That's the first important step in guaranteeing the safety of the hostages." Although the president would not authorise any rescue attempts without the families' consent, it was clear that he would not circumvent the constitution or the law to help Alberto. He could also not stop the military from searching for the kidnappers. "That is our policy."

On the way home, Alberto digested the advice he had received from everybody, encouraged by the belief that the government was willing to negotiate privately with Pablo, while aware that the president of the Patriotic Union's advice was the most realistic.

At the house with the hostages, a tall, portly boss arrived, dressed in a hood, a wool suit, a yellow tie and Italian shoes. On a mission to subdue the women, he kicked their door open and barked at a kidnapper, "I'm told you're very nervous. Let me tell you something: in this profession, the nervous get killed." He turned to Maruja. "So, you're the one causing trouble at night, coughing and making noise."

"When I'm asleep, I snore," she said calmly, "and I'm unaware I'm doing it. The room is freezing and the walls are dripping water throughout the night, so I'm unable to stop coughing."

"Do you think you can just do whatever you want here?!" he yelled. "Let me tell you something: if you cough at night or snore again, we can blow your head off." He scowled at Beatriz. "And if not your head, then your husband's and children's. We know all of their names and exactly where they live."

"You can do what you want," Maruja said. "There's absolutely nothing I can do to stop snoring. Go ahead and kill me if you want to."

"Why bring our children into it?" Beatriz asked, her eyes misting over. "What have they got to do with this? Don't you have any children?" She sobbed.

"If you really want to settle things," Maruja said, "you guys should negotiate with my husband."

Two days after the kidnapping of Maruja and Beatriz, Pablo sent a letter to the Notables, claiming that the Extraditables were holding them. On November 19, the director of *The Colombian* received a letter: "The detention of the journalist Maruja ... is our response to the recent tortures and abductions perpetrated in the city of Medellín by the same state security forces mentioned so often in our previous communiqués." Unless the situation were remedied, nobody would be freed by the Extraditables.

Visiting Francisco's father, Alberto and Galán's widow discovered him sprawled on a sofa mired in despondence. "I'm getting ready to minimise my suffering when they kill my son."

"I have a plan to negotiate with the kidnappers," Alberto said.

"Don't be naïve, my boy. You have no idea what those men are like. There's nothing we can do."

Having quit drinking and the social gatherings that he enjoyed, Alberto was preparing himself mentally to implement his plan to negotiate. At night, he drank mineral water with his son and vented his feelings. In meetings with the president's security adviser, they discussed strategies, aware that while extradition was in place, little progress would be made with the Extraditables. Perhaps he needed the courage to confront Pablo alone and engage in negotiations man to man.

Upon hearing Alberto's plan, the president's security adviser said, "Take whatever steps you want. Try anything you can. But if you want the cooperation of the government to continue, you must know that you can't overstep the bounds of the capitulation policy. Not one step, Alberto. That's all there is to it." Even with the limitations from the government, Alberto decided to soldier on.

When the hooded boss of the kidnappers showed up in expensive clothes, he didn't kick the door in or yell at the women. He showed them the Sunday papers, which quoted Alberto in agreement with the kidnappers on some issues. "Make a list of things you need," the boss said pleasantly. They wrote down cigarettes, soap, skin cream, books, toothpaste and toothbrushes, some of which arrived later that day.

During the first two days, Alberto appeared on the news eight times, convinced that anything he said would be heard by the hostages. Working in the media, most of his children included messages to Maruja in their broadcasts, including a series of instructions about staying resilient while confined.

Ten days after her kidnapping, trapped in a foul-smelling room, Maruja was telling herself that God would not send her anything that she couldn't bear. Maruja and Beatriz had been sleeping on a mattress on the floor next to Marina's bed, with a candle for light. Leaning against a wall, two kidnappers sat on the floor, observing their hostages, with hardly enough room to stretch their legs without invading the mattress. Due to a boarded-over window, it was dark, other than the light coming from the TV and the candle, which was on Marina's side. Maruja had requested that the blue light be turned off.

Every night before the hostages slept, the kidnappers shoved rags in the cracks around the door to block the light from the candle by Marina. After 6 AM, the women woke to a room lacking fresh air due to the rags. They waited without food, sometimes for hours, for the rags to be removed so that they could breathe easier. Surprisingly, whenever the women asked for coffee or cigarettes, they received them. Seeing the temporary pleasure derived from the cigarettes, Beatriz, a respiratory therapist, endured the smoke. She was almost tempted to try a cigarette after Marina said that she was looking forward to the three of them being released and later being safe at her house, smoking and drinking coffee, and joking about the kidnapping. When the kidnappers' shifts changed, they gave the women photos and knick-knacks of Our Lady of Perpetual Help and the Holy Infant.

The monotony of their routine was occasionally broken when the guards took them to the courtyard. They were allowed to walk in two pairs of thick wool men's socks, enough insulation to muffle their footsteps. Whenever they managed to fall asleep, they were fully dressed. The bags containing their belongings had expanded to include their spare clothes, medicine and hygiene products. Cigarettes were supplied abundantly. Maruja and Marina smoked over one pack a day. A TV and radio provided the latest news at low volume, while the kidnappers blasted their music. They could watch the TV from 9 AM. Awaiting the midday news, forever hopeful of coded messages from their families, they filled their mornings with soap operas and educational documentaries.

Discussing their situation, they decided that they had been housed together due to a series of errors by their kidnappers. The first house had been rendered unsafe due to the cab driver who had seen the kidnappers' car. Marina had been moved due to drunken guards attracting attention to the operation. The women resented that the wealthy Medellín Cartel had sardined them into a room with a slim bed and mattress. Even the kidnappers watching over them were suffering inhumane conditions. By listening to traffic noise, they knew they were in a neighbourhood by a highway frequented by trucks. A nearby establishment played music until late at night. Loudspeakers occasionally blasted concert music or were used to make announcements about religious or political meetings. Small aircraft coming and going suggested the presence of an airstrip.

At least once a month, a helicopter arrived. "It's bringing an army officer who is responsible for our kidnappings," Marina said. "That's why they keep Diana Turbay and Francisco Santos in other rooms in this house, so the army officer can handle all three cases each time he visits here."

One evening, yelling in the courtyard attracted their attention. "Bring it over here! Move it that way! A little higher!"

The women concluded that the boss of the house was trying to hide a corpse in a small space.

"Perhaps they have sliced up Francisco Santos," Marina said, "and they're burying the pieces under the kitchen tiles. After the killings begin, they don't stop. We are next." After a restless night punctuated by dogs barking and a rooster crowing at the wrong times, they learned that a heavy old washtub had been moved.

Maruja awoke filled with dread, her stomach in the throes of cramps induced by anxiety. Delving into good memories, she attempted to lift her spirits. As a media adviser to Galán during his earlier campaigns, she had travelled across the country with her sister, his wife Gloria, experiencing the emotional ups and downs. After relocating to Indonesia following the assassination attempt on her husband Alberto, she had returned to Colombia three times. At the end of a lunch, upon noticing Galán's strange expression, she had a premonition of his death. After she left Colombia again, on her insistence, Alberto had agreed to return to Colombia even though General Maza had warned that they were at risk of assassination. A week before their scheduled flight from Jakarta, Galán had been killed. Her husband had blamed himself for Galán's death because he had been out of the country and unable to help his friend. The loss of Galán had reopened his old wounds and from the moment he rejoined parliament, he had resumed confronting the traffickers.

In December 1989, with the government minister Carlos Lemos and a small group of parliamentarians, Alberto had to face a constitutional reform project that opened gaps of impunity for drug traffickers. His attacks had been so strong that Pablo had sent him a message stating that he had already been forgiven, but he needed "to shut his mouth." When Gaviria had announced his policy of submission, Alberto, still upset by Galán's death, had said, "The only solution to get out of this quagmire is to extradite Escobar."

Maruja's attempt to improve her mood by reliving good memories had soured thanks to the negative energy of her situation. The possibility of her own death at any moment gnawed away. Depressed, she stopped eating and speaking. Not only did the kidnappers irritate her, but also her companions. Marina had started to adopt some of the kidnappers' traits.

"Be careful," Marina said, as Maruja put a glass down.

"Why are you worried about it?" Maruja asked. "I don't believe you're the one in charge here."

Beatriz documenting every detail of their confinement bothered the guards. She was writing everything down to show her family after her release. The list she had started about her dislikes only stopped when she realised that she hated everything in the room. After the radio announced that Beatriz was a physical therapist, the kidnappers mistranslated her job title as psychotherapist and banned her from writing because they suspected she was developing a technique to unbalance their minds.

For breakfast, the hostages each received a corncake, a sausage and coffee. Lunch was lentils or beans in grey water, greasy bits of meat, a tiny lump of rice and a soft drink. Deprived of sharp instruments, they ate with spoons, while sitting on the mattress. The evening meal was leftovers reheated.

From the countryside of Antioquia, the kidnappers had only slightly more privileges than the hostages. Most of the house was off limits to them. When they slept, they were locked in a room to prevent their escape. Every month or so, they were allowed time off, which involved getting blindfolded and deposited in the trunk of a car, so that they would be clueless about the locations of the safe houses in Bogotá. Some feared that they were expendable. Well-dressed bosses in hoods made random appearances to give orders and receive reports.

The boss of the safe house was called the "major-domo" by the kidnappers. Unusually energetic for a man in his 60s, he displayed bloodshot eyes through his hood. He argued often with his wife, Damaris, who had rotten teeth, wore old clothes and sang constantly – especially salsa – at volumes that reverberated through the rooms. After starting the day with soap operas, she put the lunch ingredients into a pressure cooker, which was emptied after it whistled. Upon hearing a helicopter bringing a boss, she would spring into action and clean and hose the house to conceal the filth. Their two daughters, 9 and 7, brought friends from school to play and watch TV. On Saturdays, their teacher sometimes arrived, and other guests, which led to loud musical parties, during which the hostages were locked in their room with the TV on without any sound, unable to use the toilets.

Not only were Marina's speculations about the death of Francisco Santos unfounded, but his living conditions were better than hers. Held in the same city by a different group of kidnappers, he was treated more congenially by young men unconcerned about wrapping their heads in hoods. Although his bed was comfortable, the worst part of his confinement was having to sleep chained to it in a room with the windows boarded over, his sleep commencing by choice at 11 AM. During the night, he conversed with the kidnappers about the latest news and soccer results, watched TV with them, played cards and chess, and read newspaper accounts of his kidnapping so exaggerated that they provided an endless source of amusement to his captors. He soon started to suffer from a burning sensation in his eyes and a painful rash, but after the room and blankets were cleaned, the reaction stopped.

A thin, quiet giant guard called Monk wore a hood over his mask, which his lengthy eyelashes protruded from. For extended periods of time, he crouched down as if hypnotised. He preferred Marina, to whom he brought gifts, including religious artefacts such as a plastic crucifix on a string which she wore. As the masks had only come about after Maruja's arrival, Marina had seen the guards' faces. She described Monk as a handsome teenager with beautiful eyes.

"Chains are not allowed here," Monk said, having noticed the Virgin of Miracles medal on a chain wore by Beatriz. "You must give that to me."

"You must not take it away. It would be a terrible omen. Something bad will happen to me."

"Medals aren't allowed, because they might have long-distance electronic tracking devices inside. Here's what I'll do for you. You can keep the chain, but I need the medal. I'm sorry. These are my orders."

A guard called Spots suffered from paranoia, anxiety attacks and auditory hallucinations, and believed that his death was imminent. To avoid leaving fingerprints, he cleaned everything with alcohol. To hide his identity, he claimed to have a big scar on his face. During the night, he would raise false alarms about the arrival of the authorities. After he had put out the hostages' candle to prevent it from attracting any threats, Maruja hit her head and almost fell unconscious.

"You should know how to walk in the dark!" Spots said.

"Cut it out," she replied. "This isn't a gangster movie."

CHAPTER 2
ADJUSTING TO CAPTIVITY

Some of the guards armed with machine guns were teenagers. Displaced from the countryside, they had ended up in the slums of Medellín, where they had learned to kill. They hated authority and the lives they had been born into. They viewed crime as the only ladder up in a cruel world. They wore T-shirts, sneakers and cut-off shorts. Starting a new shift, two would arrive at 6 AM. They were supposed to alternate their sleep, but sometimes they drifted off together. Resigned to dying young, they consoled themselves by buying motorbikes and new clothes, and sending money to their mothers. They were flush with cash from collecting bounties on the police. A 15-year-old had won a prize for the most police killed. At grossly inflated prices, they bought sunglasses and jackets from the hostages.

Attempting to steady their nerves, the young guards smoked cannabis at nights or drank beer laced with a tranquilliser called Rohypnol. They played with their guns and sometimes fired them accidentally. One bullet went through a door and hit another guard in the knee. When the radio announced that Pope John Paul II wanted the hostages to be freed, a guard called the Pope "a nosy son of a bitch," which nearly provoked a shootout among the guards, many of whom prayed daily to Jesus and Mary, and asked for protection, forgiveness and success in their endeavours.

Diana Turbay's male companions, Hero Buss, Orlando Acevedo and Richard Becerra, were captives in a house overstocked with a stash of Pablo's brand-new European designer clothing. The young kidnappers boasted that they could get whatever goods the hostages wanted within twelve hours.

Out of all the hostages, Hero Buss seemed to have adapted to hardship the easiest. On a journalistic assignment in Chile, the tall German had been held captive by the military regime, which had announced that he would be shot at dawn. Having faced death and other dangers, he was able to maintain a sense of humour. "No German can live without beer," Hero Buss told the kidnappers, and three cases were promptly delivered. He convinced a kidnapper to photograph the hostages peeling potatoes.

Particularly concerned about a colleague with a heart ailment, Diana Turbay entered his room. Having recently been in hospital, he had opposed the trip. "Don't you hate me for not listening to you?" Diana said, her eyes filling with tears.

"Yes, I hated you with all my soul when we were told that we were in the hands of the Extraditables, but I've come to accept captivity as an unavoidable fate." He felt guilty for not talking her out of the excursion.

Diana and her colleagues were regularly moved to houses with different guards and conditions. The women were mostly housed separately from the men. At any time, they could be uprooted from one house to another due to the volatile nature of the kidnapping business, including whenever the police entered their neighbourhood. They often found themselves rushed along muddy paths, going up and down hills in the rain. Sometimes they were moved around Medellín by taxis, whose drivers skilfully avoided checkpoints and police patrols.

In the houses, plates, glasses and sheets were generally unwashed. Toilets could only be flushed a limited amount of times each day. Guards urinated in the sinks and showers, and slept in padlocked rooms like prisoners. Every so often, hooded bosses showed up to instruct their underlings and take reports. The mood the boss was in set the tone for the house.

Breakfast was usually a corn cake with a sausage and coffee. Lunch was beans in grey water, shreds of meat in a grease-like slop, a little rice and a soda. Cutlery was banned except for spoons. With no chairs, the captives dined on their mattresses. In the evening, they ate anything remaining from lunch. Vigilant for any updates on their disappearance, they passed time watching TV, listening to the radio and reading newspapers.

The man delegated to oversee Diana's kidnapping was Don Pacho, a thirtysomething who brought gifts, books, sweets, music cassettes and occasionally hope during his rare appearances. His underlings didn't wear hoods and went by comic-book names.

Diana was unsettled by the guards bragging about sexually assaulting strangers, and their perverse and sadistic tendencies. Occasionally, they watched movies with extreme violence and pornography, which created tension with the hostages, especially when they needed to use the toilet. Guards insisted on leaving the toilet door partially open. Sometimes the hostages caught the guards peeping at them.

Initially, the guards upset Diana by strolling around in their underwear and blasting music, which prevented her from sleeping. Over time, she convinced them to dress properly and to lower the sound. When one tried to sleep next to her, she had him leave the room. With the guards, she sometimes played Parcheesi: an Indian cross and circle board game. She helped the guards make shopping lists.

The hostages sometimes found comfort in messages brought from couriers who travelled from house to house. They delivered newspapers, toiletries and sweatsuits, which the hostages were required to wear.

At night, Diana and her friend, Azucena, sought solace from each other. They discussed news and politics, which helped distract them from their situation. They photographed each other in bed and tried to sleep until lunch arrived. They spent most of the time in a house belonging to a cartel boss, which was far more spacious than the other houses. They had a table to eat at. They listened to CDs. Assorted people visited the house. Unfamiliar women gave the hostages pictures of saints for good luck. Sometimes families with children and dogs showed up.

Watching TV, Diana saw a show filmed in her Bogotá apartment. Realising she had failed to lock a safe, she wrote to her mother, "I hope nobody is rummaging around in there." Through a TV programme, her mother reassured her.

As the news reported the kidnappings of journalists, celebrities and members of the wealthy class, Diana realised she was part of Pablo's plan to pressure the government into giving him the terms he desired for his surrender, including the end of extradition.

Leaning on religion gave her strength. She wrote prayers such as the Our Father and Hail Mary. When she wanted to speak to God or her family, she penned the words. She even prayed for Pablo: "He may have more need of your help. May it be your will that he sees the good and avoids more grief, and I ask you to help him understand our situation." When the guards found out about the diary, they gave her more paper and pencils.

After having four children with Julio César Turbay, Diana's mother, Nydia, had remarried. With Julio César Turbay making no progress with the president, Nydia became more active. She arranged masses across the country. She organised radio and TV newscasts, pleading for the release of the hostages. She had soccer matches open with the same plea. She went to meetings attended by the family members of the hostages.

An informant contacted the Colombian Solidarity Foundation, claiming that a note from a friend found in a basket of vegetables had stated that Diana was at a farm near Medellín, protected by drunken guards incapable of resisting a rescue operation. Petrified that a rescue meant certain death for her daughter, probably from police bullets, Nydia asked the informant to suppress the information.

The clue about Medellín prompted Nydia to visit Marta Ochoa – Jorge Ochoa's sister, who had been kidnapped by the M-19 – who Nydia believed was capable of contacting Pablo directly. The Ochoa sisters listened to Nydia sympathetically, but said that they couldn't influence Pablo. They complained to Nydia about the heavy-handedness of the police and gave harrowing stories of their family's suffering.

Having attempted to send a letter to Pablo via Guido Parra

and received no response, Nydia asked if they would give Pablo a letter from her. Worried that he might accuse them of creating problems for him, the sisters politely declined. Nydia viewed the encounter with optimism. Having felt that the sisters had warmed to her, she believed that a door had been opened that might lead to Diana's release and the surrender of the Ochoa brothers.

Meeting with the president, she described her visit to the Ochoa sisters. She asked him to use his power to prevent a rescue attempt and to give the Extraditables more time to surrender. He said that his policy was not to attempt any rescue without the families' authorisation. She left concerned that another branch of the government might attempt to rescue the hostages without presidential approval.

She continued her dialogue with the Ochoa sisters. Visiting one of Pablo's sisters-in-law, she heard more details of police brutality. Hoping to provoke an emotional response from Pablo, she gave the sister-in-law a letter for him in her own handwriting that she had constructed meticulously from many drafts. She addressed him as "a feeling man who loves his mother and who would give his life for her, who has a wife and young innocent defenceless children whom he wishes to protect." She said that he had achieved his goal of drawing attention to his plight, and requested that he "show the world the human being you are, and in a great humanitarian act that everyone will understand, return the hostages to us."

After reading the letter, his sister-in-law said that she was sure he would be moved by its contents. "Everything you're doing touches him, and that can only work in your daughter's favour." She sealed the letter. "Don't worry. Pablo will have the letter today."

Returning to Bogotá, Nydia was convinced that the letter would achieve its desired effect. As her ex-husband hadn't asked the president to stop the police from searching for the hostages, she decided to do so. The president declined, believing that it was OK to offer an alternative judicial policy to the Extraditables, but ceasing police operations meant stopping the hunt for Pablo. Enraged, she listened to the president harp on about the police not needing permission to act, and that he couldn't order them not to act within the limits of the law. She felt that the president didn't care about Diana's life.

Spokespeople from the families of the hostages joined the Notables, which included two former presidents. After lengthy discussions, they decided to adopt the strategy of the Extraditables by issuing public letters. In the hope of achieving progress in the negotiations, they proposed that trafficking become a collective unique crime, and that the traffickers be treated as political offenders, just like the M-19. Pablo's interest had been piqued. One of his lawyers asked the Notables to obtain a presidential letter guaranteeing his life, but they refused to ask the president.

The Notables issued a letter redefining themselves: "Our good offices have acquired a new dimension, not limited to an occasional rescue, but concerned with how to achieve peace for all Colombians."

The president approved of the peaceful objective but made his position clear: the capitulation policy was the government's only position on the surrender of the Extraditables.

Enraged, Pablo sent a letter to Guido Parra: "The letter from the Notables is almost cynical. We are supposed to release the hostages quickly because the government is dragging its feet as it studies our situation. Can they really believe we will let ourselves be deceived again?" Since their first letter, the Extraditables' position hadn't changed. "There was no reason to change it, since we have not received positive replies to the requests made in our first communication. This is a negotiation, not a game to find out who is clever and who is stupid."

In a letter to Guido Parra, Pablo detailed his goal of having the government grant him a secure prison camp. While negotiating their surrender terms, the M-19 had achieved this. He had already chosen a location. "Since this requires money, the Extraditables would assume the costs ... I'm telling you all this because I want you to talk to the mayor of Envigado, and tell him you represent me and explain the idea to him. But the reason I want you to talk to him is to get him to write a public letter to the justice minister saying he thinks the Extraditables have not accepted Decree 2047 because they fear for their safety, and that the municipality of Envigado, as its contribution to peace for the Colombian people, is prepared to build a special prison that will offer protection and security to those who surrender. Talk to him in a direct clear way, so he'll talk to Gaviria and propose the camp." He wanted a public response from the justice minister. "I know that will have the impact of a bomb … This way we'll have them where we want them."

The presidential adviser Rafael Pardo rejected the idea of treating the traffickers like the guerrillas. He believed that such political treatment and the prospect of granting a pardon was an unacceptable idea for the state and, above all, unpalatable for the international community.

Disappointed, Juan Vitta told his fellow hostages, "These are some thugs, some bastards, and all they want is to be treated the same as a guerrilla group. They want political amnesty. People like that guy Parra have already said it: 'The Extraditables are a political-military organisation or something like that. They aspire to be treated like guerrillas.' As if they were from the M-19, and that will never happen. Can you imagine that after committing all kinds of common crimes, in order to help these drug traffickers, now the government has to invent a plan to reinsert these pieces of shit?"

After the minister said no, Pablo offered more, including resolving trafficker conflicts, guaranteeing that more than a hundred traffickers would surrender and bring an end to the war. "We are not asking for amnesty or dialogue or any of the things they say they cannot give." He wanted to get on with surrendering "while everybody in this country is calling for dialogue and for treating us as political prisoners … I have no problem with extradition since I know that if they take me alive, they'll kill me, like they've done with everybody else."

Diana's father and some of the Notables confronted Pablo's lawyer. "Don't fuck with me. Let's get to the point. You've stalled everything because your demands are moronic, and there's only one damn thing at issue here: your boys must turn themselves in and confess to some crime that they can serve a twelve-year sentence for. That's what the law says, period. And in exchange for that, they'll get a reduced sentence and a guarantee of protection. All the rest is bullshit."

"Look, Doctor," Guido Parra said, "the thing is that the government says they won't be extradited, everybody says so, but where does the decree say it specifically?"

They agreed that Decree 2047 needed to be revised because it was too open to interpretation. "How soon after the decree is amended will the hostages be released?"

"They'll be free in twenty-four hours," Guido Parra said.

"All of them, of course?"

"All of them."

The noise of aircraft over the safe houses always sent the kidnappers scurrying for their weapons. Repeatedly, they told the hostages that if there were a police raid, they were under orders to assassinate all the captives. With the aircraft noises becoming more frequent, the stress of bracing for their own death was taking its toll on the hostages.

With her release getting postponed, the ups and downs sent Diana into a depression. Suffering migraines and colitis, she received no medical attention. In her diary, she wrote, "Time passes here in a way we're not used to dealing with … There is no enthusiasm about anything … I've re-examined my life up to this point: so many love affairs, so much immaturity in making important decisions, so much time wasted on worthless things … Though my convictions grow stronger about what the practice of journalism is and what it should be, I don't see it with any clarity or breadth … [My magazine] I see as so poor, not only financially but editorially. It lacks profundity and analysis."

Eventually, Azucena realised that stress had induced her

phantom pregnancy. Having clung to the possibility, she mourned its loss. Struggling to stay upbeat, she imagined getting pregnant after her release. Diana tried to remain positive with the hope that the Notables would negotiate an agreement with Pablo.

Bored with watching TV and solving crossword puzzles, Maruja and Beatriz had accepted their reality and developed coping mechanisms. After the optimism had been crushed out of Maruja, helped along by Marina's pessimism, she concluded that she would die at the hands of her captors. The realisation gave her an unexpected sense of control and an ability to endure her predicament. Refusing to believe that she would die, Beatriz attempted to minimise reality by trying not to think about it.

On November 26, 1990 – the beginning of the fourth month of Diana's captivity – Pablo decided to release one of her team. When the guards told Juan Vitta he was being freed due to illness, he thought that he was going to be shot because he had mostly recovered. "Shave and put on clean clothes." After dressing, he was instructed on what to say to the police and the media. "If you give away any clues about this location, and there is a rescue operation, the remaining hostages will be killed." He was blindfolded and transported on a maze-like journey through Medellín. His captors deposited him on a street corner.

Diana's colleague, Hero Buss, was told he would be freed on December 11. The owners of his new safe house were a couple – the wife was seven months pregnant – who wasted their bags of expense money on constant parties and lavish dinners, attended by family members and friends. The wife adorned herself with ostentatious jewellery. In between expense-money deliveries, the family would run out of food.

Hero Buss ended up in a kid's room full of mechanical toys. Amazed by the status of their hostage, they treated the large German as a celebrity, having seen him often on TV. At least thirty visitors posed for photos with him, obtained his autograph and even feasted and danced with him. It was a carefree atmosphere of unmasked people. At a time when the couple were pawning their belongings and the wife had gone into labour, Hero Buss lent them 50,000 pesos for her hospital bill. His warm welcome at the house had made him suspect that he would be held for a long time.

The day of his freedom, they returned his camera equipment and paid him back the 50,000 pesos plus 15,000 pesos for an earlier loan. Unable to find the correct shoes for his large feet, they got him a small pair that didn't fit. He had lost thirty-five pounds, so they bought him a shirt and trousers slimmer than his original clothes. His only wish that they had never granted was his request to interview Pablo.

Carrying his bags on his back, he was left by the headquarters of the newspaper, *The Colombian*, with a letter from the Extraditables, praising his human rights activism and emphasising that the capitulation policy should guarantee the safety of the Extraditables and their families. The first thing he did was ask a passer-by to take his photo.

The release of two hostages lifted Diana's spirits, which were further boosted when the guards told her and her companion, Azucena, that they were next. Having heard that before, they were sceptical. Assuming that one would be freed before the other, they each wrote a letter for the other to deliver to their family.

To counteract Marina's negativity, Maruja challenged her remarks with optimistic predictions, which amused the guards. When the wife of the kidnappers' boss, Damaris, did not go shopping for the household necessities, Maruja and Beatriz interpreted it as a sign of their imminent release, which would happen on a sunny day, and include a party at Maruja's apartment. With her culinary knowledge, Maruja detailed the menu. They would get dressed together and help with each other's make-up.

"Don't tell anyone it's my birthday tomorrow," Maruja told Beatriz. On the TV, a programme featuring Maruja's children gave her birthday away to the kidnappers, who were moved by her family's emotional appeals.

"Villamizar looks so young and nice," a guard said. "He loves you so much."

"Can you introduce us to your daughters, so that we can take them on a date?" one asked.

Pablo told the Ministry of Justice the exact wording he required in Decree 2047 and convinced the government to make the changes. "We are willing to modify that decree," Gaviria said in December 1990, "because we are interested in bringing peace to the country. We are interested in having those Colombians who have committed crimes submit to our justice system. For that reason, over the course of this week, we are going to shed as much light as possible on the decree and eventually incorporate a few modifications."

Maruja's 53rd birthday, on December 9, brought the elections to the Constituent Assembly and fresh hopes of getting released to the hostages. Having prepared answers for the media, Maruja envisioned herself at a press conference, followed by spending time with her family. At 11 AM, the boss and Damaris appeared in high spirits, with champagne and a birthday cake. Glasses were passed around, and everyone congratulated Maruja before singing "Happy Birthday." Although touched by their efforts, she felt as if she were in a netherworld separated from her family, only able to watch them on TV. As the jittery day ended without her freedom, she refused to be disheartened, convinced that her husband would secure her freedom.

As the guards relaxed the rules, Maruja and Beatriz enjoyed more liberty to stand, move around, change the TV channels and pour coffee. They were disappointed in the food still coming in skimpy portions of soup, beans, lentils and scraps of meat. Maruja stopped using pillows to stifle her coughs. Intimidated by the kidnappers waving guns and boasting about earning rewards for killing police, Maruja attempted to persuade them to protect the hostages in the event of a police raid, which would earn them reduced sentences in court in the event of their capture. Resigned to dying in a shootout, they at first resisted, but over time they kept their guns wrapped in cloth and stopped pointing them at the hostages.

Occasionally, Maruja became so frustrated that she yelled at the guards to kill her, and she attacked Marina for making gloomy predictions, which included that armed killers were on standby in a nearby car-repair shop. After Marina called some TV journalists sons of bitches because she had not been mentioned in their show, an enraged Maruja yelled at her to show respect.

"Your captivity is going to be a long one," the hooded boss said. "You will not be freed by Christmas or the New Year." The news sent the hostages into a tailspin. Maruja had a problem with her veins that caused leg pains, and random pain across her body made her constantly shift positions. Guards who didn't like her attitude banned her from using the toilet for one day. When she was finally allowed into the bathroom, nothing emerged due to chronic cystitis. In future bathroom visits, blood emerged.

Beatriz had breathing difficulties and an intense stabbing pain from a bleeding stomach ulcer. "I'm in so much pain," she said in a weak voice, "I need an emergency visit to the bathroom."

As unscheduled bathroom visits were off limits, Spots contemplated the predicament for a while. "OK. But I'm taking a huge risk." The next day, he obtained medication, which eased her cramps.

The arrival of new guards disrupted their routine. The biggest one had hairy black skin bordering on fur, so they nicknamed him Gorilla. Due to his size, he had difficulty manoeuvring around the small rooms, and he often knocked over things. He had massive muscles and hands, and a deep voice incapable of whispering. He strutted around in a ski mask, gym shorts and a tight shirt that revealed his ripped physique. Beatriz and Gorilla didn't get along.

With Christmas approaching, a priest arrived to perform the ancient Christian tradition of devotional prayer. While the hostages were locked in their room, Damaris and the family prayed and raised glasses of apple wine. The children received sweets and joined in the carol singing. The priest sprinkled and circulated holy water, splashing gallons to purge the house of its sins. After he had left, Damaris entered the hostages' room. Taking the women and guards by surprise, she threw water at the walls, the mattress and the TV.

"What are you doing?" Maruja asked.

"It's holy water," Damaris said. "It's to ensure that nothing bad will happen to us."

On their knees, with water raining down, the guards made the sign of the cross.

On December 13, whispers and noise in the house roused Diana, who leapt from bed, expecting to be freed. Energised, she woke Azucena, and they both packed. While Diana showered, a guard told Azucena that only she was going, so she got dressed.

After emerging from the shower, Diana gazed at her companion, her eyes glistening with anticipation. "Are we going, Azu?"

Breathing deeply, Azucena lowered her head. "No, I'm going alone." Azucena started crying.

Reeling as if stabbed in the heart, Diana mustered the courage to say, "I'm so happy for you. Don't worry. I knew it would be this way." She gave Azucena a letter for her mother, asking Nydia to celebrate Christmas with Diana's children. They hugged, walked to the car and hugged again. Azucena got inside. Diana waved.

On the way to the airport, Azucena heard her husband on a radio broadcast. Asked what he had been doing when he had learned that she was going to be released, he said he had been writing a poem for her. On December 16, they celebrated their fourth wedding anniversary.

On December 17, Diana's cameraman, Orlando, was in a room he had recently been moved to after complaining about the smell and having to sleep on the floor. Ruminating on the cause of the fresh bloodstains on the mattress – either a stabbing or torture – was nauseating him. Having learned on TV about the release of some of the hostages, he took his mind off the conditions by convincing himself that his release was next.

His door opened. In walked the boss in charge of Diana's house. "Put clothes on. You're leaving now."

With hardly any time to dress, and convinced he was going

to be killed, he was given a statement for the media and his eyes were covered. The boss drove him through Medellín, gave him 5,000 pesos for a taxi and dropped him off at 9 AM. Unable to hail a cab, he called his wife. "Slim, it's me."

At first, she didn't recognise his voice. "Oh my God!" In the afternoon at the airport, she sliced through a crowd of journalists and failed to recognise her plump, pale husband sporting a dark, unwieldy moustache. Finally reunited, they kissed. During Orlando's captivity, they had decided to have a second child. After a couple of nights of being around too many people wanting to speak to Orlando, they conceived.

Francisco Santo assumed that he would not get released because Pablo had freed some of the least important hostages, while holding onto the three major ones: the daughter of an ex-president, the son of the founder of the most prestigious newspaper and Galán's sister-in-law. Although the releases gave hope to Beatriz and even Marina, Maruja couldn't shake a depression exacerbated by the approach of Christmas, which she despised so much that she never sent cards or gifts, and rolled her eyes when people sang carols. When the boss and his wife brought a Christmas dinner, Maruja took sleeping pills to avoid the festivities.

Diana kept abreast of the news via TV, radio and newspapers, but missed the enjoyment of discussing it with Azucena. In her diary, she wrote, "It isn't easy to describe what I feel at each moment: the pain, the anguish, the terrifying days I've experienced." Increasingly, she mulled over dying in a rescue attempt, while hoping her release would be "pretty soon, now."

The house boss stopped having long conversations with Diana and bringing newspapers. Having requested to meet Pablo, she rehearsed what she would say to him, convinced she'd be able to get him to negotiate. Hearing her mother on TV or radio gave her hope. "I have always felt she is my guardian angel." She was convinced that her mother's determination would result in a Christmas release.

On Christmas Eve, a party at the house holding Diana included barbecued meat, alcohol, salsa music, coloured lights and fireworks. Assuming it was her leaving celebration, she expected to be told to pack her belongings. On Christmas Day, the guards gave her a lined leather jacket, which she believed was to keep her warm in the cold weather during her freedom. She envisioned her mother getting supper ready and a wreath of mistletoe at home with a welcome message, but watching all the holiday lights getting turned off crushed her.

The next day, her family appeared on a Christmas TV show, including her two children – who had grown in her absence – and brothers and sisters. Even though the family hadn't been in a celebratory mood, it had been arranged due to her letter delivered by Azucena. Nydia, too, had anticipated Diana's release that day.

Diana wrote, "I confess my sorrow at not being there, not sharing the day with all of them … But it cheered me so. I felt very close to everyone, it made me happy to see them all together."

As usual, her thoughts shifted to her situation. Why wasn't the government more actively pursuing the surrender of the Extraditables if it had satisfied their requests? "As long as that is not demanded of them, they will feel more comfortable about taking their time, knowing they have in their power the most important weapon [the hostages] for exerting pressure on the government." She compared the negotiations to a game of chess. "But which piece am I? I can't help thinking we're all dispensable." She had lost faith in the Notables: "They started out with an eminently humanitarian mission and ended up doing a favour for the Extraditables."

CHAPTER 3
HOSTAGE MURDERED

On New Year's Eve, Damaris arrived with breakfast. "Tonight, we'll celebrate with a big party with roast pork and champagne." The prospect of another celebration without her family intensified Maruja's depression. With Beatriz in a funk, Marina expressed joy at the news, as if their roles had been reversed and she were now the optimistic one. Her sprightly mood lifted the guards' spirits.

"We must be fair," Marina said. "The guards are away from their families as well. It's our job to make their New Year's Eve as happy as can be. I've got an idea. Why don't we wear the three nightgowns I've got here for good luck in the New Year?" She turned to Maruja. "OK, darling, which colour would you like?"

"It's all the same to me," Maruja said.

"I think green suits you best. You have the pink." Marina handed a nightgown to Beatriz. "I'll have the white one. As we have no mirror, let's do each other's make-up, so we look pretty for the party." She dug in her bag for a make-up case.

"Putting a nightgown on is one thing," Maruja said, "but do you seriously expect me to paint myself like a crazy woman under these circumstances? No, thanks, Marina. I won't do it."

"Well, I will," Marina said, shrugging. On the bed, she sat down. Using candlelight to see, Beatriz applied blush, eyeshadow and daring lipstick, to add colour to Marina's anaemic face, which restored enough of her beauty to surprise her roommates.

At the party, the hostages and four masked guards spoke in their normal voices – except for the house boss, who maintained protocol by whispering even though excessively drunk.

Spots handed Beatriz a bottle of aftershave. "This will help you all smell good when you receive one million hugs on your release day."

"That looks like a gift from a secret admirer," the boss said, frightening Beatriz.

Maruja admired Marina's ability to improve the atmosphere by shelving her own woes. While the guards raised their masks to drink, Marina told jokes. It grew so hot that the guards asked the hostages to face the other way, while they temporarily removed their masks to gulp air. At midnight, church bells rang and the noise blended with the sirens of fire engines. The TV played the national anthem, while everyone crammed on the bed and mattress, dripping sweat.

"Everyone stand up and sing with me," Maruja said. After the song, she lifted a glass of apple wine. "Here's to peace in Colombia." By 12:30 AM, with the food and drink depleted, the party ended. The sight of the new shift of familiar guards relieved the hostages.

Having expected to be released on December 31, Beatriz was crushed by the reality of the New Year starting. When Maruja looked at her, she sobbed. Tension was so high, they stopped communicating in the tiny room. With her roommates' health deteriorating, Marina drew on her energy reserves to massage Maruja, who was still discharging blood into the toilet. Massaging their legs with moisturising cream became a ritual for all three roommates that distracted them from their predicament.

Beatriz noticed that the inventory of cream had run low. "What will we do if the cream runs out?" she asked, concerned that the absence of their ritual would drive them insane.

"Well, we can always request more," Maruja said sarcastically. "Or should we just make a decision when the time comes?"

Beatriz exploded, "How dare you talk to me like that! It's your damn fault I'm in here!"

"If you don't shut up, I'll lock you in separate rooms," a guard said.

Fear rippled through them as they contemplated the possibility of getting attacked alone, sexually or otherwise. The guards had recently been watching violent movies with sexual content and porn movies, and sharing stories about raping strangers. Catching a guard peeping on her in the bathroom, Beatriz had slammed the door on his fingers.

Marina received a boost when her photo was shown in a TV campaign. But in future campaigns, it was removed, which disheartened her. Her roommates suspected that it had been removed because the campaign managers thought that she was dead.

On January 12, 1991, a young, graceful doctor arrived wearing a yellow silk mask and holding a large leather bag brimming with equipment. After examining each roommate, he checked their blood and pee samples. He whispered to Maruja, "I am one of the most embarrassed people in the world having to see you here. I want to say that I'm not here voluntarily. I was a great friend and supporter of Galán. I voted for him. You don't deserve to be suffering like this but try to endure. Calmness is good for your health." Unable to fathom why he was there, Maruja was sceptical. "You are both suffering from intense stress and the onset of malnutrition. You need a more balanced, vitamin-enhanced diet. Maruja, you have circulatory problems and a bladder infection." After prescribing medication to Maruja and Beatriz, he told Marina, "Take better care of your health." He handed each woman a box. "Each contains twenty tranquillisers. Take one in the morning, one at noon and another before you go to bed. There are also powerful barbiturates for emergency situations. If you take a quarter of a pill, you will fall unconscious before you can count to four." The women trembled at the prospect of the situations he had in mind.

Attempting to restore the health of the hostages, the kidnappers allowed them to walk around the courtyard after midnight, but the fresh air and the movement was counteracted by the stress of the guards pointing guns at them. The feeble women were too weak to walk and out of practice. To stop herself from falling, Maruja kept touching the wall. The guards and Damaris helped them acclimatise to the courtyard. In the following days, their bodies and attitudes rapidly responded to the exercise. After two weeks, Maruja was swiftly circling the courtyard up to 1,000 times.

Moonlight allowed the women to observe the area around the courtyard. In a decrepit section were clothes on washing lines, discarded packing cases and household items. Newspaper covered the windows of a second-storey building, which the women assumed was the guards' sleeping quarters. Beyond a kitchen door and a door to their room was a board gate to a pen with lambs and hens, a possible escape route guarded by a mean German shepherd. The dog barked at Maruja, but over time it warmed to her and allowed her to pet it.

For unknown reasons, Marina opted to go out to the courtyard on her own, accompanied by Monk, who had been rotated back in as a guard. After the TV programmes stopped for the day, they walked for one hour. Upon their return, Maruja and Beatriz went to the courtyard.

After exercise one evening, Marina returned disturbed. "I saw a man dressed in black, with a black mask, watching me from the laundry area." Discrediting it as a hallucination, her roommates didn't react. During exercise, they saw there was insufficient light to see anyone in the laundry area. Besides, any stranger would have set off the German shepherd. Monk claimed it was a ghost only visible to Marina.

Three days later, Marina returned more disturbed. "The man in black is back. For a long time, he watched me, and he didn't care that I was looking back at him, either." Monk denied the presence of the man in black, but outside, bathed in the spooky moonlight, Maruja and Beatriz were unsure.

Marina was so terrified that she stopped taking walks. Her fear transmitted to Maruja, who awoke to an image of Monk in the candlelight, in his usual squatting position, but with his mask transformed into a skull. She suspected that the apparition of

Monk had something to do with the anniversary of her mother's death.

Bedbound, Marina complained of the return of a back pain that she presumed had been cured. Mired in gloom, she depended on her roommates. Although they carried her to the bathroom, held food and drinks for her, adjusted her pillow to enable her to watch TV and doted on her in every way possible, no appreciation was ever expressed by Marina, only negativity. "I'm so sick and you two won't even help me after everything I've done for you." She occupied her hours praying and preening her nails. Eventually, she just lay in bed doing nothing but occasionally crying. "OK, now it's all in God's hands." An impromptu pep talk by the doctor failed to resurrect her. Reabsorbed in her prayers and nail filing, she offered no verbal appreciation when Maruja tried to comfort her, but she did proffer a freezing cold hand.

The negotiations were going well until Pablo's beloved Prisco Gang ran into trouble. In a shootout with the police intelligence branch called the DIJIN, Armando Prisco ran out of ammunition and received a bullet to the temple. Presumed dead, he was abandoned, and the papers reported the government's victory. The authorities had underestimated the medical skills of his doctor brother, who managed to get his body into a clinic and resurrected him.

During the presumption of his boss's death, one of his underlings, Asylum, had spent twenty million pesos of Armando's money. Disgraced and under threat from the Priscos, he told the police where Armando was recovering. They raided the estate of Llano Grande and, finding him in a wheelchair, they shot Armando in front of his family enough times to prevent him from rising from the dead again. Next, Asylum handed them Ricardo Prisco. They shot the gang's leader in the Conquistador neighbourhood. Then Asylum took them to Jorge Humberto Vásquez, the boss in charge of holding captive Diana and her companions.

"The only thing that has been democratised in this country is death," Pablo announced. "Before, only the poor died violently. Starting now, the powerful will, too."

On January 23, a guard stormed into the room of Francisco Santos. "Look, this shit is all fucked up. There was a massacre against the Priscos, and the boss is mad. He's going to start killing hostages – first Marina, second Richard, third Beatriz, fourth Maruja, fifth Diana and sixth you. One every eight days. But do not worry, because the boss says that this government will not take more than three dead."

Diana overheard the guards discussing the death of the Priscos. One was crying.

"And what do we do now with the merchandise [hostages]?" a guard asked.

"We'll get rid of it." A statement from the Extraditables had been prepared listing the order in which the hostages would be killed. The words instilled Diana with so much fear that she couldn't sleep. She was told that they would soon be changing houses.

The rate at which they were going to kill hostages motivated Francisco to write to his family. He filled out six sheets of notebook paper, writing clearly and in lowercase with a steady hand despite the gravity of his situation: "My only wish is for this drama to end as soon as possible, regardless of the outcome, so that we may all have some peace at last." He expressed gratitude to his wife for helping him grow as a man, a citizen and a father. He regretted spending so much time at work instead of at home. "I take this remorse with me to the grave." For his children, who were only babies, he wrote, "Tell them about me when they can understand what happened and accept with some equanimity the needless pain of my death."

After expressing gratitude to his father, he asked him "to take care of everything before you come to join me so my children can receive their inheritance without major difficulties." Next, he progressed to what he described as the boring but fundamental part. He wanted the family to be unified and financially secure. Regarding his life insurance with *The Time*, he wrote, "I ask you to demand what they promised because it would not be fair if my sacrifices for the people proved to be completely useless." He worried about family rivalry tearing apart *The Time*. "It would be very sad, after this sacrifice, if *The Time* were broken up or sold to outsiders." Finally, he thanked his wife for all the good shared memories. Deeply moved by his letter, the guard guaranteed that it would be delivered.

Unknown to Francisco, he only had four hours left to live, because Pablo had moved him to number one on the kill list. When Marta Ochoa found out, she sent a message to Pablo urging him not to kill Francisco, because the act would reduce the country to ruins. Pablo never responded, nor did Marta know whether he had read her message, but Francisco was reprieved, and an irrevocable order was issued to kill and dump Marina.

On January 23, 1991, Monk entered the room where the women were watching TV. "We're taking Granny to another house," he said cheerfully.

Marina was in bed, her lips devoid of colour and her white hair a tangled mess.

"Get your things together, Granny. You have five minutes."

He stooped to help her up. Her mouth opened but no sound emerged. She stood, grabbed her bag and floated towards the bathroom like a ghost.

While she was inside, Maruja said, "Are you going to kill her?"

"You can't ask anything like that! I told you: she is going to a better house. I swear."

After the women requested to speak to the boss, another guard arrived and confiscated the TV and radio, which the women viewed as a bad omen. The guards said they would collect Marina in five minutes.

Taking her time, Marina emerged in a pink sweatsuit, men's socks and her original shoes, mildewed and too big for her shrunken feet. Under the sweatsuit, she wore a scapula with a plastic cross. "Who knows, maybe they're going to release me."

"Of course they are."

"That's right. How wonderful!"

Marina asked if they had messages for their families. She put some aftershave behind her ear and rearranged her hair without a mirror. Sat on the bed, she smoked slowly, as if resigned to her fate.

"If you have a chance to see my husband and children," Beatriz said, to prevent herself from crying, "tell them I'm well and love them very much."

"Don't ask me to do that," Marina said, gazing into space. "We know I'll never have the chance."

The women gave Marina water and powerful sedatives, but her trembling hand was unable to hold the glass. Maruja held the water, so Marina could swallow the pills. Marina's big eyes told Maruja that they were all aware of what was about to happen. After giving her a pink wool hood, they hugged and kissed, and said goodbye.

"Don't worry," Maruja said.

"God bless you," Beatriz said.

With a stoic expression, Marina approached the guards. They rotated the hood, so that she couldn't see. With her walking backwards, Monk steered her out of the house. Stood still, the women remained speechless as they listened to a car start and drive away. Among dense traffic heading north from Bogotá, Marina was in the trunk. One of the hit men would later say, "I felt regret to kill that old lady who was paying for her brother's mistakes." At the murder scene, he backed away, while his partner used a gun with a silencer to kill her in the trunk by shooting her in the head.

Thirty minutes later, Monk returned in a bad mood. "What have you done with Marina?" Beatriz asked.

"After walking outside with her, two new bosses were waiting for us in the garage. I asked them, 'Where are you taking her?' They were angry at me and one yelled, 'You don't ask questions here, you son of a bitch! Get back in the house and leave Marina with Barabbas.'" A guard called Barabbas had doted on Marina and despised Maruja. During his explosions, Barabbas headbutted walls and kicked the TV.

They believed Monk because they knew that he respected Marina as if she were his grandmother, and if he had participated in her murder, he wouldn't have returned so soon. Barabbas, on the other hand, had boasted about killing people. In the middle of the night, the haunting sounds of a wounded animal disturbed the women. Investigating the source, they found Monk crying. In the morning, he refused breakfast and said that he was sad because they had taken Granny.

The prolonged absence of their TV and radio made the women suspicious. When Damaris showed up at the house, and accompanied the women on their nightly walks, Maruja asked about Marina.

"I'm taking care of her," Damaris said. "She always thinks of you and sends you both her best."

"What happened to Barabbas?"

"He hasn't come back here because he is now in charge of my security."

Every time they interacted with Damaris, her well wishes from Marina grew more effusive, and she always added that Marina was just marvellous. While Maruja feared the worst, Beatriz didn't want to think about what might have happened. Struggling to remain sane, she told herself that Marina was alive.

On January 24, 1991, a corpse was discovered north of Bogotá, sat in an upright position against a barbed wire fence, with her arms extended. Her outfit was intact except for her shoes, which had been stolen. The pink hood, still positioned with its eyeholes at the back of the head, was encrusted with blood due to six bullets having been fired from a close distance. Most of them had entered the left side of the face and the top of the skull. One had entered the forehead. The crowd watching the magistrate examine the corpse was impressed by the white hair, the well-manicured hands and nails, and even the quality of the underwear. Unable to identify Marina, the Institute of Forensic Medicine tagged the corpse NN and sent it to a recently dug mass grave, which was to hold 200 bodies.

The beginning of 1991 saw violence escalate across Colombia. As well as cartel violence, guerrilla groups were bombing and kidnapping and murdering. Pablo issued a statement condemning the police for their practice of snatching young men from the Medellín slums. He claimed that at any time of the day, ten boys would be kidnapped at random, taken to a basement or an empty lot and shot dead without any questions asked. The police were operating under the assumption that the boys worked for Pablo or eventually would or supported him in some way. To back up his claims, he referred to international human rights organisations that were documenting the abuses committed by the authorities.

To insulate themselves from the escalating mayhem and due to increasing pressure from their female family members, the Ochoa brothers decided to turn themselves in. In December 1990, the senior trafficker Kiko Moncada submitted to Pablo's will to bring a message to Fabio Ochoa Jr: if Fabio surrendered, he would be killed. They needed to be unified around extradition, about which Pablo remained stubborn. Despite the threats and warnings, Fabio intended to proceed. He wrote a letter to the justice minister: "Promise me that you will not extradite me and that you will not leave me with legal messes to fuck me up, and I will surrender." Aware that the authorities were under instructions not to capture him but to kill him, he viewed surrendering in accordance with the decree as a unique opportunity.

Marta Ochoa played a key role in the negotiations. Each brother surrendered a month or so apart, from December 18, 1990 to February 16, 1991. At different times and places, the Director of Criminal Instruction of Medellín personally collected them. In Itagüí maximum-security prison, they ended up in a fortified building at the top of a steep narrow street in an industrial suburb of Medellín. They passed time making leather crafts. Years later, Jorge Ochoa admitted that they had surrendered to save their own skin. Although they had surrendered against Pablo's wishes, he now used them as negotiators with the government.

Even though Decree 3030 – issued on December 14, 1990

– established that a prisoner convicted of multiple crimes would serve the amount of time only for the crime carrying the longest sentence, there was still ambiguity over extradition. Technically, the Ochoa brothers could have been extradited, which was unacceptable to Pablo. The new decree included procedures and time limits pertaining to evidence from overseas for use in Colombian trials.

Pablo saw problems with the decree: the conditions for non-extradition were uncertain, there was a fixed time limit on pardonable crimes and there was an accelerated exchange of evidence with the US authorities to facilitate extradition hearings. The new decree was criticised by many parties, including the family members of the hostages.

To Alberto, the new decree looked like a step backwards because it was tougher than the first. There was speculation that the more reactionary members of the government were responsible for its harshness. They had mistakenly taken the release of four journalists and Pablo's softer stance in his communications as a sign of weakness. With Pablo holding onto key hostages and the Constituent Assembly possibly about to abolish extradition, his strength was intact. The decree was criticised so heavily that a third decree was drafted.

While negotiations continued, Pablo, having just turned 41, planned to celebrate Christmas with his family. With Medellín famous for its street decorations, people mobbed La Playa Avenue, the banks of the river and the Nutibara Hill to see thousands of coloured lights forming figures that made the city look completely calm. Staying in an apartment in the city centre near La Playa, Pablo took his wife and children out to see the decorations, confident that they would be unnoticed among the thousands walking around.

CHAPTER 4
EX-PRESIDENT'S DAUGHTER KILLED

Diana's mother viewed the surrender of the Ochoa brothers as a positive development. As soon as the first Ochoa, Fabio, had surrendered, Nydia, her daughter and granddaughter went to visit him in prison, accompanied by five members of the Ochoa family, including Marta.

In Fabio's cell, they were greeted by Fabio's father. Now 70 but with a face still exuding charm, Fabio Sr lavished Nydia with praise for her brave efforts to free Diana. He wanted her to ask the president to extend the time limit for surrender in the new decree. Unable to do so, he recommended that they put the request in writing. He offered to help her however he could.

When it was time for her to leave, the younger Fabio said to Nydia, "Where there is life, there is hope."

After getting Diana's letter from Azucena in Bogotá, Nydia visited the released hostage, Hero Buss, who said that after his first week of captivity, he hadn't seen Diana, but the guards had told him that she was well. His biggest concern was a rescue attempt. "You cannot imagine the constant threat that they'll kill you. Not only because the law, as they call it, is there, but because they're always so edgy, they think the tiniest noise is a rescue operation." He recommended that she continue to lobby against a rescue and for a change to the time limit on surrender.

Since Pablo's announcement about killing hostages, Nydia had been envisioning dark scenarios. She pressed senior government officials to rely on intelligence rather than launch a rescue. But her efforts were unable to fix her shattered heart, a pain aggravated by a feeling of an imminent tragedy and a radio broadcast by the

Extraditables pledging to wrap the hostages' corpses in sacks and drop them off at the presidential palace if the decree remained unchanged.

She left a message: "I implore you to ask the president and the members of the Council on Security if they need to find bags of dead hostages at their door before they change the decree."

When the president said that Decree 3030 needed more time, Nydia replied, "A change in the deadline is necessary not only to save the lives of the hostages, but it's the one thing that will make the terrorists surrender. Change it and they'll let Diana go."

The president refused because he didn't want to reward the Extraditables with what they wanted by taking the hostages. "Democracy was never endangered by the assassinations of four presidential candidates or because of any abduction," the president later said. "The real threat came at those moments when we faced the temptation or risk or even the rumour of a possibility of an amnesty."

Disappointed in her ex-husband for not being more proactive, Nydia decided to write a letter to the president in the hope of him taking more action, but she needed divine inspiration first. Cloistered in a room with a statue of the Virgin Mary and candles, she prayed all night. At dawn, she started writing multiple drafts – some of which she tore up – while sobbing endlessly.

"I don't pretend to be composing a public document. I want to communicate with the president of my country and, with all due respect, convey to him my most considered thoughts, and a justifiably anguished plea ... The country knows, and all of you know, that if they happen to find the kidnappers during one of those searches, a terrible tragedy might ensue ..." If the president didn't amend the decree, "This would mean that the distress and anguish suffered not only by the families, but by the entire nation, would be prolonged for endless months ... Because of my convictions, because of the respect I have for you as First Magistrate of the Nation, I would be incapable of suggesting any initiative of my own devising, but I do feel inclined to entreat you, for the sake of innocent lives, not to underestimate the danger that time represents."

The Extraditables issued a statement about the murder of the Prisco Gang, which included two brothers and the man in charge of Diana's captivity, Don Pacho. They claimed that the police had used the usual excuse of a gunfight to kill Pablo's associates in cold blood. One brother had been slain in front of his young children and pregnant wife; the other in his wheelchair – he had been paralysed during a previous assassination attempt. Within a week, a second captive would be murdered. The statement was the realisation of Nydia's fears. She had a sense that they were going to kill her daughter, and there was nothing that she could do to motivate the people who could prevent it.

Convinced that executions were imminent, Alberto called the president. "You have to stop these raids."

"No," the president said. "That isn't why I was elected."

Slamming it down, Alberto almost broke the phone. He wondered who Pablo would order to be killed first. At his request, former presidents joined the Notables in their call for a peaceful political solution and condemned the violent methods used by the Extraditables.

Around dawn on January 21, 1991, Diana wrote, "It's close to five months, and only we know what this means. I don't want to lose faith or the hope that I'll go home safe and sound." After the death of Marina and the release of Azucena, Diana had requested to share a room with Richard to combat her loneliness. Their nocturnal existence consisted of listening to the radio until dawn and sleeping in the daytime. With the guards tense since the death of the Priscos, Diana and Richard had been moved twice in the hope of preventing police raids.

Around 11 AM on January 25, the mechanical noise of propellers intensified as four combat helicopters homed in on the house holding Diana. Supposedly acting on an anonymous tip about armed men in the area, a military-style raid involving over 100 troops had been arranged in the hope of capturing senior cartel members.

A guard appeared at Diana's door. "The law's all over us." Fear froze the four flustered guards. The hostages expected to be shot because they had been told many times that that would happen if there were a raid.

With the guards yelling at her to hurry, Diana brushed her teeth and put on the clothes she had been captured in, now all too big due to her weight loss. With the helicopters buzzing, she was pushed towards an exit and given a large white hat to make her look like a farmworker. They put a black shawl over her. Her colleague Richard was wearing his leather jacket and carrying his camera equipment.

"Head for the mountain!" a guard yelled. "Run!"

Running, the guards fanned out, ready to train their weapons on the helicopters. With the sun beating down, Diana and Richard dashed across a cornfield towards a steep rocky path. Helicopters appeared. Gunfire erupted. Richard dived.

"Don't move! Play dead!" Diana fell facedown and felt a warm liquid running down her hip. "They killed me. I can't move my legs. Please look at my back. Before falling, I felt something like an electric shock at my waist."

Raising her shirt, Richard saw a hole in her body above the left hip bone. "You've been shot." A high-velocity explosive bullet had shattered her spinal column. She had life-threatening internal bleeding.

The shooting grew louder. "Leave me here. Go save yourself. Run!"

Richard fished a picture of the Virgin Mary out of his pocket and put it in Diana's hand. To a chorus of gunfire, they prayed. With their guns pointed at Richard and Diana, two troops approached.

"Don't shoot!" Richard said.

"Where's Pablo?"

"I don't know. I'm Richard Becerra. I'm a journalist. This is Diana Turbay. She's wounded."

"Prove it."

Richard displayed an ID. Some farmhands emerged from the vegetation and helped them put Diana on a sheet and carry her, conscious and in agony, to a helicopter. On board, Richard saw one of the kidnappers, handcuffed. Days later, the kidnapper's corpse would be found.

Ex-president Turbay's phone rang. A military source said that Diana and Francisco had been rescued by the Elite Corps. He notified Alberto, who congratulated him, while realising that the only hostages left for Pablo to kill were Maruja and Beatriz. Listening to the radio, Turbay heard no news. He soon found out that Diana had been seriously wounded and Francisco was still in the hands of the Extraditables.

The first Nydia heard was that Diana was safely hospitalised, undergoing routine treatment. While everyone else was optimistic, she responded, "They've killed Diana!" Heading for Bogotá in a car, fixating on radio updates – the last of which said Diana was in intensive care – she sobbed.

After changing clothes, she went to the airport and made a call. "They killed Diana, Mr President, and it's your doing. It's your fault. It's what comes of having a soul of stone."

"No, Señora," the president said calmly, happy to share the good news. "It seems there was a raid, and nothing is confirmed yet, but Diana is alive."

"No. They killed her."

"How do you know that?"

"Because I'm her mother and my heart tells me so."

The Turbay family boarded a 30-year-old presidential plane for Medellín. When they landed, a presidential adviser came on board with an update. In the helicopter to Medellín, Diana had lost consciousness. They had cut open her chest and massaged her heart manually. Emergency treatment had failed to stop the bleeding. She was dead.

At the hospital, Nydia almost collapsed in front of her naked daughter drained of colour on a bloodstained sheet with a massive incision in her chest. Afterwards, tortured by grief, she held a press conference. "This is the story of a death foretold." She detailed her appeals to the president. While holding the Extraditables responsible, she said that the guilt should be shared equally by the government and the president, "who, with lack of feeling, almost with coldness and indifference, turned a deaf ear to the appeals that there be no rescues and that the lives of the hostages not be placed in danger."

The media reported her statement. The president called a meeting. He wanted to issue a denial of Nydia's claims, but instead it was decided that the senior members of the government would attend the funeral. Before the funeral, Nydia sent Diana's letters to the president. Richard told Nydia about the now deceased kidnapper he had seen handcuffed on the helicopter, so she now knew that the police had known where Diana was being held hostage. Both agreed that the government had unnecessarily delayed Pablo's surrender to modify the policy of subjugation.

In the crowded Primatial Cathedral in Bolívar Square, the president got up and walked towards Nydia, intending to shake her hand, his every step followed by the eyes of the mourners and the lenses of the media. Convinced Nydia would turn away from him in disgust, he held out his hand. Cameras clicked and lights flashed. Relieved that he hadn't attempted to hug her, she shook it gingerly. The mourners included the former presidents López and Pastrana, and the US Ambassador. Going to the cemetery amid a blanket of grey drizzle, the coffin was covered with the Colombian flag.

After the mass, Nydia asked to see the president to give him new information. Although he feared she was coming to pluck out his heart, he agreed to see her. Wearing black, she entered his office. "I've come to do you a favour." Having learned that the president hadn't ordered the fatal raid, she asked for his forgiveness. Convinced that he had been deceived, she now believed that the purpose of the raid was to free the hostages, not to capture Pablo. The authorities had obtained the location of the house holding the hostages by capturing and torturing one of Pablo's gang, the kidnapper Richard had seen on the helicopter. After taking troops to the house, the kidnapper had been shot, left at the scene and accounted for as someone killed in a shootout. "Find out if the man who was handcuffed on the helicopter is the same man who appeared dead days later."

The attitude of the president – whom Nydia later described as a block of ice – reduced her to tears and provoked her into relaunching her earlier attacks. "Just think about it. What if your daughter had been in this situation? What would you have done then?" Without giving him any time to answer, she said, "Don't you think, Mr President, that you were mistaken in your handling of this problem?"

"It's possible." She shook his hand and bolted out.

The police claimed that Diana had been shot in the spine by one of the kidnappers. Pablo's version of events matched Nydia's. He said that the police had tortured two of his men, whom he named and for whom he provided ID numbers. Running away from the house, Diana had been shot by the police. Several innocent farmhands had also been shot and accounted for as criminals killed in a gun battle.

The police denied the existence of the man handcuffed on the helicopter. They claimed it had been a routine operation and that the man found dead days later had been a peasant at the scene whom they had questioned. That version of events collapsed after Officer Lino Pinzon was punished for having tortured a man into confessing Diana's location, killing him afterwards and putting a gun on him to generate the appearance of combat. The family of the deceased won a substantial settlement from the government.

Pablo decided to execute Asylum for betraying the Priscos. The commander of the remaining fifteen members of the gang summoned him to a meeting, which Asylum saw as an opportunity to further double-cross them by bringing the police. Hoping to use them as human shields, he arrived with his wife and children, but the foot soldiers had no qualms about shooting him regardless of his family. Knowing it was an ambush, they used AR-15s to repel the police and escape.

On January 30, 1991, the Extraditables announced that the order to execute Marina Montoya had been issued on January 23. "If the men in charge of the order forgave her, her family must know. If they complied with the order, then the police must know. If she was executed, we do not understand why the police have not yet reported finding her body." The statement caught the eye of the pathologist who had performed the autopsy on Marina. She was located in a mass grave, next to the corpse of a boy who was wrapped in her pink sweatsuit. Her son identified her distinctive hands. Due to her unusual dress, characteristics and gunshot wound in the neck, the police were accused of hiding the corpse. It was believed that such a dramatic news headline would have forced the government to stop raids on the cartel.

At his wits' end, Alberto listened to the news around the clock. If Marina had been killed days ago, another execution was imminent. Out of his sister Beatriz, his wife Maruja and Francisco, he feared that his sister would be next. He badgered the president and Rafael Pardo for updates. "You invented the policy of submission to justice," he told them, "but the decrees issued so far are not clear enough. To save Beatriz, a decree is needed that says that if Escobar turns himself in to justice and confesses to a crime, he should not be extradited. A new decree must be issued or they'll kill everybody in sight."

On January 28, Rafael Pardo called Alberto. "The final version of the decree is ready for the president's signature. It was delayed because all the ministers had to sign it, and the communications minister was absent. I reached him by phone and said, 'Mr Minister, either you're here in half an hour to sign the decree or you're not a minister anymore.'"

The deaths of Diana and Marina swung more people in favour of a peaceful settlement. If Gaviria continued to stall Pablo's surrender, he risked being viewed as hard-hearted by the public. If he rushed into a settlement, he risked it being viewed as an act of contrition for Diana's death. Convinced that further delays would multiply the government's problems, he signed Decree 3030 on January 29.

On January 30, Gaviria called Alberto: "January 25 was a terrible day for everyone."

After thanking the president, Alberto called Pablo's lawyer Guido Parra. "I hope you're not going to start any shit now over how bad this decree is."

"No. I have already studied it carefully. There are no problems at this end. Just think how much grief it could have saved us if it had come out earlier."

"What's the next step?"

"Nothing. They'll all be released within forty-eight hours."

The Extraditables announced, "We will respect the lives of the remaining hostages." They said one hostage would be released right away.

Alberto rushed to meet Guido Parra. "What do they mean just one? You said they'd release all of them!"

"Relax, Alberto. It's a matter of a week."

The negotiations were stalled by Pablo's concerns about the continued killings of slum kids by the police, an alliance between General Maza and the Cali Cartel to kill his workers, and the safety of his family and associates after he surrendered.

CHAPTER 5
HIGH-VALUE HOSTAGE RELEASED

Having no TV or radio prevented Maruja and Beatriz from learning about the deaths of Marina and Diana. Pressing the guards for information produced contradictory stories. With no news to watch, they grew restless. The guards gave them magazines that focused on entertainment, not news, and replaced the blue light bulb with a regular one that the women could turn on to read for an hour in the morning and an hour at night. Having adjusted to near darkness, they found the brightness and heat from the bulb unbearable. While Beatriz focused on crossword puzzles, Maruja pretended to sleep on the mattress, so desperately depressed she could barely eat.

In late January, a young guard whose work was finished at the house said goodbye to the women. "I've got something to tell you if you promise you won't reveal who told you." The women agreed. "They killed Diana Turbay." Fear snapped the women from their lethargy. If they killed Diana, then surely they would be next. While Beatriz tried to dispel the thought, Maruja trembled.

Days later, while Maruja was playing dominoes with a guard, Gorilla approached, tapping his chest. "There's a funny feeling here. What could it be?"

"Either gas or a heart attack," Maruja said.

Gorilla dropped his sub-machine gun and stood with his hand on his chest. "My heart hurts! Dammit!" With a crashing sound that attracted the boss and his wife, he fell facedown onto the breakfast leftovers. A tiny guard attempted to help the massive man. Obstructed by his gun, he gave it to Beatriz and told her that she was now responsible for Maruja.

Lacking the combined strength to lift Gorilla, the boss, Damaris and the guard dragged him into the living room, watched by the newly armed Beatriz, and Maruja, who was eyeing Gorilla's gun. Having received military training, both women imagined holding their kidnappers at gunpoint, but did not succumb. Gorilla was never seen again.

By February, Maruja had convinced herself that Pablo would release Beatriz first, while she would remain in captivity. On February 2, during the nightly walk, Damaris said that she had brought make-up for their release. Back in the building, Beatriz shaved her legs.

Two new hooded bosses arrived. "A communiqué from the Extraditables announced the release of two hostages," one told the women. "But there still may be problems. Remember how on December 9 you thought you were going to be released also." Every time the bosses returned, their moods were positive and their comments optimistic, which lifted the women's spirits until one of them said in the evening, "Don't worry, ladies. It'll be very quick," which frightened the hostages for several days. Three days later, one announced, "One hostage will be released, probably Beatriz, because Francisco and Maruja are being held for higher things."

On February 7, the bosses arrived early. "Beatriz is going. Maruja has to wait another week." While words poured from Beatriz's mouth, irritating her captors, Maruja couldn't help wondering whether her husband had coordinated the release of his sister over her, which manifested an anger that lasted for a few days.

At night, Maruja instructed Beatriz on what to say to Alberto, so that her life would not be imperilled. She worried about him acting impulsively and the police attempting to rescue her. "Don't tell him anything that could identify the house."

"Don't you trust my brother?"

"More than anybody in the world, but this is between us and no one else. Promise me that nobody will find out. Could you also ask him whether my blood-circulation medicine has any side effects?" That night in her mind, Maruja began to draft her will. Her gloom was such that the guards reassured her that nothing bad would happen.

At 7 PM the next day, the two bosses arrived for Beatriz. "We've come for you." Remembering those same words that had been told to Marina before her execution filled Beatriz with dread. Longing to hear them state that they were letting her go, she tried to trick them by asking whether they were releasing Maruja, too.

"No questions! How am I supposed to know that?" one said.

"One thing has nothing to do with the other. This is political," the other said.

In a schoolgirl's miniskirt, Damaris arrived with cake and drinks. The hostages were told the breaking news: the Extraditables had kidnapped two prominent industrialists in Bogotá.

"After living for so long on the run, Pablo wants to surrender," a boss said to reassure the women. "It's rumoured he's been hiding in sewers. We'll bring the radio and TV back in time for Maruja to see Beatriz with her family." Maruja believed them, because on the night of Marina's execution, only hit men had arrived – not bosses, who appeared to be making genuine preparations – and there was no cake. "You've got ten minutes to get ready while we drink coffee," a boss said.

"Can I get a mirror to apply my make-up?" Beatriz asked Damaris, still fretting about getting killed. Having lacked a mirror for three months, the women rushed to the one brought by Damaris, unable to recognise themselves due to weight loss, malnutrition and depression. "That's not me!" Beatriz said. The large white light bulb getting turned on compounded their shock, while highlighting their anaemic faces and limp hair, which Beatriz felt compelled to comb before assessing the make-up situation.

"What's got into you?" Maruja asked. "You're so pale, you'll look terrible if you apply that make-up."

Instead of make-up, she splashed on aftershave, swallowed a tranquilliser, yanked her hair into a ponytail, and put on a pink sweatsuit, and her original flat shoes that had gained mildew under the bed.

"We're going to put sticky tape over your eyes so that you can't see our faces or the route."

"But that will tear off my eyebrows and lashes when I remove it. Wait. I can help you." Over each eyelid, she positioned cotton to cushion the tape.

Hoping to prevent Beatriz from crying, Maruja hid her emotions. "Tell Alberto not to worry, and that I love him and the children a lot." She kissed her friend, and tried not to think about what it would soon be like to be alone with four guards. After Beatriz departed, she listened to the vehicle's engine fade. When no TV or radio arrived, she knew that whether Beatriz was dead or alive would remain a mystery.

Hidden on the floor, Beatriz felt the jeep traverse rough terrain. After it arrived on a smooth road, a kidnapper threatened her. "There'll be a mob of journalists waiting for you. Remember to be careful. A wrong word could end your sister-in-law's life. You never saw us or talked to us, and the drive took more than two hours."

"I'd like to ask a favour," Beatriz said, trembling uncontrollably at the prospect that she was getting set up to die. "Maruja needs medicine for her circulatory problems. If we send it, will you make sure she gets it?"

"Affirmative. No problem."

"Thank you. Your instructions will be followed. I won't cause any trouble."

When numerous vehicles could be heard, the kidnappers whispered, "There are lots of checkpoints here. If we're stopped, I'll say you're my wife, who we're taking to the hospital. They will see how pale you are."

"What about the patches on my eyes?"

"You had an operation. You'll sit next to me and I'll put my arm around you. We'll drop you off at a certain spot. You need to get out fast and slowly count to thirty. Then remove the tape, walk, don't look back and get the first taxi." He handed her money. "It's 5,000 pesos for the taxi." Thirty minutes later, the car stopped. "If you tell the media you were with Marina, we'll execute Maruja." Clumsily, they manoeuvred Beatriz onto the ground.

"It's OK. I'm fine now." After hearing two cars drive away, she realised she was in the middle of the street and removed the blindfold. The night was clear with hardly any stars. Recognising the neighbourhood, she looked at the houses, hoping to find one occupied, so that she could call home.

A yellow cab pulled up. "Taxi?"

After getting in, she assumed that the well-dressed driver was part of Pablo's organisation. He took her address and slowed down when approaching her house to assess the media situation, but no journalists were there. "Six hundred pesos, please."

"Do you have change for 5,000?"

"No."

"I'll go in to get change."

Inside, an old porter yelled, hugged her and paid the driver. Her youngest son shouted "Mama!" and her 15-year-old girl careened towards her screaming and clung to her neck. As Beatriz could only whisper, her daughter asked why she was talking like that. Half-asleep after drinking a whiskey in bed, her husband, Dr Guerrero, heard the children screaming, appeared in his pyjamas and hugged Beatriz. Having rehearsed the moment mentally numerous times, neither of them cried.

Beatriz telephoned Alberto. "Where are you?" he asked.

"At my house."

"Perfect. I'll be there in ten minutes. Before then, don't talk to anybody." With his son driving, Alberto arrived in record time, eager to obtain the latest news about his wife and to help his sister prepare for the arrival of the police and the media.

"Believe me, Maruja is OK. Things are difficult, but bearable. She's incredibly brave. Do you have Marina's telephone number?"

"They killed her."

Beatriz finally sobbed. After she had run out of tears, she was instructed on telling a story – about a three-hour drive from the temperate zone – that would not endanger the other hostages. With Alberto adamant about preventing a rescue attempt, she described the house accurately to him. He filed the information away in case a rescue became the only option. After sleeping, she spoke to the media, amid a sea of flowers, managing to withhold clues about the real location.

Back at the kidnappers' house, Damaris appeared. "Beatriz is home safe. She was careful not to say anything that could do anyone any harm. She is with her family and their entire house is overflowing with people."

"If that's true, why can't I have a radio?" Growing hysterical, suspecting that Beatriz had died, she recklessly challenged the guards, who attempted to calm her.

"We'll try to get you a radio."

Later, the regular boss appeared. "Beatriz is in a safe place. The entire country has seen her on TV with her family."

"I want a radio so that I can hear her with my own ears."

"I promise to bring you one."

At midnight, still without a radio, Maruja took two tranquillisers to counteract her anger and fell into a deep sleep.

Safe at home, Beatriz was recovering when she received a call. "The name of the medicine!"

The familiar voice spread a chill through her body. "What medicine?"

"The medicine for the señora," said the boss of the house, the husband of Damaris.

"Vasoton. How are things?"

"I'm OK, thank you."

"Not you. Her."

"Don't worry. She's fine."

After hanging up, overwhelmed by memories, she sobbed. During a TV interview, she detailed her release in the hope that Maruja would hear her and be reassured.

CHAPTER 6
OCHOAS HELP HOSTAGE'S HUSBAND

"Your wife's release is a matter of three days," Pablo's lawyer Guido Parra told Alberto. After three days, nothing happened, so Alberto returned to the lawyer, who responded, "The increase of murders committed by the police in the slums of Medellín has complicated the matter. Until the government ends those barbaric methods, it'll be difficult to release anybody."

"That wasn't part of the agreement," Alberto said. "Everything was based on the decree being explicit, which it is. It's a debt of honour and nobody can play games with me."

"You don't know how fucked up it is being a lawyer for them. My problem isn't whether or not to challenge them. My problem is that if things don't turn out OK, they'll kill me. What should I do?"

"Cut the bullshit and talk straight. What's going on?"

"If the murders by the police don't stop and nobody is held responsible and punished, they'll never free her."

Exploding, Alberto cursed Pablo. "You need to get lost because the man who is going to kill you is me!"

Having believed El Patrón, Alberto left the meeting feeling crushed and defeated. Now he had to break the news to the remaining hostages' family members, to whom he had been upbeat about the negotiations. In a meeting with the politician Rafael Pardo, Alberto said, "Imagine how I feel. For years, Pablo has been my family's cross and mine. First, he threatened me. Secondly, he made an attempt on my life. It's a miracle I escaped. He continued to threaten me. He assassinated Galán. He kidnapped my wife and sister, and now he wants me to defend his rights."

The setback made him realise that there was only one way to get his wife back: to fly to Medellín and negotiate with Pablo in person. He decided to focus on the drug lord surrendering rather than him freeing the hostages. Employing the same strategy as Diana Turbay's mother, he planned to visit the Ochoa brothers in prison. He sought permission from Rafael Pardo.

"You have the president's approval," the minister said, "but it's not an official visit. It's an exploratory one. You can make no agreement in exchange for government concessions. The government is only interested in the surrender of the Extraditables within the limits set by the capitulation policy."

Guido Parra's usefulness to the cartel was near its end. Pablo denied authorising the guarantees the lawyer had made to Alberto, who no longer trusted Guido Parra. Pablo had ordered the lawyer to destroy the letters in which he had described Francisco's kidnapping, but Guido Parra had given the originals to Francisco's father, who was the director of *The Time*. Aware that the breach might end his life, he moved overseas, only to be killed three years later.

The police reprisals in the aftermath of Diana's death had complicated Pablo's surrender. The murder rate in Medellín had surged to twenty a day. Hordes of armed young men were assassinating police, and branches of the police were flouting the law to torture and kill anyone on the streets. With guerrilla violence escalating, the City of Eternal Spring was a battlefield, with Pablo hiding amid the chaos. Unintentionally, Alberto had become the government's olive branch. The effort he exerted to earn his wife's freedom increased her value as a hostage to Pablo, who viewed him as the ideal mediator. Their individual struggles had interlocked their fates.

Seeking advice, Alberto visited Diana's mother, who described her experience, including her meetings with the Ochoas. Nydia gave him a letter for Pablo, which she hoped would prevent others from feeling her sorrow. She wrote that she understood that raiding criminals was a function of the government, but when it came to hostages, raids were unnecessary because everybody knew the tragic outcomes, such as what had happened to Diana. "For this reason, I come to you, my heart overflowing with pain, forgiveness and goodwill, to implore you to free Maruja and Francisco ... Give me your word that you did not want Diana to die."

After reading the letter, Pablo was astonished by her lack of blame and anger. Although he didn't respond, he later wrote, "How it grieves me that I did not have the courage to answer her."

Escorted by eight bodyguards, six from the Medellín police and two from the DAS, Alberto arrived at the maximum-security Itagüí prison. He passed through three checkpoints, travelled down a corridor with adobe walls and up slender stairs with yellow pipe railings to the third floor, where the Ochoas had turned their quarters into a workstation for manufacturing leather products, including horse saddles. Most of the family was present, including the women.

As it was lunchtime, food was served that had been prepared at Hacienda La Loma, the Ochoas' main residence. The canteen was at the end of a courtyard, with exercise equipment and posters of movie stars on the walls. At a dining table with a dozen spaces, everybody ate and praised the food.

After eating, Alberto described the breakdown in his negotiations with Guido Parra. "I'm convinced that only direct contact with Pablo Escobar will save Maruja. We must stop this barbarism and not make any more mistakes. Firstly, I assure you that there is no possibility of an armed rescue attempt. I prefer to talk, to find out what's going on and what people want."

Jorge Ochoa described his family's losses and suffering, how difficult it had been to surrender and his fears that extradition would not end. "It's been a hard war for us. You can't imagine what our family and friends have suffered. Everything has happened to us." He named family members who had been kidnapped and murdered.

74

"It's been as hard for me as for you. The Extraditables tried to kill me in 1986. Even at the ends of the earth, they pursued me. They abducted my wife and sister. I'm not here to complain. I'm just pointing out that my family has been equally victimised. It's an abuse, and the time has come for us to begin to understand each other." The family listened in silence as the two men spoke.

"We can't do anything," Jorge said. "Nydia was here. We understood her situation but told her the same thing. We don't want any problems."

"While the war lasts, you are all endangered even behind these fortified walls. If it ends now, you'll have your father and mother, your entire family intact. But that won't happen until Escobar surrenders and Maruja and Francisco are freed safe and sound. I assure you that if they're killed, you, your families, everyone will pay."

Over the three-hour conversation, the two men earned each other's respect. The Ochoas appreciated Alberto's direct approach and analysis.

"OK, then," Jorge said. "We'll send Pablo your message and tell him you were here. I advise you to visit my father at La Loma. He'll enjoy speaking to you."

With two bodyguards and all the Ochoas who could leave the prison, Alberto arrived at the entrance to La Loma, and walked a kilometre along a path with leafy trees. Security men appeared and challenged his two bodyguards. After everybody had calmed down, Alberto was allowed into the main house to speak to Fabio Sr, who was sitting on a terrace with a view of never-ending fields, surrounded by female family members in black mourning clothes, and plenty of food and drink.

Aware that Fabio Sr was up to speed on the three-hour conversation in the prison, Alberto was more succinct. He emphasised how more war would only hurt the large wealthy family, who were not cut out for murder and terrorism. "Presently, your three sons are safe, but the future is unpredictable, so it's in your best interest to achieve peace, which is only possible if Escobar surrenders."

In five minutes, Fabio Sr summed up his thoughts in brief sentences. "No matter what's done, in the end, the most important element is missing: talking to Escobar in person. The best thing is to start there. You're the right man to try it because Pablo only trusts men whose words are as good as gold. You are one of those men, but the problem is proving it to him."

At 6 PM, Alberto left, satisfied with the response from the Ochoas. They all had the same goal as the government of getting Pablo to surrender. Returning to Bogotá, he was excited to tell the president about his day, but upon arrival, he learned that Gaviria's cousin and childhood friend had died.

On Friday, four hooded armed men had snatched his cousin from a country estate. The president did not know who was responsible. On Saturday at dawn, Gaviria had gone diving on an island where he had been scheduled to attend a conference. Afterwards, he had learned that his cousin had been buried alive in a coffin in a field, his corpse had been retrieved, and traffickers were not suspected. Unable to fly due to his diving, he couldn't return to Bogotá. At 4 PM, ignoring medical advice, he had returned to Bogotá to arrange the funeral, on what he later described as one of the hardest days of his life.

Unable to make any progress with the president, Alberto received help from Jorge Ochoa, who wrote Pablo a letter urging him to surrender. He vouched for Alberto, describing him as a serious, believable and trustworthy Santanderean.

Immediately, Pablo responded: "With that son of a bitch Alberto, there is nothing to talk about."

Marta Ochoa and Jorge's wife, Maria Lia, asked Alberto to attend another meeting at La Loma. Travelling alone, he got a taxi in Medellín. The young driver asked if he was scared, and he smiled in the mirror. "Don't worry," the driver said. "Nothing will happen to you while you're with us. How could you think such a thing?" The remark boosted his confidence, which enhanced an instinct that he had the protection of a supernatural force.

Despite Pablo's attitude, the Ochoas urged Alberto to

persevere. Thirty-eight times he visited the prison, convincing the Ochoas that an acceleration of the war would sweep them all away. One time, he lost his cool and lashed out: "Ask Escobar what else does he want? Either he frees them or we end up killing each other!" Pablo responded that he needed to calm down, because the release of the hostages would come quickly. The Ochoa women became Alberto's guardian angels and helped him to overcome his scepticism. Jorge informed Pablo that guarantees for his life and safety were in place, and he would not be extradited. Receiving no reply from Pablo, the Ochoas asked Alberto to write directly to El Patrón.

On March 4, 1991, Jorge helped Alberto draft a letter, which opened by stating that respect for human rights was necessary in achieving peace. "There is a fact, however, that cannot be ignored: those who violate human rights have no better excuse for continuing to do so than citing the same violations committed by others." He pointed out how he and his family had been targeted over the years, including the murder of his sister-in-law's husband, Galán. "My sister-in-law, Gloria ... and I do not understand, and cannot accept so many unjustified and inexplicable attacks." True peace would only be found if Maruja and the hostages were released.

Two weeks later, Pablo responded: "I regret that I cannot oblige you." He pointed out that members of the Constituent Assembly in agreement with the hostages' families were against considering extradition unless the captives were freed. This was inappropriate because the kidnappings could not be thought of as a way of pressurising members of the Constituent Assembly since they pre-dated the election. "Remember, Alberto, extradition has taken many victims, and adding two more will not change the process or the continuing struggle very much." Although he conceded that they wanted the same thing – to protect their families – he wanted justice for the 400 young people murdered in Medellín by the police. The kidnappings were justifiable to pressure the government to punish the guilty police. Surprised that no public official had contacted him directly, he said that pleas for the hostages' freedom would be useless because the lives and safety of the families and associates of the Extraditables were at stake. "If the government does not intervene and does not listen to our proposals, we will proceed to execute Maruja and Francisco, about that there can be no doubt."

From the response, Alberto understood that surrendering was still on the table, but Pablo was holding out until his higher demands were satisfied. Alberto met with the president, who took notes on the situation. The prosecutor general revealed that he was about to publish a report on Diana's death, holding the police accountable, and he was indicting three troops from the Elite Corps. Separately, eleven officers whom Pablo had named had been investigated and charged. This was great news to Alberto, as it seemed the government was willing to proceed in a way more conducive to Pablo's expectations.

On April 3, 1991, the prosecutor general's office published an investigative study into the circumstances surrounding Diana's death. Although the report did not acknowledge that the bullet that killed Diana had been fired by the police, it did state that the police had abducted and murdered a local person who had just left his house to get a taxi, and it cited two other unexplainable deaths. It recommended that members of the unit that had raided the house holding Diana should be held accountable for the three deaths.

The report inspired Alberto to send a second letter to Pablo and a letter to Maruja. To convey how difficult it was for the president to control the branches of the government such as the army, he described the government's three divisions: executive, legislative and judicial. He agreed with Pablo denouncing human rights violations committed by the police, and insisting on guarantees for his safety, and that of his family and associates. "I share your opinion that you and I are engaged in essentially the same struggle: to protect our families' lives and our own, and to achieve peace." He asked Pablo to form a joint strategy.

A few days later, Pablo replied: "I know that the country is divided into president, Congress, police, army, but I also know that the president is in charge." The next four pages described police atrocities. He stated that the Extraditables had no intention of killing Diana and had not done so. She had been removed from the house dressed like a worker to help her escape. "A dead hostage has no value … Don't worry about statements to the press demanding my extradition. I know that everything will work out, and that you will bear me no grudge because your battle to defend your family has the same objectives as the one I am waging to defend mine."

In earlier correspondence, Pablo had expressed embarrassment for kidnapping Maruja, and Alberto had offered to exchange himself for Maruja because they were the ones doing battle, not her. Pablo had declined him.

Refraining from public functions, Alberto spent hours on his terrace gazing at where he thought Maruja was being held, attempting to communicate with her telepathically. He contributed to the TV campaign *Colombia Wants Them Back*, which focused on the details of captivity provided by Beatriz.

After a famous harpsichordist announced that he would get on his knees to beg for the hostages' release, Pablo responded, "Thirty million Colombians can come to me on their knees and I still won't let them go." In a letter to Alberto, Pablo praised *Colombia Wants Them Back* for championing respect for human rights.

In early March 2001, Alberto received a message from the Ochoas: "Come immediately. Something serious is going to happen." Pablo was threatening to explode fifty tons of dynamite in Cartagena's historic district, 100 kilos for each young person killed in Medellín.

"Now we're not fighting for Maruja, but to save Cartagena," he told the president.

"Thank you for the information," Gaviria said. "The government will take steps to prevent the disaster, but under no circumstances will I submit to blackmail."

In Medellín, Alberto and the Ochoas convinced Pablo to hold off. El Patrón wrote that for the time being, nothing would happen to the hostages, and that he had postponed exploding bombs in large cities, but if the police atrocities continued beyond April, he would leave no stone standing in the ancient and noble city of Cartagena de Indias.

Concerned about surrendering, some of his men asked, "If you let the hostages go, who will comply with you?"

"Alberto – his word is gold," Pablo said.

Without Beatriz and denied TV and radio, Maruja was losing her mind. Having remained strong to bolster her roommates, she started to crumble in the tiny rancid room. She embarked on a hunger strike and exploded on the guards regardless of the consequences, yelling loud enough for passers-by to hear. From the guards' reactions – threats they failed to carry out – she realised they had been instructed to keep her alive at all costs, which gave her a sense of power.

To pacify her, the boss arrived with a TV and radio. "You'll learn something now. Marina Montoya is dead."

Her heart hurt for Marina. "Murderers! That's all you are: murderers!"

The doctor arrived. "Beatriz is home safe."

"I don't believe it until I see it with my own eyes. You haven't been back, which I understand because you must be ashamed of what you did to Marina. What happened? Was she condemned to die?"

"It was a question of taking revenge for a double betrayal. Your case is different. It's political."

"At least tell me what happened to Marina. Did she know?"

"I swear she didn't."

"How come? How could she not know?"

"She was told she was going to another house. They asked her to get into the trunk of a car. She was shot in the back of the head. She couldn't have known anything."

Images of Marina's final moments haunted Maruja, who planned to swallow all her sleeping pills if her death sentence arrived. Seeing Beatriz on the news brought about a temporary joy until she noticed some changes in Beatriz's apartment, including that it had been painted distastefully. "How stupid the decorations are! It's just the opposite of what I said!" She wanted to chastise whoever was responsible.

Sleeping in Marina's bed, she could smell her and even heard her whispering. One night, Marina grabbed her arm and said her name into her ear, and she believed that Marina's presence was real.

Pulling Maruja from the brink were the messages from her family conveyed by the media. After the messages stopped for over a week, she felt abandoned, and remained on the bed facing the wall, eating and drinking barely enough to stay alive, plagued by cramps and shooting pains in her legs that she didn't report to the guards.

New guards replaced the shift that worked with Barabbas, including an overweight one who danced to salsa for hours after breakfast. Young, talkative and well-mannered, they invited her to play Nintendo and encouraged her to abide by the doctor's orders, to stay healthy for the sake of her family and to resume the nightly walks, during which she played with the German shepherd.

"Don't think I'm going to try anything stupid," Maruja said. "I won't do anything disallowed because I know this business will be over soon and turn out fine. That's why it's senseless to put so many restrictions on me."

She was allowed to speak normally, to move around the room and to go to the bathroom outside of the schedule. From the TV programmes directed at the hostages, she adopted exercises in confined spaces. Watching *Colombia Wants Them Back* cheered her up.

When more of the Prisco Gang died in February, including one of the doctors who had tended to the hostages, tension rose in the house as everyone expected Pablo to order a retaliatory assassination, just like he had done in January when Marina had been executed in response to the murders of some of the Prisco brothers.

One of Pablo's men aimed to avenge the Priscos by detonating a bomb by the policemen stationed outside of the Plaza de Toros La Macarena bullring in Medellín, with a capacity of 15,000 people. On February 16, 1991, the event started with music. The stadium was packed with people enjoying snacks and alcohol when the bullfight began. Outside, spotting a female he was acquainted with, the bomber waited for her to drive by before pressing a detonator. The ground shook and day turned into night as smoke blocked the sun. There was a chorus of screams, the stench of charred flesh, a man on fire running and twisting and turning, yells for help from people trapped under cars and booths, and dozens silently slumped, some dead, others wounded. The dead included three musicians from the Marco Fidel Suarez band, who had entertained Pablo for years. The traffickers had financed their rise and accompanied them to rodeos and parties.

With the police unable to protect the people of Medellín, popular militias had formed linked to the guerrilla groups. Mostly young people, these armed men confronted murderers, robbers, rapists and other criminals. Their popularity increased when they defended neighbourhoods from the government-backed extermination squads who were killing young people on the basis that they were the foundation of Pablo's empire. When the street gangs Pablo controlled victimised poor neighbourhoods, the militias stepped in.

To strengthen his power, Pablo decided to make peace with the militias to whom he had lost men and territory in Medellín. He arranged to meet 40-year-old Lucho, who belonged to the ELN guerrilla group. Lucho hated the Medellín Cartel's Fidel Castaño, whom he blamed for the deaths of trade unionists, students, leftist activists and human rights defenders. A big man with the voice of an anxious teenager, Lucho agreed to meet Pablo, but didn't expect much. Tension was palpable at the meeting. Pablo mentioned some of his men who had fallen at the hands of the ELN.

"Man, Pablo, what a shame," Lucho said. "We shot the people of the La Caseta band who worked for the Priscos, for being pigs. The situation was very simple: these boys made a living by carrying an AR-15 rifle. Assaulting supermarkets, doing mischief and stuff here in the commune, so, we didn't stand for that."

"How come my people were assaulting poor people with these guns?" Pablo asked. "We gave them to them so they could make a living in the wealthy neighbourhoods, in El Poblado, to go out and earn ten or twenty million pesos, so how come? It's hard for me to control so many people. You do not know what they'll do with the guns, but if they start stealing in our community, brother, we have to kill them." He defused the mood by reminiscing about the times when they had both studied at the Lyceum of the University of Antioquia, including the fights and the pranks. When the energy in the room had changed, he emphasised their common ground. "I am an anti-oligarchic anti-imperialist type and I identify with you. I do not agree with the fact that they mistreat the poorest people and that's why the work of the militias seems good to me."

Having dreamt of being recognised as a revolutionary, he left satisfied that the truce would lead to him building a great army in Medellín, comprising of his neighbourhood gangs allied with the militias. Although it did evolve, he did not have time left on earth to realise its fulfilment. After the meeting with Lucho, neighbourhood parties celebrated the truce.

Pablo told the government that he was prepared to surrender if twenty police were fired, including their leader, Colonel Oscar Peláez Carmona, due to atrocities committed against women and children. He offered to release hostages and explosives, and to order groups of hit men to disarm. Believing that it would demoralise the entire police force, the government refused to dismiss the twenty even though evidence existed of irregularities, but it did agree that Pablo could find his own secure prison.

"I'm not trying to scare you," the boss told Maruja, "but something serious happened. Since last night, a butterfly has been on the courtyard gate. After they killed the other Priscos, the exact same thing happened. For three days, a black butterfly stayed on the bathroom door."

"What does that mean?"

"It's a terrible omen because that's when they killed Marina."

"Is the present butterfly black or tan?"

"Tan."

"That's a good omen. Only the black ones are unlucky."

The impact of the death of the Priscos was counteracted by a rumour that the Constituent Assembly had found problems with extradition. Public opinion was so against extradition that even when Gaviria visited America on February 28 and expressed his resolve to maintain it at all costs, Pablo was undisturbed.

Maruja was playing dominoes with the guards, when the salsa dancer announced that a new crew of guards, including Barabbas, was replacing the young guards the next day. They arrived noisily, with Barabbas pointing his sub-machine gun at Maruja and yelling at the guards to search the room and find secret hiding places. Monk put on a serious air as they tore the room apart, including the mattress, rendering it lumpy and hard to sleep on.

Exasperated by Barabbas pointing his weapon at her head, including waking her up by pressing its barrel against her temple, Maruja said, "I'm not gonna die just because you fired a bullet by mistake. Take it easy or I'll complain."

He ignored her request. "You rich motherfuckers. Did you really believe you'd run things forever? Not anymore. Dammit. It's all over!"

"You kill your friends!" she screamed. "Your friends kill you. You all end up murdering each other! Find me one person who can say what kind of animals you are." Screaming savagely, Barabbas punched the wall, damaging his wrist.

With the boss of the house coming home increasingly late after cheating on his wife, fights between the couple were often.

After a punch knocked her through a window, Damaris and her children left. The demoralisation spread to the guards, whose drug smoke filled the house, and they performed loud antics. Maruja warned that they would attract the police, and they responded, "Let them come and kill us."

Stress caused her hair to start falling out. With everyone behaving so loudly and chaotically, she ignored the rules by talking in her normal voice and going to the bathroom whenever she liked. After a hooded guard burst into the bathroom when she was showering, she grabbed a towel and screamed so loud that the guard froze, as if expecting her noise to draw the police. Silently, he backtracked out.

The chaos ended in March when two new hooded bosses reinstalled the young guards and Damaris returned. In April, Maruja received a letter from her husband, on the back of which Pablo had scribbled: "I know this has been terrible for you and your family, but my family and I have also suffered a great deal. But don't worry, I promise that nothing will happen to you, whatever else happens … Don't pay attention to my press communiqués, they're only to keep up the pressure."

An important boss arrived, who had only visited a few times. "If Escobar isn't willing to spend at least fourteen years in prison," Maruja told him, "the government won't accept his surrender."

"Why don't you write him a letter? It could be helpful." He fetched a pencil and paper. While she chain-smoked and wrote, he paced the room.

She thanked Pablo for his kind words, which had made her feel safer, and for the respect that she had received from him. If he would accept the decree, she hoped that he and his family would have a good future in a peaceful Colombia. In the night, after taking a sedative, she dreamed that she was in a futuristic western movie in which Pablo jumped from a helicopter and used her as a shield against incoming bullets.

Alberto returned to La Loma. Cradling a whiskey and sitting in his throne-like chair, Fabio Sr sympathised with his plight. "We won't screw around anymore with letters. At this rate, it will take a hundred years. The best thing is for you to meet with Escobar and for the two of you to agree on whatever conditions you like."

In a letter to Pablo, Fabio Sr proposed that Alberto be transported to him in the boot of a car. Pablo responded, "Maybe I'll talk to Alberto, but not now."

Alberto tried to broker a month's truce from the National Police, who refused to halt operations against the cartel criminals. The police told Alberto, "You're acting at your own risk and all we can do is wish you luck."

CHAPTER 7
DIVINE INTERVENTION

In Catholic Colombia, many worshippers, including cartel hit men, sought inspiration from a programme called *God's Minute*. It was hosted by Father Garcia, a white-haired octogenarian with worldly brown eyes and a slim face, who had debuted on TV in 1955. Before the evening news, he would appear in a black habit with a clerical collar and deliver a sixty-second homily with a social message. Generations of Colombians watched his broadcasts.

In harmony with his teachings, he lived in a tiny vicarage room with numerous unrepaired leaks, where he slept sparsely on wooden planks with a sheet produced by nuns, who had sewn together miniature house-shaped bits of cloth. He shunned pillows and hardly ever replaced his clothing. In a restaurant, he once approached a woman with a diamond ring and told her that it was worth enough to build 120 houses for the poor. The next day, she mailed it to him.

He had won forty-six awards for arranging charitable events. He raised money to build *God's Minute* housing projects in the slums. During national disasters, he led fundraising campaigns. Since 1961, he had hosted the Banquet for a Million, at which celebrities paid a million pesos for a cup of soup and a roll of bread served by a beauty queen. He once outraged the puritanical by sending a fundraiser invitation to the actress Bridget Bardot, who was renowned for her sex appeal.

On April 12, 1991, Father Garcia set off to visit a doctor famous for developing a chemical malaria vaccine in 1986 and donating its patent to the World Health Organisation. He wanted the doctor to help him set up an AIDS clinic. On the journey, he was accompanied by an old friend and confidant, who had financed his chapel and many of his projects.

"Listen, Father," his friend said. "Why don't you do something to move this thing along and help Pablo Escobar turn himself in?" Much later, the friend claimed that his request that day had been inspired by God, and that, "It was like Father was floating. During the interview [with the doctor], the only thing on his mind was what I had said, and when we left, I thought he looked so excited that I began to worry."

With the priest in such a rapturous state, his friend took him to rest at a holiday home in the Caribbean. Sleeping little, he jumped up in the middle of meals to go on long walks of contemplation. "Oh, sea of Coveñas!" he yelled at the tide. "Can I do it? Should I do it? You who know everything: will we not die in the attempt?" After the walks, he would return as if hypnotised, eager to discuss the answers received from God.

By April 16, his mind had fixated on a plan. On April 18, Father Garcia arrived at the TV studio at 6:50 PM. Pablo's workers watched the man they considered a saint deliver a message to their boss:

"O sea, O immense sea! O solitary sea, which knows it all! I want to ask you a few things. Answer me. You keep the secrets. I would like to build a grand institute for the rehabilitation of sicarios in Medellín. What do you think, O sea? Speak to me, you who keep secrets. I would like to speak with Pablo Escobar, on the edge of the sea, here exactly, both of us seated on this beach.

"They have told me you want to surrender. They have told me you would like to talk to me. Oh sea! Oh sea of Coveñas at five in the evening, when the sun is setting! What should I do? They tell me he is weary of his life and its turmoil ... Tell me, oh sea: can I do it? Should I do it? You who know the history of Colombia, you who saw the Indians worshipping on this shore, you who heard the sound of history: should I do it? Will I be rejected if I do it?

If I do it, will there be shooting when I go with them? Will I fall with them in this adventure?"

Afterwards, the priest was inundated with messages from across Colombia. A swarm of journalists started to shadow his movements. The public was divided. Some believed he was acting on behalf of God. Others thought that he was insane and that he had crossed a line that separated beliefs in redemption from naiveté.

"He is a lifeline thrown by God," Fabio Ochoa Sr said. "A saint could be a means to attract a warrior, especially a believing warrior, like Pablo." The old man also knew that Pablo's family, especially his wife, needed to be convinced. If Pablo's entourage felt insecure, El Patrón would lash out with dangerous behaviour.

The next day, the priest arrived unannounced at the prison holding the Ochoas, who trusted in his divine powers. As the negotiations required a degree of secrecy, the Ochoas were concerned about his high profile. They referred him to Fabio Sr, who told him that Pablo would be amenable to his idea and that the traffickers – who generally believed in the Virgin Mary, the Holy Infant and assorted saints – would be more likely to surrender if Father Garcia were to bless such activity. Two days later, the priest announced that the hostages would be freed soon and that he was communicating with the Extraditables.

With Pablo still holding Maruja, and the president having commissioned Alberto to negotiate the release of the captives, the politician had paid close attention to the priest's broadcast. *God's Minute* had convinced Alberto that Father Garcia could play an important part in the negotiations. In recent months – with media interest in Pablo's possible surrender escalating – Alberto's letters to Pablo had achieved nothing. El Patrón was still insisting on the police being held accountable for the murders of slum kids and claiming that General Maza had been behind the assassination of the presidential candidate, Luis Carlos Galán, for which Pablo had been blamed. "Tell Doña Gloria that Maza killed her husband, there can be no doubt about it."

Pablo continued to accuse Maza of allying with the Cali Cartel. Maza responded that he wasn't going after the Cali Cartel or even drug traffic, but after traffickers committing terrorism. Maza sensed that Pablo was going to call for his resignation as a condition of his surrender.

With Maza opposed to concessions for the Medellín Cartel, Gaviria arranged a meeting with him at the Palace of Nariño to explain the particulars. After disagreeing with the president's approach, Maza said, "These guys are going to lead you and the whole country to disaster. There are many things that make me think that this is going to collapse." Years later, Maza said that Gaviria's decision was, "the worst thing that could have happened to the Colombian legal tradition."

Many books on Pablo have portrayed his battle with Maza as evil versus good. The reality was more complex. On November 25, 2010, Colombian prosecutors issued an arrest warrant for Maza for his involvement in Galán's murder – as detailed in part two of this four-book series. The prosecutors claimed that Maza had intentionally reduced Galán's bodyguards to enable the assassination of which Pablo had been accused. Presently, Maza is still serving a thirty-year sentence. Pablo had told Alberto the truth about Maza's role as a co-conspirator.

In meetings with Pablo's lawyers, Francisco's father patiently listened to the details demanded in the new decree. Previously, Hernando Santos had fiercely opposed concessions to traffickers. He represented an aristocracy that had always acted out of convenience instead of principles. Years later, Hernando said, "The fact that Escobar had put the state in check shows how weak our State was but also shows how powerful, how intelligent and how sharp Escobar was. What the guerrillas had tried for forty years, this guy did in three or four: open the floodgates towards a democratisation of the country with a new constitution." To end extradition, Pablo wanted the stamp of the Constituent Assembly on the decree, which had happened with the peace agreement with the M-19. United against extradition, rival cartels used influence and money to buy the votes of the constituents.

Alberto went to see Father Garcia at the TV studio. They visited the Ochoas in prison. In a cell, the priest dictated a letter in the exact same manner he delivered his TV sermons. He invited Pablo to join him in bringing peace to Colombia. In this endeavour, he hoped to be accredited by the government, so that Pablo's "rights, and those of your family and friends, will be respected." He asked the boss not to make impossible demands on the government. He concluded with, "If you believe we can meet in a place that is safe for both of us, let me know."

Three days later, Pablo responded. He requested disciplinary sanctions against the police he had accused of murdering the slum kids. He agreed to surrender and to confess to a crime even though no evidence existed anywhere in the world of any crime alleged to have been committed by him. Although disappointed that Pablo hadn't agreed to meet him, the priest provided a unique opportunity to obtain good conditions for Pablo's surrender and a guarantee for a negotiation. El Patrón viewed Father Garcia as a means to remedy the insecurities of his closest people.

After corresponding with Pablo in secrecy for five months, Alberto appreciated the priest getting involved. An old friend of the family, Father Garcia was a native of Cuzco like Alberto. His main concern was the priest's high profile, including the journalists camped outside of his vicarage. On May 13, 1991, Alberto received a letter from Pablo, requesting that he take the priest to the Ochoas at La Loma and keep him there for as long as possible. It could be days or months, because Pablo needed to examine every detail of the operation. If any security issues arose, negotiations would collapse.

On May 14 at 5 AM, Alberto showed up at the priest's study, where he was hard at work. "Come, Father, we're going to Medellín."

Fabio Sr was away, so the Ochoa sisters welcomed the priest. After breakfast, Marta Ochoa said that the priest would soon be seeing Pablo. He was delighted until Alberto clarified what that meant. "It's better for you to know from the very beginning,

Father. You may have to go alone with the driver, and nobody knows where he'll take you or for how long."

The risk upset the priest. Pacing, he prayed and fumbled with his rosary beads. Occasionally, he glanced out of the window in case his transport had arrived. Resisting the urge to make a call, he said, "Fortunately, there's no need for telephones when you talk to God." He refused a sumptuous lunch. Resting on a canopy bed, he couldn't sleep. At 4 PM, he appeared in Alberto's room. "Alberto, we'd better go back to Bogotá." With difficulty, the Ochoa sisters convinced him to stay. As the sun set, he insisted on leaving, but was rebuffed by the majority.

Although Father Garcia was adept at many things, he was useless at removing his contact lenses. That job was entrusted to his faithful secretary, Paulina, who had been working for him since she was a teenager and even after marrying and having a son, had continued to attend to his daily needs. She usually travelled everywhere with him and handled the delicate matter of his lenses. On this occasion, the Ochoa sisters helped the troubled priest extract his lenses.

Expecting Pablo to send a car in the dead of night, Father Garcia and Alberto couldn't sleep. In the morning, despite many attempts, nobody was able to put in the priest's lenses, which upset him so much that he didn't arrive for breakfast. Finally, a woman in charge of the ranch managed to get them in.

After gazing out of the window in a bad mood, Father Garcia sprang from his chair. "I'm leaving! This whole thing is as phoney as a rooster laying eggs." Persuaded to stay until lunch, he resumed eating and talking in a friendly way. He announced that he was going to take a nap. "But I'm warning you, as soon as I wake up, I'm leaving." Hoping to come up with a strategy to detain him beyond his nap, Marta made some calls, but none were productive.

Around 3 PM, a car arrived. Alberto rushed to the priest's room. "Father, they've come for you."

The half-awake priest shook off his fright and made the sign of the cross. "Kneel down, my boy. We'll pray together." After praying, he stood. "Let's see what's going on with Pablo."

Outside, Alberto told the driver, "I'm holding you accountable for the father. He's too important a person. Be careful what you people do with him. Be aware of the responsibility you have."

The driver's face pinched with disdain. "Do you think that if I get in a car with a saint, anything can happen to us?" The driver had the priest put on a baseball cap to disguise his snowy hair.

In the passenger seat, the priest removed the cap, tossed it out of the window and yelled at Alberto, whose face was crinkled with concern, "Don't worry about me, my boy. I control the waters."

It rained so much on the journey that they breezed through all the police checkpoints not under Pablo's control. After being on the road for over three hours and changing cars three times, they arrived at a house near Sabáneta with a massive swimming pool and sports facilities. In a garden, Father Garcia was approached by twenty armed men, whom he berated for not surrendering and for living sinful lives. On a terrace, Pablo had a beard and was dressed casually. Believing that Father Garcia was a saint, he displayed upmost respect.

"Pablo, I've come so we can straighten this out," the priest said, as if El Patrón were a lost sheep.

In the living room, they sat opposite each other in armchairs. A drop of whiskey steadied the priest's nerves, whereas Pablo drank fruit juice. Due to his age and bad memory, he asked Pablo to jot down his conditions. When Pablo was finished, the priest examined the list and crossed some conditions out, stating that they were impossible. With a stroke of a pen, the priest had eliminated things Pablo had been stuck on for months, such as his grievances with the police accused of killing slum kids. The document ended up a combination of Pablo's conditions modified by the priest's scrawl, with the addition of further clarifications by Pablo.

"Are you responsible for killing four presidential candidates?" Father Garcia asked.

"I've not committed all of the crimes attributed to me ... The Extraditables have Maruja in normal conditions and good health.

The hostages will be released as soon as the terms for surrender are arranged ... I acknowledge the president's good faith and willingness to reach an agreement."

As the priest stood to leave, a contact lens fell out. He struggled, but couldn't put it back in. Pablo also tried and failed. As did the staff. "It's no use. The only one who can do it is Paulina."

"I know who Paulina is and exactly where she is," Pablo said, taking the priest by surprise. "Don't worry, Father. If you like, we can bring her here." Father Garcia said he needed to leave, so putting it back in would have to be postponed. "Will you bless this little gold medal?" Pablo asked, pointing below his neck.

In the garden, surrounded by bodyguards, the priest blessed Pablo's medal. "Father," a bodyguard said, "you can't leave without giving us your blessing." Around the priest, they all kneeled, including Pablo. After blessing them, he urged them to renounce crime and help to bring peace.

At 8:30 PM, he arrived at La Loma on a tranquil night with the stars bright. After the car parked, he sprang out with the dexterity of an athlete and into the hands of Alberto. "Take it easy, my boy. No problems there. I had them all on their knees." For the rest of the evening, he was in a sprightly mood. He wanted to jump on a plane and meet the president, but the Ochoa sisters convinced him to rest. In the middle of the night, he paced around the house conversing with God.

On Thursday, May 16, at 11 AM, Father Garcia – the public negotiator – and Alberto – the real negotiator – landed in Bogotá, where Alberto told his son that his mother would be released in three days. For the first time since the kidnapping, Alberto attended a party, where his natural high confounded the guests, who believed that he had placed too much trust in the drug lord. By this time, Alberto roughly knew where his wife was being held. He was so fearful of a raid ending her life that he had insisted on Beatriz remaining indoors and not speaking to the authorities.

The priest was besieged by journalists. "If we don't defraud Pablo, he'll become the great architect of peace. Deep down, all

men are good, although some circumstances can make them evil."
Contradicting the media's portrayal of El Patrón for the previous
two years, he said, "Escobar is a good man." *The Time* claimed
that the priest had a private letter from Pablo which would be
delivered on Monday – it was the notes that Pablo and Father
Garcia had scribbled.

CHAPTER 8
FINAL HOSTAGES RELEASED

Francisco's father asked Pablo's ex-girlfriend, Virginia Vallejo, to intervene. She replied that she had no idea where he was or how to contact him. During an interview, asked whether she would ever see Pablo again, she responded that it had been years and that the interviewer should ask Pablo himself – if that were possible, because he rarely granted interviews. Two days later, he called her, demanding to know why she had said such ugly things about him. She said she was fed up being asked about him and she wondered how many of the thousands of homicides he had ordered.

"After the Constitutional Assembly is held," he said, "everything will go back to normal. The public is tired of war."

She pointed out that the Cali Cartel had bribed 60 per cent of Congress, so how could he control the Constitutional Assembly? He said his lead guaranteed absolute victory, but he couldn't talk about it on the phone. Changing the constitution would abolish extradition.

"Congratulations on your friend, Santo's proverbial efficiency."

"He's not my friend. He's my errand boy. After the assembly is over, I won't need him ever again."

She updated Pablo on her failed relationship with a German, his evil mother and the prenuptial agreement she had refused to sign. Pablo said on a magazine cover she had looked horrible and too old.

"On TV, I look better than ever, much better than you. I'm 41 and look 30." She pointed out that they had published that ugly picture because Pablo had kidnapped the owner of the magazine. She berated him for terrorising her prospective employers.

He said that she was much better off than being a slave for tyrants. The man she had abandoned would soon want her back, because she was so addictive. She deserved to be happy.

"He's coming in a few days," she said, "but I can't bear the scrutiny of his mother for the rest of my life." He suggested that she become a businesswoman, said goodbye and hung up.

Pablo sent a message to Alberto, confirming that his wife would be released on Monday at 7 PM. On May 21 at 9 AM, Alberto would have to return to Medellín as part of Pablo's surrender.

The Extraditables issued a statement the day before the presidential meeting: "We have ordered the release of Francisco Santos and Maruja Pachón." Journalists descended on Alberto's house.

On Sunday, May 19, at 7 PM, Maruja learned about the Extraditables' announcement, but she remained sceptical until her door burst open. "It's over! We need to celebrate!" yelled the boss of the house, accompanied by Damaris.

"Shouldn't you wait for a direct official order from one of Pablo's men?"

"I'm expecting the official order before I go to bed."

Her captors' enthusiasm was contagious. Contemplating recent events – including the escalation of grandiose claims in the news about Father Garcia, and the increased amount of her friends appearing in broadcasts of *Colombia Wants Them Back* – Maruja considered putting on the clothes she had worn on the night of the kidnapping, because she didn't want to speak to the media in a depressing sweatsuit. As the night progressed, the news hysteria subsided, and the official order never arrived. Assuming that she had deluded herself, she swallowed a cocktail of sleeping pills and woke up on Monday, confused as to who she was and where she was being held.

While his wife's mood cycled, Alberto's faith in her release was unwavering. At 9 PM on Sunday, a radio station claimed that Maruja had been dropped off in the Salitre district. While most of the reporters raced from his house to find her, Alberto was unmoved. "They'd never release her in an isolated place like that where anything could happen to her. For sure it will be tomorrow in a safe place." A journalist asked why he was so confident about that. "It's Pablo's word of honour." To lock up for the night, he asked the remaining journalists to leave. Not wanting to miss any developments, they slept in vehicles outside.

On Monday, the 6 AM news announced that Father Garcia would be hosting a press conference at noon after meeting the president. The hostages' imminent release was the headline of the day.

"You'll be released this afternoon," Maruja was informed by a low-ranking boss at 9 AM.

"What about the ring that was taken from me on the first night?"

"Don't worry. All your things have been kept safe."

"I am worried because it wasn't taken here, but in the first house, and I've never seen that man again. Was it you?"

"No. I already told you to take it easy, because your stuff is safe. I've seen them."

Damaris offered help. "I can buy you anything you need."

"Can I get lipstick, eyebrow pencil, mascara and new stockings, because my original ones were torn on the first night."

Later, in the absence of any new developments, the boss was disheartened. "As so often happens, there may have been a last-minute change of plan."

Ignoring him, Maruja showered, put on her original clothes and listened to the rumours and speculation on the radio, and the voices of her excited children and friends. The guards stopped cleaning to watch developments. They tried to bolster her spirits as the afternoon unfolded without her release, but her mood soured.

Up at 5 AM, the president focused on the news headlines and adjusted his schedule to meet his advisers, whom he told, "OK, let's finish this assignment."

One adviser relayed General Maza's belief that Pablo would not surrender without a pardon from the Constituent Assembly but added that such a pardon would be useless to Pablo, whose enemies such as the Cali Cartel had condemned him to death. "It might help him, but it's not exactly a complete solution." Pablo's main concern was being housed in a prison that would protect him and his people. Worried that the priest might convey an impossible demand from Pablo that would sabotage the negotiations, the advisers recommended that the president not attend the meeting on his own, and that he issue a statement immediately after the meeting to quell speculation.

The special meeting commenced at noon. Father Garcia was accompanied by two clerics and Alberto, who brought his son. With the president were his private secretary and a senior politician. While the meeting was photographed and videoed, Father Garcia detailed his discussion with Pablo, and expressed a belief that the boss would surrender and free the hostages. He produced the notes from the meeting – rumours of which had achieved great heights. Pablo's main condition was that the prison be the one he had selected in Envigado.

Studying the notes, the president expressed dismay over Pablo not promising to release the hostages but only agreeing to bring the matter up with the Extraditables. Alberto smoothed things over by pointing out that it was Pablo's strategy to not provide any written evidence that could be used against him. The priest wanted to know what he should do if Pablo requested his presence at the official surrender.

"You should go, Father," the president said.

"Who would guarantee my safety?"

"No one can provide better guarantees than Escobar for the safety of his own operation." The president asked Father Garcia to tread lightly with the media to prevent them from quoting anything that might upset Pablo.

The priest agreed. "I've wanted to be of service in this, and I am at your disposal if you need me for anything else …" The meeting lasted for twenty minutes and there was no press release. After the meeting, and lunch with his son, Alberto slept.

Pablo sent the priest a letter from Manuela, who asked for protection for her father and family. Dropping previous requirements, such as the dismissal of police, Pablo's communication focused on the conditions of his incarceration. He didn't want to be with the Ochoas because that prison was susceptible to attack.

Watching the news, Maruja was dismayed by the lack of developments. Still on a high, Damaris allowed her to choose lunch. "Anything other than lentils," Maruja said. With no time for Damaris to go shopping, Maruja ended up with lentils anyway.

At 6 PM, her husband received a call: "She'll arrive a few minutes after seven. They're leaving now." Alberto had a porter check that his car was in the garden with his driver on standby. He selected a dark suit and a light-coloured, diamond-patterned tie.

Maruja's door opened and two bosses entered. She recalled how this had been the moment Marina had been led to her death and Beatriz to her freedom. Her pulse accelerated as she waited for the announcement. "We're going. Get ready. Move it!"

Having repeatedly fantasised about this moment, she decided to prolong it. "What about my ring?"

"I sent it with your sister-in-law," the low-ranking boss said.

"That's untrue. You told me that you had seen it after that."

Damaris and her husband handed over Maruja's personal belongings, including gifts she had received from the guards such as Christmas cards, magazines and books. The young guards gave her pictures of saints, and asked her not to forget them, to pray for them and to do something to improve their lives.

"I'll do anything you want," Maruja said. "If you need me, get in touch and I'll help you."

One boss extracted something from his pocket. "What can I give you to remember me by? Here's the bullet we didn't shoot you with."

With her mask raised as high as her nose, Damaris kissed and hugged Maruja. After getting hugged by the boss of the house, she received a filthy hood, which they put on with the eyeholes at the back of her head, just like they had done to Marina before her execution. Unable to see, she was guided out, gagging on the stench of the hood, and placed on the back seat of a car.

"Rest your head on his knees, so no one can see you from outside. There are several checkpoints. If we're stopped, your hood will be removed, and you must behave yourself." In the living room, Alberto waited with family and journalists, while Maruja travelled along a rough road, guarded by three men. After fifteen minutes, one said, "We need you to lie on the floor now." The luxury car stopped for five minutes. On a regular road, the car joined the noisy commuter traffic. Forty-five minutes into the journey, the car stopped. "Now get out! Move it!"

"I can't see!" she yelled, resisting the hands attempting to eject her from the car. A strong hand prevented her from trying to remove her hood.

"Wait five minutes before you take it off."

Getting pushed out of the car, her weight carried her forward as if she were falling off a cliff. Listening to the car speed away, she removed her hood to see if she were on a street. A car made a U-turn and approached her. Assuming it had been sent by the kidnappers to complete her release, she walked towards the driver's side. "Please. I am Maruja Pachón. They just released me." The driver escorted her to the nearest house to use the phone. The mother of the house and the children shrieked with joy and hugged Maruja, who requested alcohol, which she drank in one gulp. After misdialling her own number twice, she got through to her daughter.

"Mamma, where are you?"

Alberto leapt from a chair and grabbed the phone. "What do you say, baby? How are you?"

"Fine, sweetheart. No problems."

After scribbling down the address, he confirmed it with the mother. "Thanks a lot. It's not far. I'm leaving now." He descended the stairs two at a time and sprinted across the lobby with a mob of journalists stampeding behind. Other journalists darted at him, causing a collision in the doorway. "Maruja is free! Let's go!" In the car, he slammed the door, startling the driver. "Let's go pick her up." Having received the address so rapidly, the driver went the wrong way. "Watch what you're doing! We must arrive fast! Don't get lost or I'll cut off your balls!" While the convoy following him got stuck in traffic, he arrived at the street in a record fifteen minutes. Spotting journalists attempting to enter the property, he identified the house and sliced through the mob.

"This way." The mother pointed upwards.

Alberto charged up the stairs and burst into a children's room full of dolls and bicycles. He reversed into the room opposite, where Maruja was sitting on the bed in the same chequered jacket she had disappeared in. They hugged with an intensity stoked by her 193-day absence, until a deluge of journalists snapped them back to reality. Smiling, Alberto said, "Your colleagues."

Maruja didn't recognise herself in a mirror. "I spent six months without looking at my reflection. I look awful." She displayed swollen fingers. "I didn't realise because they took my ring."

"You look perfect." With his arm around her shoulder, Alberto escorted out his malnourished wife, whose large brown eyes gleamed with love and relief. In the living room, a frenzy of camera flashes stunned Maruja. "Take it easy, guys. It'll be easier to talk in my apartment."

While President Gaviria drove to Alberto's apartment, the kidnappers prepared to release Francisco Santos. When Alberto and Maruja reunited with her son outside of the apartment in the proximity of the spot she had been kidnapped from, all three of them finally sobbed, while their neighbours saluted her return.

Aware of Maruja's release, Francisco was dwelling on what might happen to him when a guard without a blindfold entered the room, grabbed his arm and took him to the first floor. Surprised to see the house had been emptied, he asked what was going on. "We've moved the furniture out in a truck, so we don't have to pay the last month's rent." The guard cackled.

The kidnappers hugged and thanked him for teaching them so much. He said they had taught him plenty, too. In the garage, he was told, "Hold a book over your face as if you're reading it. If on the road, we see the police, you must leap from the car so that we can escape. The most important thing of all is that you must never say that you were in Bogotá, but that you were three hours away down a horrible highway. If you tell them where you were, we're going to have to kill all of the neighbours to prevent them from identifying us."

By a police kiosk, the car stalled. While the kidnappers sweated, attempts to restart it failed. Eventually, it started back up. Two blocks away, they took his book, gave him 6,000 pesos for a taxi and let him out on a street corner. Refusing his pesos, a young taxi driver drove him home. To get through the crowd outside, the driver blasted the horn and yelled playfully. Expecting to see that Francisco had become a shadow of his former self, the media were shocked by his weight gain and zest for life.

CHAPTER 9
EL PATRÓN SURRENDERS

Behind the scenes, lawyers for both sides distilled the negotiations down to three issues: the location of the prison, the guards and the involvement of the police and army. As the prison holding the Ochoas could have been car bombed, Pablo had refused that suggestion. Out of forty staff, Pablo would get to select half of the guards, all of whom would come from Antioquia. He would decide who would attend the surrendering, and whether there would be any journalists. He would surrender by helicopter, with the priest and Alberto aboard.

"I do not go alone without the priest in that helicopter," Pablo told Alberto. "They knock him down and I have to go hand in hand with him to the heavens. No, you give me cover, too."

"Carlos Gustavo Arrieta and the Director of Criminal Instruction, Carlos Eduardo Mejía, also wanted to attend."

"Let them come, but we put them in another helicopter." He told his men that he would use the officials as a decoy: "If there is an attack, we will shoot them first."

He had wanted to convert a convent in El Poblado into a prison, but the nuns had refused to sell it. A proposal to reinforce a Medellín prison was also rejected. The remaining option was the Municipal Rehabilitation Centre for Drug Addicts on property called La Catedral del Valle, stationed on a mountainous slope over the Honey Valley, 7,000 feet above sea level, which would give the guards and the occupants a bird's-eye view of any threats. The area was foggy in the evening and at dawn, which made a surprise raid from the air more difficult and provided a means for the occupants to slip away unnoticed. They could easily lose their pursuers in the surrounding forest, which was teeming with wildlife, such as armadillos, sloths and huge, iridescent butterflies.

The building and 30,000 square metres of land had been registered in the name of one of Pablo's friends, a trusted old ironmonger. Pablo wanted only local guards and for the police and army to have nothing to do with it. The mayor of Envigado approved the transfer of the building into a prison called the Cathedral.

It had cement floors, tile roofs and green metal doors. Formerly a farmhouse, the administration section included three little rooms: a kitchen, a courtyard and a punishment cell. It had a big dormitory, library, study and six cells with their own bathrooms. The large dayroom included four showers, a dressing room and six toilets. Motivated by Father Garcia's blessing of the project, seventy men had been working around the clock, remodelling it. Due to its inaccessibility, mules had brought furnishings: water heaters, military cots, tubular yellow armchairs, potted plants …

Despite its secure location, Pablo wanted bodyguards inside the prison, just in case anything happened. "I won't surrender alone." He wouldn't abandon his associates to be slaughtered by the Elite Corps, while omitting to say that by keeping his network close, he could continue to run his operation. As added insurance, he and Roberto buried weapons near their designated cells. "One day we'll need them," he told his brother.

The night of his wife's release, Alberto stayed up until dawn chatting with her. After an hour's sleep, he set off for Medellín. At La Loma, he met Monkey, one of two men, including Jorge Ochoa, whom Pablo had authorised to finalise the negotiations. Monkey was tall, blond and had a golden moustache.

The phone rang. "Dr Villa, are you happy?" Pablo asked Alberto. "I thank you for coming. You're a man of your word and I knew you wouldn't fail me. Let's start to arrange how I'll turn myself in."

Monkey and Alberto visited the Cathedral. They found a wide comfortable construction with a view that Pablo didn't want obstructed. From outside, it appeared austere, with only concrete visible. They discussed security concerns as they examined a double fence over nine feet high, with fifteen rows of electrified barbed wire. Out of the nine watchtowers, the two at the entrance were being reinforced. The cells had grills, tables, tubular beds and a cement area with an electric grill and a two-burner gas stove. Alberto frowned upon the Italian tiles in Pablo's bathroom, so he issued an order: "Remove that shit! This is a prison!" After the inspection, he said, "It seemed to me a very prison-like prison." He hadn't noticed that the switch for the 10,000-watt fence was in Pablo's room.

An arrangement with Pablo had been made whereby Alberto would receive an anonymous call: "In fifteen minutes, Doctor." Then he would go to his upstairs neighbour, Aseneth, and take a call from Pablo. As her house was a jumble of writers and artists, who came and went throughout the day and night, it was considered a safe place to call.

One evening, Alberto didn't get to the phone on time. Aseneth answered, "He doesn't live here."

"Don't worry about that," Pablo said. "He's on his way up."

Alberto tried to tell Aseneth what was going on. She covered her ears. "I don't want to know anything about anything. Do whatever you want in my house, but don't tell me."

At La Loma, Maruja thanked the Ochoas for facilitating her release. Alberto mentioned that her emerald and diamond ring, taken by the kidnappers, had not been returned as promised. Monkey's offer to buy a new one was declined because Maruja wanted the original due to its sentimental value. Monkey promised to refer the matter to Pablo, who successfully ordered it to be returned.

The president's fear of the priest saying a word that might threaten the negotiations at the last minute was realised during a broadcast of *God's Minute*. The 83-year-old called Pablo an unrepentant pornographer and an abuser of minors, and demanded that he remove himself from the hands of the devil and return to God's path. The about-face astounded the viewers. Enraged, Pablo believed that something seismic had occurred. As the priest's blessing had cajoled his men into surrendering, he was now faced with a rebellion. Demanding an immediate public explanation, he refused to surrender.

Perplexed, Alberto wondered whether the priest's mind had started to crack, as it wasn't the first time that he had rambled out of reality. Or maybe Pablo's enemies had encouraged the outburst to torpedo the surrender. Alberto hustled the priest over to La Loma to speak to Pablo on the phone. Out of the various explanations he offered, the acceptable one was that an editing error had made him appear to say pornographer. Having recorded the conversation with the priest, Pablo played it to his men, which satisfied them.

Government demands presented the next challenge. The politicians wanted more say in the selection of the guards. They wanted army and National Guard troops to be on patrol outside the Cathedral. They wanted to cut down trees to make a firing range adjacent to the Cathedral. Citing the Law on Prisons, which prohibited military forces from going inside a jail, Pablo rejected the idea of combined patrols. Cutting down trees would permit helicopter landings and a possible assault on the prison, which was unacceptable. He changed his mind after it was explained that the removal of the trees would provide greater visibility, which would give him more time to respond to an attack. The National Director of Criminal Investigation was insisting on building a fortified wall around the prison in addition to the barbed wire, the prospect of which infuriated Pablo.

On May 30, 1991, newspapers began reporting the terms of surrender. What caught the public's attention the most was the removal of General Maza and two prominent police leaders. After meeting the president, Maza sent him a six-page letter, saying he was in favour of Pablo's surrender: "For reasons known to you, Mr President, many persons and entities are intent upon destabilising my career, perhaps with the aim of placing me in a situation of risk that will allow them to carry out their plans against me." He suspected that the government had negotiated his position away, even though there was no official evidence of it.

Pablo informed Maza that their war was over. There would be no more attacks. His men were surrendering. He was turning in his dynamite. He listed the hiding places for 700 kilos of explosives. Maza was sceptical. He asked the president, "How come you're going to take him to his natural refuge, where he hid for at least five months while we chased him?"

Losing patience with Pablo, the government appointed an outsider as the director of the prison, not a local person as had been requested. They assigned twenty National Guards to the prison, who were also outsiders.

"In any event," Alberto said, "if they want to bribe someone, it makes no difference if he's from Antioquia or somewhere else."

Not wanting to make a fuss, Pablo agreed that the army could guard the entrance. The government offered assurances that precautions would be taken to ensure that his food wasn't poisoned. Policies and procedures for the prison were determined by the National Board of Prisons. Prisoners had to wake up at 7 AM. At 8 PM, they had to be locked in their cells. Females could visit on Sundays from 8 AM until 2 PM. Men could visit on Saturdays. Children could visit the first and third Sunday of each month.

On June 9, 1991, Medellín police started to implement security measures, including removing people from the area who didn't live there. Two days later, Pablo asked for a final condition: he wanted the prosecutor general to be present at his surrender.

Pablo lacked the official ID necessary for a surrendering person. To get citizenship papers, he was supposed to go to an office at the Civil Registry, which was impossible for a man with so many enemies. His lawyers asked the government to issue citizenship papers without him having to make an appearance. The solution proposed was for him to identify himself with his fingerprints and to bring an old notarised ID, while declaring that his new ID had been lost.

On June 18, Juan Pablo and Manuela called their father from Miami and excitedly described the recent days they had spent in Los Angeles, San Francisco and Las Vegas.

"Tomorrow I'm going to turn myself in," Pablo said to his son, "because I already know that the new constitution will not include extradition." Juan Pablo expressed concerns that his father might be falling into a trap. "Don't worry, son. Everything has gone to plan. I can no longer be extradited." After Manuela got on the phone, he said, "Soon my problems will all be in the past. Before long, we'll all be living together again. On the news, you will see that I'm in a prison, but don't worry, because it is my decision to go there."

On June 18, Monkey called Alberto at midnight, waking him up. Alberto took the elevator to Aseneth's apartment, where a party with accordion music was in full swing. Wrestling his way through the revellers, he was stopped by Aseneth. "I know who's calling you. Be careful, because one false step and they'll have your balls." She escorted him to her bedroom, where the phone was ringing.

Above the ruckus, Alberto heard, "Ready. Come to Medellín first thing tomorrow."

On June 19, Pablo asked his wife to go home and get her things in order, so that she could meet him at the Cathedral.

At 5 AM, Alberto appeared at the dwellings of Father Garcia, who was in the oratory finishing mass. "Well, Father, let's go. We're flying to Medellín because Escobar is ready to surrender."

Aboard a Civil Aeronautics plane were representatives of the government. Travelling with the priest was his nephew, who assisted him. They were met at the Medellín airport by Marta Ochoa and Jorge Ochoa's wife, Maria Lia. The officials went to the capitol building. Alberto and Father Garcia headed for Maria Lia's apartment.

Over breakfast, the surrender arrangements were finalised. The priest was told that Pablo was on his way, employing his usual evasion techniques, travelling sometimes by car and at other times walking around checkpoints. His imminent surrender unnerved the priest so much that one of his contact lenses fell out and he stood on it. To remedy his despair, Marta took him to an optician to get a pair of glasses. On the way there and back, they were stopped at numerous checkpoints, where the guards saluted Father Garcia for bringing peace.

At 2:30 PM, Monkey showed up and said to Alberto, "Ready. Let's go to the capitol building. You take your car and I'll take mine."

At the building, the women waited outside. Putting on dark glasses and a golfer's hat, Monkey disguised himself. Misidentifying Monkey, a bystander called the government to report that Pablo had just surrendered at the capitol building. About to leave the building, Monkey received a call on a two-way radio notifying him that a military plane was heading for the city, carrying injured soldiers. To keep the airspace open for Pablo, Alberto had the military ambulance rerouted and repeated his order to keep the sky clear.

"Not even birds will fly over Medellín today," the defence minister wrote in his diary.

After 3 PM, a helicopter lifted from the capitol building's roof with the National Director of Criminal Instruction, the prosecutor and a cameraman. Ten minutes later, an order was despatched to Monkey's radio.

Boarding a second helicopter with two of his closest men, Otto and Mugre, Pablo appraised the passengers: Monkey, Alberto, Father Garcia and Luis Alirio Calle, the only reporter invited because Pablo admired his honest daily TV broadcast about solidarity, peace, hope and religion. He offered his hand to Alberto. "How are you, Alberto?"

"How's it going, Pablo?"

Smiling, he thanked Father Garcia. "What are you doing here?" he said to Monkey. "Do you want to get yourself killed?" He sat next to his bodyguards. His friendly tone left the passengers wondering whether he had praised or chastised Monkey. Smiling,

Monkey shook his head. "Ah, Chief." Turning to the reporter, he said, "At last I meet you, man, Luis Alirio."

Based on Pablo's tranquillity and self-control, Alberto's first impression was that Pablo possessed a dangerous level of confidence bordering on the supernatural. Monkey was unable to close the helicopter door, so the co-pilot did it.

"Do we take off now?" the pilot asked.

"What do you think? Move it!" Pablo said, briefly dropping his polite mask. As the helicopter ascended, Pablo said to Alberto, "Everything is fine, isn't it?"

"Everything's perfect." For five minutes, Alberto braced for the helicopter to be blown out of the sky as it flew towards Treasure Hill, between El Poblado and urban Envigado. Gazing at the view, Pablo saw the La Paz neighbourhood and the mountains where he had played as a child, and from where years later he had commanded a war against those officials whom he felt had unjustly persecuted him.

"I'm going to turn on my tape recorder," the reporter said.

"Tell the president that I'm not going to disappoint him in anything," Pablo said for the tape. "He knows that people are going to start slandering about me committing crimes from here and all those things ..."

As they flew, a radio broadcast announced that the government's position on extradition had been defeated in the Constituent Assembly by a vote of fifty-one to thirteen, with five abstentions. It was official confirmation of Pablo's demand for non-extradition. The reversal on extradition had come about at a time when President George HW Bush was mustering support for the invasion of Iraq. Colombia had used its seat on the United Nations Security Council to vote against the attack. Bush had wanted the Colombian government to reverse its position. Dozens of traffickers had been extradited to America, which was still providing arms and soldiers to Colombia. In a quid pro quo fashion, the Colombian president had voted to attack Iraq, while reversing its policy on extradition.

After 3 PM, Victoria, Hermilda and Aunt Ines set off for the Cathedral, while listening eagerly to radio stations for any news. Approaching the prison, they prayed that everything would go smoothly.

Monkey directed the helicopter pilot to a soccer pitch by tropical flower gardens. "Put it down over there. Don't turn off the engine."

As it descended, 100 armed bodyguards arranged by Roberto formed a circle to protect Pablo, who helped the priest get off the helicopter. Wearing tennis shoes, faded blue jeans, a blue checked shirt and a light-blue jacket, the bearded boss with long hair walked with a carefree stride. Overweight and tanned, he said goodbye to and hugged the nearest bodyguards, some of whom were crying. He told Otto and Mugre to come with him.

Pablo spotted a government cameraman recording him. "Turn off your equipment!" Fifty nervous guards in blue uniforms were brandishing guns. He responded like thunder: "Lower your weapons, damn it!" They were lowered before their commander issued the same order. They walked to a house containing the official delegation, more of Pablo's men who had surrendered and his wife and mother, who was sobbing. "Take it easy, Ma," he said, patting Hermilda on the shoulder. He guaranteed Victoria that her suffering was over. He said that he lived for her and the kids, all of whom deserved to live peacefully. She gazed at him with hope that he had left his past behind.

"Nothing wrong is going to happen to Pablo," Alberto said. "Don't worry. I give you my word."

"Thank you," Pablo said.

The prison director shook Pablo's hand. "Señor Escobar. I'm Lewis Jorge Pataquiva."

Pablo pulled up a trouser leg, revealing a SIG Sauer 9 mm pistol with a gold monogram inlaid on a mother of pearl handle. The spellbound crowd watched him remove each bullet and throw the gun to the ground. The gesture was designed to show confidence in the warden, whose appointment had worried him. "Will you sign the delivery certificate as a witness?" he asked Alberto. On a portable phone, he told his brother that he had surrendered, and then he acknowledged everyone. Addressing the journalists present, he said his surrender was an act of peace. "I decided to give myself up the moment I saw the National Constitutional Assembly working for the strengthening of human rights and Colombian democracy."

The journalists wrote about Pablo:

"I had thought that he was a petulant, proud, disciplined man, one of those who is always looking over his shoulder. But I was wrong. On the contrary, he is educated. He asks permission if he walks in front of a person and is agreeable when he greets someone."

"You can see that he is someone who worries about his appearance. Especially his shoes. They were impeccably clean."

"He walks as if he had no worry in the world. He is very jovial and he laughs a lot."

"He had a bit of a belly, which makes him look like a calm man."

"I'm here," said Carlos Arrieta, the attorney general, taking Pablo's hand, "Señor Escobar, to make certain your rights are respected."

Pablo thanked him. Having seen a TV show about Arrieta, Pablo had enjoyed the part which showed the attorney general playing with his daughter. Having been at war with the government since his daughter's birth, he had been unable to spend any proper time with her. "Do you know why I did this?"

"No. Why?" Arrieta asked.

"One day I want to play with Manuela just like you did with your Camila." The attorney general was impressed by his desire to be a good father.

Pablo took Alberto's arm. "Let's go. You and I have a lot to talk about." In an outside gallery, they both leaned against a railing. "I apologise for what I have done to you. Know that neither I nor any of my men will ever touch you or your family again. I apologise for the pain I've caused your family. Both sides have suffered much in this war."

The words surprised his bodyguards. "You are the only person to whom the boss has ever apologised," one said.

"Leave us alone to talk," Pablo told them.

"Why was Luis Carlos Galán killed?" Alberto asked.

"The fact is that everybody wanted to kill Dr Galán. I was present at the discussions when the attack was decided, but I had nothing to do with what happened. A lot of people were involved in that. I didn't even like the idea, because I knew what would happen if they killed him, but once the decision was made, I couldn't oppose it. Please tell Doña Gloria that for me," he said, referring to Galán's widow. Alberto later stated that Pablo had told him that a unanimous decision had been made to kill Galán by politicians, members of the Colombian Congress, paramilitary groups and the Cali Cartel.

"Why was an attempt made on my life?"

"A group of your associates in Congress had convinced me that you were uncontrollable and stubborn and had to be stopped somehow before you succeeded in having extradition approved. Besides, in that war we were fighting, just a rumour could get you killed. But now that I know you, thank God nothing happened to you."

"Who in Congress said those things about me?"

"No. I'm not going to give you names, but you know who they were."

"Why did you kidnap my wife and sister?"

"I was kidnapping people to get something and I didn't get it. Nobody was talking to me. Nobody was paying attention, so I went after Doña Maruja to see if that would work." He said that the negotiations had convinced him that Alberto was a brave man of his word, and he was eternally grateful for that. Even though he was not expecting them to ever be friends, he assured Alberto that nothing bad would ever happen to his family. "Who knows how long I'll be here, but I still have a lot of friends, so if any of you feels unsafe, if anybody tries to give you a hard time, you let me know and that'll be the end of it. You met your obligations to me, and I thank you and will do the same for you. You have my word of honour." He asked Alberto if he would give further reassurances to his mother and wife, who were having sleepless nights as they suspected the government had arranged for him to be murdered in prison.

After leaving the Cathedral, Alberto went to Itagüí prison to thank the Ochoas. Some of Pablo's men took him on a tour of the city. Fascinated by how they lived and their belief systems, he stayed out drinking with them until 7 AM. For an entire day, he slept at the Ochoas' La Loma property, before returning to Bogotá.

Forty-one-year-old Pablo underwent the medical examination required for new prisoners. Courteously, he answered questions asked by Marta Luz Hurtado, the Director of Criminal Instruction of Medellín. After his fingerprints had been taken, she asked, "Did you have surgery on your fingers?" Displaying his hands, he laughed. The actor from *The Godfather*, Gianni Russo, has described in his book and interviews witnessing Pablo burning his fingertips. His health was documented as that of "a young man in normal physical and mental condition." He said that the scar on his nose was due to an injury from playing football as a child. The only abnormality found was congestion in the nasal mucous membranes.

To obtain imprisonment, he cited a crime that he had been found guilty of by the French authorities: acting as a middleman in a drug transaction arranged by his cousin, Gustavo. He issued a statement: "That country's penal code … gives one the right to apply for a revision of their case, when they appear before their national judge, in this case a Colombian judge. This is precisely the objective of my voluntary presentation to this office, in other words, to have a Colombian judge examine my case." Rather than plead guilty to a crime, he had surrendered to appeal the French conviction.

In court in Bogotá, he declared his job title as "livestock farmer," and added, "I have no addictions, don't smoke, don't drink." He said he had done an accounting course and, while incarcerated, he was going to obtain a college degree. "I wish to clarify that there may be people who might try to send anonymous letters, make phone calls or commit actions in bad faith under my name in order to harm me. There have been many accusations, but I've never been convicted of a crime in Colombia."

"Do you know where they got the 400 kilos of cocaine?" the judge asked, referring to his conviction in France.

"I think Mr Gustavo Gaviria was in charge of that."

"Who is Mr Gustavo Gaviria?"

"Mr Gustavo Gaviria was a cousin of mine."

"Do you know how Mr Gaviria died?"

"Mr Gaviria was murdered by members of the National Police during one of the raid-executions, which have been publicly denounced on many occasions."

"Let's talk about your personal and family's modus vivendi, and the economic conditions you've had throughout your life."

"Well, my family is from the north-central part of Colombia, my mother is a teacher at a rural school and my father is a farmer. They made a great effort to give me the education I received, and my current situation is perfectly defined and clear before the national tax office ... I have always liked to work independently and, since my adolescence, I have worked to help sustain my family. Even when I was studying, I worked at a bicycle rental shop and other less important jobs to support my studies ... Later, I got into the business of buying and selling cars, livestock and land investments. I want to cite Hacienda Nápoles as an example of this – that it was bought in conjunction with another partner at a time when these lands were in the middle of the jungle. Now they are practically ready to be colonised. When I bought land in that region, there were no means of communication or transport, and we had to endure a twenty-three-hour journey. I say this in order to clarify the image that people have that it's all been easy …" Asked if he had originally started in business with other people, he said, "No. It all began from scratch, as many fortunes have started in Colombia and in the world."

"Tell the court what disciplinary or penal precedents appear on your record."

"Yes, there have been many accusations, but I've never been convicted of a crime in Colombia. The accusations of theft, homicide, drug-trafficking and many others were made by General Miguel Maza, according to whom every crime that is committed in this country is my fault."

After he denied any involvement in the cocaine business, the judge insisted that he must know something about it. "Only what I see or read in the media. What I've seen and heard in the media is that cocaine costs a lot of money and is consumed by the high social classes in the United States and other countries of the world. I have seen that many political leaders and governments around the world have been accused of narco-trafficking, like the current Vice President of the United States [Dan Quayle], who has been accused of buying and selling cocaine and cannabis. I have also seen the declarations of one of Mr Reagan's daughters, in which she admits to taking cannabis, and I've heard the accusations against the Kennedy family, and also accusations of heroin dealing against the Shah of Iran, as well as the Spanish president. Felipe González publicly admitted that he took cannabis. My conclusion is that there is universal hypocrisy towards drug-trafficking and narcotics, and what worries me is that from what I see in the media, all the evil involved in drug addiction is blamed on cocaine and Colombians, when the truth is that the most dangerous drugs are produced in labs in the United States, like crack. I've never heard of a Colombian being detained for possession of crack because it's produced in North America." He had a point: the journalist Gary Webb discovered that the CIA had facilitated the importation of tons of cocaine into America, some of which had contributed to the crack epidemic. George HW Bush and other senior politicians had been deeply involved in covert drug activity while using Pablo's operation as a smoke-screen (explored in my books *American Made* and *Clinton Bush and CIA Conspiracies*).

"What is your opinion, bearing in mind your last few answers, on narco-trafficking?"

"My opinion, based on what I've read, I would say that cocaine [will continue] invading the world … so long as the high classes continue to consume the drug. I would also like to say that the coca leaf has existed in our country for centuries and it's part of our aboriginal cultures …"

"How do you explain that you, Pablo Escobar, are pointed out as the boss of the Medellín Cartel?"

Avoiding the question, he referred the judge to a statement he had submitted on videotape. "Another explanation I can give is this: General Maza is my personal enemy … [He] proclaimed himself my personal enemy in an interview given to *The Time* on the eighth of September, 1991. It is clear then that he suffers a military frustration for not capturing me. The fact that he carried out many operations in order to capture me, and they all failed, making him look bad, has made him say he hates me and I am his personal enemy …"

The court heard a list of traffickers who had claimed that Pablo was their boss. "I don't know any of these people," he said. "But through the press, I know about Mr Max Mermelstein. I deduce that he is a lying witness, which the US government has against me. Everyone in Colombia knows that North American criminals negotiate their sentences in exchange for testifying against Colombians … I would like to add to the file a copy of *Semana* magazine, which has an article about Max Mermelstein, to demonstrate what a liar this man is: 'Escobar was the chief of chiefs. The boss of cocaine trafficking wore blue jeans and a soccer shirt, was tall and thin.'" Pablo stood to display his short, stout body. "I ask you to tell me, am I a tall and thin person? For a gringo to say that one is tall, you would suppose that man to be very tall."

From all over the world, hundreds of journalists requested direct interviews, which Pablo refused, while allowing a few to post him questions. *The Colombian* published his first prison photo, which showed him with a white poncho and a long beard, but hid the almost fifty pounds weight gain from over two years. He wrote a public statement for the media, which he recorded on tape: "After seven years of persecution, abuses and struggles, I wish to serve all the years of jail necessary to contribute to the peace of my family, to the peace of Colombia, to the strengthening of respect for human rights, to the strengthening of civil power and the strengthening of democracy in my beloved Colombian homeland."

The attitude of the police was expressed by Colonel Naranjo: "When Escobar imposed conditions and surrendered, the police did not feel totally mocked. Some people believe that the police did not receive that surrendering well. But we understood that if he turned himself in, it was the same as having captured him and, in any case, the institution was not able to contain terrorism anymore. The police rested when he surrendered. In general, that first phase was irrational. People believed that only the police – and not the whole of society and institutions – was responsible for combating Escobar."

CHAPTER 10
PRISON LIFE

With some of the millions he had smuggled into prison, it wasn't long before El Patrón started to modify his surroundings. Cash was stored in milk cans inside containers of salt, sugar, rice, beans and fresh fish, which were classified as food rations and permitted. Extra money was buried near the soccer field and in underground tunnels accessible by trapdoors in the cells. When his men needed paying, helicopters transported cash out.

With officials from the Ministry of Justice and the National Bureau of Prisons frequently visiting, Pablo lobbied them for a doctor, a social worker and areas to work. He wanted to study law or journalism, but universities kept rejecting his application.

With his own surveillance system, he monitored the four sides of the prison and installed checkpoints on the access road. With the approval of the prison director, Homero Rodríguez, a.k.a. Rambo, an Israeli military specialist, he converted the prison into a club.

The centre of the prison became a game room with two pool tables, fitness equipment, a roulette table, games such as chess and parquet, and several motorbikes. The cabins had double beds, bookshelves, lavish bathrooms, stereos, refrigerators, TVs and VCRs. He added a bar, lounge and disco, where he hosted parties and weddings. Famous people, models, politicians and soccer players danced and cavorted. He installed a sauna in the gym, and jacuzzis and hot tubs in the bathrooms.

A sliding door replaced his cell's bars. Two adjacent cells produced an office. The only people allowed into his quarters without pre-authorisation were his family and his delivery driver Limón, who had worked for Roberto for twenty years, and was an official employee of the municipality of Envigado. Those waiting to see him remained outside of his office. When not receiving visitors, he spent hours handwriting responses to letters, using a cheap pen and with a dictionary on hand. A journalist in Medellín received a letter of safe passage to be presented to anyone threatening him. A communications student with an illustrious surname who wanted to write a biography about Pablo was instructed to postpone the book idea and establish a friendship. To a TV presenter who detailed her emotions, he described how excited he became upon receiving drawings from his daughter, about the long trips that Manuela had taken to visit him. He admitted writing poetry and requested some books by Tolstoy. The hundreds of letters he wrote had his signature, fingerprint and a request for forgiveness for any spelling mistakes. They were posted in traditional envelopes with red and blue stripes.

Years later, one of the freed hostages, Pacho Santos, commented on Pablo's writing ability: "As an editor, I would not have changed a comma in his letters and communications. He wrote in a simple, direct, perfectly coherent language and did not say another word than what he had to say."

An area in his living room included a bar, fridge, small table, kitchenette and valuable paintings. His paperweights were little soldiers, a gift from a guard's wife, and a rumour circulated that the soldiers represented people he wanted to kill. His bedroom included a double bed below a gold-framed portrait of the Virgin Mary, a library, a fireplace, a closet that looked out onto a cove (which stored weapons) and a bathroom with a tub. In a corridor, on one side of the cell, was the control panel for the lights, the foghorn and the electricity of the outer fence. At the front was a terrace with a view of Medellín – and a few metres away was Manuela's dollhouse. One of the biggest benefits was the time he could spend with his family.

Large items such as computers and big-screen TVs – on which they watched *God's Minute* – were smuggled in by Limón's truck, with crates of soda disguising the contraband. Limón brought women in, too. Despite rules restricting visits to official days, people were always sneaking in, as the checkpoint guards had been bribed. Vans with fake walls held up to twenty people. It was ideal for those who wanted to keep their visits a secret, such as criminals and politicians. Allocated a $500,000 a month budget, Popeye paid the guards at the six checkpoints. Coloured pieces of paper convertible into cash at a bank in Envigado were used for bribery at the rate of approximately $100,000 monthly. As well as cash, the guards received gifts, including refrigerators and TVs, which Limón shopped for.

Pablo's extensive record collection was there, including albums signed by Frank Sinatra from when he had visited him in Las Vegas, and Elvis records purchased during a Graceland trip. His books ranged from bibles to Nobel Prize winners. He had novels by Gabriel García Márquez and Stefan Zweig, a prominent Austrian writer from the 1920s. His movies on videotape included *The Godfather* trilogy and films starring Chuck Norris. He also loved the series *The Untouchables*, which he watched three times.

Most of the prisoners had posters on their walls, whereas Pablo hung valuable paintings. His closet was full of neatly pressed jeans, shirts and Nike sneakers, some with spikes on in case he had to flee. He never tied the laces of his sneakers – it was said that if he did, then an emergency was imminent. In case of danger from above the prison, a remote control allowed him to turn off all the internal lights. Communications were a priority. He had cellphones, radio transmitters, a fax machine and beepers. Roberto has denied claims by authors that Pablo used carrier pigeons. Further up the slope, cabins were built for privacy with females and as hideouts in case the prison was attacked. They were painted brightly and had sound systems and fancy lamps. Paths were made into the forest to allow a quick getaway and to enable the prisoners to enjoy fresh air.

Women with high heels, silicone enhancements and their hair dyed blonde were smuggled into the Cathedral for sex, with Pablo preferring teenagers. He would order his men to find the most beautiful girls from the colleges of Medellín. Working for Pablo, a madam who helped to coordinate beauty pageants provided him with catalogues of girls, naked and clothed, and if he saw somebody attractive on TV, she would send the person an invitation to the Cathedral with the enticement that they would earn a car or something valuable.

She would tell Pablo, "I have this girl who will have sex for this amount." The girls earned up to three million pesos for each visit, and those who performed well were invited back. For each girl provided, the madam earned one million pesos. TV models and divas received up to twelve million pesos per visit. Money made inaccessible women available to men from poor backgrounds, who delighted in soiling the privileged and beautiful. During the police raid of the Cathedral, sex toys and blow-up dolls were photographed. Popeye claimed that the sex toys had been used by girls performing lesbian shows and the orgies were compensation for a workforce who needed to destress.

As the location included a direct sightline to his family's home, he mounted a telescope so he could see his wife and children while talking to them on the phone. His daughter's playhouse was filled with toys. He said that his main motivation to come to an agreement was to restore his family life.

His mother was the first to attend the regular Sunday family visits. She arrived with the family's favourite food, including tamales, and religious images for the chapel. At noon, Father Garcia arrived. Delighted with the chapel, he heard confessions from Pablo, Roberto and some of Pablo's men. All the prisoners and their families attended the mass hosted by the priest. Pablo made a large donation for his social projects.

The visits exposed Pablo's drug habit to his sister. While tidying up the library in his room, Luz Maria discovered cannabis. After she asked what it was, Popeye constantly joked that the boss's sister didn't know what weed was. For Christmas, Pablo's wife brought lobster and caviar, and his mother contributed fritters and custard sweets. To satisfy them both, he put the caviar inside of the fritter and ate it. Popeye pointed out that Pablo's solution would be good material for a book he hoped to write. The boss responded that dead people don't write books.

The soccer field was renovated, night lights installed and wires positioned above it to sabotage helicopter landings. Despite having a bad knee, Pablo played centre forward. His men made tactful allowances such as passing him the ball to score winning goals. The professional teams who came to play were careful never to win. He had a replacement on standby in case he grew tired. When he regained his energy after resting, he would resume. The guards served the players refreshments. Sometimes his lawyers had to wait hours to see him if he was on the field.

The introduction of two chefs known as the Stomach Brothers addressed his concerns about getting poisoned. They prepared his favourites, including beans, pork, eggs and rice. He had installed exercise equipment such as weights and bikes for the prisoners to get in shape, but as they were no longer on the run and had access to endless food and alcohol, they started to gain weight. The Cathedral became known as "Club Medellín" or "Hotel Escobar." *Hustler* magazine published an illustration of Pablo and his associates partying in prison, throwing darts at a picture of President George HW Bush. Pablo obtained the illustration and hung it on his wall.

As if it were a religious kingdom, the Cathedral was full of Catholic images and symbols in which Pablo acted as a feudal overlord. His drive for family, hierarchy and lavish rituals contrasted with the debauchery of his underlings. Surrounded by yes-men, he began to believe that he was the future of Colombia.

With the government protecting him instead of hunting him down, his cocaine business thrived. Father Garcia tried to broker peace with the Cali Cartel. He arranged for Pablo to speak to its leaders, who were offering a peace agreement plus $3 million to end the war. Some of his men urged him to accept the deal, but others opposed it. "No, boss, you are already safe, and you can bend them from here," Big Gun said. Those in support of total war knew that Pablo's money would flow faster to them because they would perform more hits. He was the chief of a clan of warriors who died with detachment, a course that would eventually swallow him. As if he were defending his pride, he demanded $5 million from Cali. No progress was made because they were all too stubborn.

"I don't believe a word of those two," Pablo told Roberto, referring to the brothers Gilberto and Miguel.

News of Pablo's resumption of criminal activity and affairs with women devastated Victoria, who withdrew from him and decided that her role as a mother was only to maintain the relationship between Pablo and their children. To her, it was incomprehensible that he would violate his promise for those he had claimed were the most precious to him. The increasingly chaotic atmosphere at the prison made his family uneasy. Hermilda warned that if he kept having so many visitors, he would not last there another year. After he insisted that nothing bad would happen, she called him hard-headed.

To address legal problems, he had thirty lawyers working almost full-time. He was facing an indictment for being the intellectual author of the murder of the presidential candidate, Galán. During a raid of one of his properties, paperwork was found linking him to the assassination of the journalist, Guillermo Cano. On September 25, 1991, one of his men, La Quica, was using a payphone in New York when he was arrested for traveling with a fake passport. La Quica and two others offered no resistance to the police. Although he gave the fake name Esteban Restrepo-Echavarria, his fingerprints matched records provided by Colombia. Believed to be in the country as part of a hit on Max Mermelstein, a witness in the Barry Seal murder case, La Quica was held without bail and accused of being a player in the bombing of Avianca Flight 203. Eventually, charged with "conspiracy to import and distribute cocaine, substantive importation of cocaine, participating and conspiring to participate in a racketeering enterprise, engaging in a continuing criminal enterprise, various offenses relating to the bombing of a civilian airliner and the extraterritorial murder of two citizens of the United States," he would receive ten life sentences plus forty-five years, all to be served consecutively.

When he wasn't meeting his lawyers, Pablo was usually on the telephone or reading. He tried to learn Mandarin. He received endless letters from people asking for help, business advice and money. If their stories checked out, he often sent cash to them. People gathered at the prison gate with notes, seeking his assistance. At nights, he sat in a rocking chair and watched the lights come on in Envigado, while thinking about his family.

Near the end of September, Gaviria summoned Alberto to the Palace of Nariño. He arrived with his wife Maruja and his sister Gloria Pachón. "Escobar confessed his participation in the export of cocaine to France," the president said. "It's an offense that has already been condemned by a Paris court, and we're going to need to release him within a few months because there is no way to condemn him for other crimes. There is no evidence. The only person who can convince him to confess to a crime of such importance is you."

Realising that the president needed to give Pablo a bigger sentence to improve his standing in the international community, Alberto went to the Cathedral. "If you do not stay in jail for at least ten years, this cannot stand. If you get out, everything will ignite because neither the United States nor Colombia can stand for you to be freed quickly."

"For how many presidential terms do you think I'll have to stay?"

"At least three. Gaviria, the next and another, at least ten years."

Silently, Pablo contemplated. "With you leaving as an ambassador for the Netherlands, who will liaise with Gaviria for me?"

"I'll find someone in the government to fill that role."

Days later, Pablo's legal team arrived at the Cathedral. At noon, he rose and dressed in jeans, a short-sleeved shirt and a sapphire-coloured watch. In the early afternoon over breakfast, he considered what to say about his sentence. During the meeting, a lawyer offered him an ostentatious gold bracelet. Studying it, Pablo calmly said, "First of all, I have nothing to buy it with, but also, if I buy it from you, they will all say that I am a Mafioso." Everyone laughed.

After complaining about his unfair treatment, the lawyers measured their words because they were aware of Pablo's knowledge of the laws, the codes of procedure and the jurisprudence of the Supreme Court of Justice. The meeting ended with him accepting that he would serve a minimum of ten years, after which he would live a normal life with his family and enjoy his wealth.

After dismissing the lawyers, he received the ELN guerrilla Lucho, who had been smuggled into the Cathedral in the double bottom of a small truck. Lucho found Pablo with cardboard boxes full of cash. "You see, the commander of this military base changes every month, and when the new one arrives, I'll buy him for thirty million pesos." Holding up a photo album with a tree diagram of his hit men, Pablo said, "This was a gift from an army officer. It's the album that the military was using to decide who to allow in and out of the Cathedral."

A feast prepared by the Stomach Brothers arrived: beans, rice, chorizo, egg, ground beef, salad, ripe plantains and black pudding. In-between devouring food, Pablo talked: "Look, Lucho, man, you are well placed. The most loyal people are the people of the communes. On the other hand, the most corrupt class in Colombia are the politicians, and there they have the power to protect themselves and their interests." The two agreed that it was necessary that their men in the neighbourhoods kept the peace. "I have twenty Uzi sub-machine guns for you."

After Lucho left, Pablo was informed that some men acting suspiciously outside of the Cathedral had been detained. "Bring them in for questioning." During a speedy kangaroo court, Pablo determined that they were spying for Cali and sentenced them to death. After they had been executed, he sent one of his US-trained pilots to bomb Cali Godfather Miguel at his house in the Ciudad Jardín neighbourhood, but the helicopter crashed outside of Cali.

He sent Tyson to kill Cali Godfather Pacho: "I hope he dies with his soccer shoes on." Fifteen men stormed the Villa Legua estate near Cali and killed twenty-two people, but Pacho was absent. Pacho would eventually die with his soccer shoes on, but five years after Pablo's death.

On the day of the Feast of the Virgin of Mercy, the patron saint of the traffickers, Pablo rose at 1 PM and read newspapers. He was told that a woman called Claudia was waiting, but he couldn't see her yet, because he had scheduled a soccer game: the traffickers versus members of Atletico Nacional and Deportivo Independiente Medellín. Despite the rain, he dressed in the German national team's colours, with a number nine on his back, and tied the laces of his black and white Nikes. On the pitch, he greeted some World Cup players, including the goalkeeper René Higuita, a.k.a. El Loco (The Madman), whom he admired for his flamboyant style and behaviour. While goalkeeping, he had developed a unique scorpion kick, which wowed the world at Wembley Stadium, England, two years after Pablo's death.

Despite his weight and a bad knee, Pablo regularly played soccer for hours. The visiting team scored three goals in fifty minutes, but after an hour and a half it was drawn. The visitors scored two more goals, but the traffickers pulled back by the end. From outside of the penalty area, Pablo scored the equalising goal, so that the game finished 5-5. Years later, when the goalkeeper was asked whether he had dived the wrong way on purpose to allow the ball into the net, he responded with a smile and said that Pablo had scored the goal and what more could he say.

After the game and spending an hour in the bathroom, Pablo emerged wearing a wool poncho given to him by Father Garcia. He stopped in a corridor to play with a bird that had landed on his shoulder. At 4 PM, Claudia spotted him with the indigo bunting. She had come to ask Pablo – the godfather of her marriage – to intervene on her behalf. She wanted to leave her trafficker husband without getting killed for doing so. So that he could hear her story, they sat.

"You know I married at 15 years old. I lived a horrible life. I never spent eight days in my house. It was from here to there, fearing we would get detained, accompanied day and night by an entourage of bodyguards. It was a year and a half that felt like fifteen years. Every day, I lived so many things that it seemed forever. Every day, I saw a gang of men coming over, one day with their wives and the next day with their lovers. They had weapons coming and going. The phone rang constantly. The TV could not be turned on because the ads about rewards appeared. No, no, I was like, uh, impregnated with it all. That hectic life, that bustle. How tired I became! Like a skeleton.

"I became pregnant. I had an abortion because I felt it was the right step after an argument, but for him there were no reasons. The idea of divorce made him angry, and he went from threats to actual attacks. One night, they broke into my mother's house, then I decided to go to Cali and there I suffered another attack."

Although he had listened attentively, Pablo was reluctant to go against his men in family matters. "And so? What am I supposed to do? Do you want to stay here and live with me?"

"It would be foolish for me to come here to act as a maid."

"So, what can I do? Why are you so upset?"

"If I leave this place, I will die like a chicken in a corner."

"What chicken? Stop talking like that! Don't you think you should go back to him?"

"No. I'm not crazy."

As one of Pablo's men had vouched for Claudia's plight, he took pity on her. "You have faced things very well. You have the ability to get out, and there are very few people who have that ability. I'm going to help you." El Patrón sent her husband his reasons for helping her, and her life was spared.

Years later, after Pablo's death, Claudia said, "Pablo was only bad because he thought he was God. He once said, 'I dispense justice myself, period.' But there was a balance in how he was not entirely good or bad. The bad guys liked him because he was bad and the good ones because he was good. Everyone liked him. I liked him because of the sense of justice he had."

On December 1, 1991, he celebrated his forty-second birthday with a party in the Cathedral, where his guests ate stuffed turkey, caviar, pink salmon, smoked trout and Russian salad while live music played. His gifts included a red jacket bought by Victoria in Spain and a Russian fur hat from his mother. Photographed wearing it, he declared it would be a symbol of his identity "like Che Guevara's beret." At night, the kids watched the inmates release coloured balloons.

In early 1992, the attorney general's office published photos taken at Hotel Escobar, including of waterbeds, jacuzzis, big-screen TVs ... The embarrassed president commissioned an investigation, but the justice minister found that the furnishings were legal because each prisoner was allowed a bed and a bathtub, and TVs were permitted for good behaviour.

"I want all of these things taken out immediately!" the president said. "Tell the army to go in there and take everything. Escobar has to know we're not kidding."

No government department wanted the job. "No way," the minister of defence said. "I cannot do it because I don't have the people." When it was pointed out that he had 120,000 troops, he still refused. Due to the deal struck with Pablo, the police couldn't do it. The DAS said that they couldn't act because they were only allowed inside the prison in the event of a riot.

In the end, a lawyer was told to take a truck and some workers, and to go to the prison and get the goods. "What have I ever done to you?" the lawyer responded. "Why'd you give me this assignment?" Banking on the truck not being allowed to enter the prison, so he could turn around and go home, the lawyer set off. When he arrived, the prison gate opened and Pablo waved them in.

Upon being told why they were there, Pablo said, "Certainly. I didn't know these things bothered you. Please, take everything out." He and his men helped them carry the goods until everything was gone. The lawyer rushed to his boss with photos of the bare prison. While the president was examining the photos, the goods were heading back to the Cathedral.

When the government tried to build a maximum-security prison based on the American model to transfer Pablo to, no construction company would accept the job. One said, "We're not going to build a cage with the lion already inside." Finally, a company owned by an Israeli security expert attempted to do it, with supposedly incorruptible workers from afar. Watching the work crew, Pablo's men wrote down their licence-plate numbers, and eventually attacked them, causing many to quit. The project was abandoned.

While in the Cathedral, Pablo wanted to preserve his legend in literature and the media. An illustrator from Medellín, Guezú, had a cartoon published in *The Time* called The Epistle of Pablo, showing him heaven-bound with wings and a saintly aura, with his characteristic lock of hair, and with Father Garcia blessing him. Pablo commissioned Guezú to make a book containing the cartoons and caricatures of him published since 1982, the year he made a splash in politics. While talking, Guezú noticed that on the walls of Pablo's room hung his wanted posters.

Travelling Colombia, Guezú gathered pictures, which were brought to the Cathedral. Lying on the bed, barefoot, Pablo examined the cartoons one by one and even accepted some lampooning him. In *Hustler* magazine, he is in a prison called the Medellín Club, holding a joint with three half-naked women and firing a gun at President George HW Bush on TV. Its caption says, "Pablo, leave something for us." He admired a cartoon by Velezefe published in *The Colombian* in 1984, which shows a raid on his estate, and one of his giraffes with its neck in a cloud, and on its head above the cloud is Pablo. In July 1991, *Semana* published a drawing of him on its cover, which he asked to be replicated.

Obsessed with archiving everything about him, he had his private secretary maintain a room full of articles and books. In a video, he narrated the history of his social projects, which she claimed had been obstructed by people like Lara Bonilla, Guillermo Cano and Galán. Besotted by the idea of his own greatness, he studied the republican history of Colombia in the nineteenth century. He saw himself as a chieftain and believed that he was similar to the early guerrillas.

The publication of the book was taking too long, so he asked Guezú to accelerate things. When it was done, one of his assistants went for the book, only to have it confiscated by DAS agents, whom Pablo had to bribe to retrieve it. Finally, he ordered the publication of 500 copies of *Pablo Escobar Gaviria en Caricaturas 1983–1991*. He chose a leather binding, added his signature and thumbprint to the cover, and included some text criticising the War on Drugs. His family and friends received them as gifts with personal messages. He intended to write an autobiography that would clarify his role in the biggest crimes he was blamed for, including the assassination of Galán.

Some of what he wrote ended up in the hands of the authorities:

"The sale of cigarettes, aguardiente, weapons, votes, public sector jobs, patronage, import licences, grants, joints of cannabis or a dose of cocaine, is something totally and completely obscene."

"Neither divorce nor prostitution are bad in themselves. They are simply rather undesirable solutions, but necessary to avoid greater problems. Personally, I could not care less, because I do not have a problem with them."

"All those stimulants and antidepressants, all those synthetic drugs from the big legal laboratories abroad – legal they say, because they believe that they solve everything – they are more dangerous and more deadly and more addictive than cocaine. But they don't say that, because they are produced by them. The problem is that, speaking in monetary terms, cocaine left them behind and it is the first time in history that they haven't had the guts or the imagination or the power that we have."

He told *Semana*, "Legalisation is the solution to finish with the drug traffickers. Education is [necessary] to finish with drugs."

The elite police sent the government reports warning about his activity: "In the Cathedral, people enter without authorisation, and from there, Escobar has reorganised the drug trafficking network, kidnapping and attacks are ordered, and it is even insistently rumoured that Pablo leaves his cell to go to the city." The government paid no attention. With the nation fixated on economic turmoil and power outages, El Patrón in jail was the president's only trophy.

Years later, the former hostage, Francisco Santos, said, "The great mistake of the Gaviria government was forgetting who that gentleman was, not appreciating who it had in jail, not realising that Escobar was the most villainous of the bandits, and that he was always going to be like that. Pablo was a criminal by heart. He could not do anything different from what he did, and it was inevitable that the situation would end up like it did. Crime was his reason for being, it was a natural thing, his genetic essence, or I do not know … but that was what took him to the grave. It is just that not only was he a great bandit – which is a very nice term – but also a murderer and a shameless person who could steal candy from a child. That is what it means to be a bandit: being able to do the smallest thing and jump to the biggest thing without any problem."

CHAPTER 11
BOMBING THE CATHEDRAL

The Cathedral provided the Cali Cartel with a direct target to strike, so the godfathers decided to bring back the mercenaries. Their leader, David Tomkins, was in England. After the Galán assassination on August 18, 1989, the authorities went from house to house hunting down anyone associated with the traffickers. Tomkins and McAleese had been in an apartment outside Cali, which had housed Gilberto and Miguel's mother. With a raid imminent, they moved by jeep around security checkpoints to another apartment.

Worldwide media had published the story of the failed raid on Hacienda Nápoles, putting their lives in danger, so they had fled to Panama. Disturbed by the developments, the entire team of mercenaries wanted to complete the mission but couldn't return to Colombia. Two team members who had dropped out of the mission made the mistake of doing media interviews. One appeared on CNN. In a UK interview, a team member's face and voice were disguised, but when the interview was shown overseas, his disguises were lifted. He ended up shot in both knees and in a wheelchair. Due to the government's crackdown and the media leaks, the godfathers postponed the operation. In September 1989, the team ate a farewell meal with Cali's head of security, Jorge Salcedo, at a restaurant in Panama, and then flew home.

On September 13, 1989, the US government went public about a witness who had defected from the Medellín Cartel. It was a doctor whom Tomkins had trained during a previous mission financed by the Medellín Cartel. On a screen, Tomkins' picture was identified by the doctor, who said that Tomkins was an explosives instructor and the leader of the foreign mercenaries. He blamed Tomkins, the mercenaries and their training programmes for the surge in violence in Colombia.

Two US Senate investigators showed up at Tomkins' house in England, insisting that he and McAleese testify in Washington. After refusing, he notified Jorge. The next year, they asked Tomkins to testify again at a hearing about arms trafficking, mercenaries and drug cartels. The Cali Cartel didn't object, so on February 27, 1991, Tomkins testified about his missions in Colombia in 1988 and 1989, including the failed attempt to kill Pablo. At the hearing, Tomkins refused to name anyone involved.

In 1991, at the US Embassy in London, the DEA told Tomkins that the US government was offering millions for Pablo's assassination. They wanted him to get hired by Pablo, so that Tomkins could kill him. With the failed attempt to kill Pablo in the news, Tomkins replied that Pablo would certainly hire him only to torture and murder him. The DEA said they hadn't thought of that.

In July 1991, Tomkins met Jorge in Panama City. Tomkins learned that the prison consisted of concrete blocks, a roof of asbestos sheeting, dorm-style cells and Pablo's wing. The surrounding area was booby-trapped with anti-helicopter wires, which were only removed to allow permitted landings. Cyclone-wire netting under the roof prevented anyone getting in from above. The biggest threat though, Jorge told Tomkins, was the machine-gun posts.

As Pablo had built defences against the standard methods of assault, Tomkins was going to decline the mission. Then he considered bombing the Cathedral, using helicopters dropping drums of C-4. By remote-control detonating a couple of hundred kilos of C-4 at both sides of the building, the men inside would be cooked alive. After listening to the plan, Jorge offered his own. He knew a pilot keen to sell some 500-pound bombs.

Jorge flew to Guatemala to negotiate a price for four Mk-82 bombs from an El Salvadoran colonel who knew Cali's intentions.

He wanted $600,000. Jorge said it sounded expensive, but he would relay it to the godfathers. Before leaving, he asked whether $500,000 was acceptable.

In need of a small ground-attack bomber, Tomkins asked a former CIA contractor whom he had met before. He was put in touch with a seller and all three met in Miami. A deal was agreed, and Jorge arrived. The seller and his technician showed Jorge and Tomkins the plane. The lack of ID markings and the presence of a six-barrel machine gun in its nose made Tomkins and Jorge suspicious. Intending to do background checks, they filmed the seller and the technician.

Jorge left the country. Tomkins stalled the seller by paying a $25,000 deposit and arranging a meeting the next week to conclude the transaction. The seller offered Tomkins a range of military equipment, which he had not requested. The cartel established that the technician was a former DEA agent and that the seller had been compromised.

On Sunday, Tomkins fled to England. He contacted the seller and apologised for his sudden departure. Working with US Customs as part of Operation Dragonfly, the seller tried to entice Tomkins back to inspect another plane. The former CIA contractor who had brokered the deal was a confidential informant who received a percentage of the money or assets confiscated in sting operations.

While the bombing mission stalled for lack of a plane, Pablo was planning further attacks against Cali. A cousin of godfather Miguel's fourth wife revealed that a family member visiting from Medellín had asked too many questions about the godfathers, including the names of their children's schools, how they were transported to school and details of other properties that the fourth wife frequented. The godfathers sent a Cali police sergeant to arrest the inquisitive family member. The police brought the man to one of Pacho's ranches. He was escorted into a living room full of bodyguards. Sitting around with glasses of orange juice, the godfathers ceased their small talk to examine the new arrival, whose face glossed over with sweat.

In a hostile tone, Gilberto asked why the man had so many questions about their children. The captive acted clueless. Gilberto cited the questions about their children's schools. The captive claimed that he was just curious and apologised for being rude. Cutting him off, Gilberto accused him of working for Pablo. With a pained expression, the captive protested that he would never betray them. Softening his voice into a coaxing tone, Gilberto said he understood that the captive had no choice because he lived in Medellín, and Pablo had threatened him and his family. The captive fell back on his curiosity excuse.

Gilberto sprang up, demanded a fork and yelled that he was going to remove the captive's eyeballs as punishment for lying. The bodyguards grabbed the captive and dragged him to a dining room, where there was a large polished table. Everybody moved into there. Standing at the end of the table, Gilberto demanded that the captive be brought to him. The bodyguards shoved the captive forward. One handed the godfather a fork.

Sobbing, the captive broke down. He had done it because Pablo had threatened to kill his entire family, including his baby. He would rather die than hurt the godfathers and their families. After resting the fork on the table, Gilberto ushered everybody back into the living room. In the dining room, the captive revealed everything to the godfathers and Jorge. He had been to the Cathedral a few times, which is where Pablo had sanctioned the fact-finding mission. Not wanting the captive to die, Jorge asked Miguel to intervene, because the man had details about the interior of the Cathedral, which could help the bombing mission. Miguel instructed the captive to tell Jorge everything.

Although the information provided was helpful, Jorge wanted to get inside the Cathedral to get a feel for the place. The cartel bribed the authorities to allow Jorge onto a police helicopter that had been scheduled by Pablo to transport a judge and a court reporter to the prison.

On the morning of the flight, Jorge put on a disguise: a green jumpsuit with three stripes, indicating the rank of police captain; a big helmet with a radio microphone, sunglasses and well-polished boots. He asked the pilot to approach the Cathedral in a way that would provide the best view of the grounds. He noticed the absence of a section of perimeter fence behind the building, which the prisoners could easily escape through if attacked. Seeing the playhouse for Pablo's daughter and imagining the underground bunker, Jorge sensed that Pablo had prepared countermeasures for a raid.

Jorge believed that the bombing mission would end in disaster, but the godfathers were so gung-ho that he had to tread carefully. He alerted Miguel to the risks: dropping bombs on a mountain-side target was far more imprecise than on flat land. Bombing what was technically classified as government property would be classified as terrorism, which could result in a government crackdown on the cartel. Miguel told Jorge to get on with the damn job.

Using the media and legal documents filed with the attorney general, the cartel leaked information about Pablo's luxuries to cause public outrage. The prison director was fired, and the job offered to a childhood friend of Jorge, who urged him to decline the directorship, not just because he would have no real power, but also because of the threat of getting bombed. A code word was arranged, so Jorge could alert his friend when the bombing was imminent.

With the civil war in El Salvador ending, the bombs had to be purchased quickly, otherwise the transaction would become impossible. Jorge visited Miguel to get the cash. He found the godfather meticulously wrapping $500,000. Taking possession of a red and gold box, Jorge said that it was heavy. The godfather's frown silenced him.

Jorge put the box in a shopping bag and boarded a plane. In El Salvador, a sergeant who was an aide to the colonel selling the bombs got on board. After the passengers had left, Jorge gave the sergeant $500,000. The sergeant left with the money, took $20,000 and gave the rest to the colonel.

Jorge told the airport officials that he was in El Salvador on business-seeking opportunities in orange-juice exportation. He checked into a hotel, where his passport was photocopied. The following morning, he met Nelson, the local leader of Cali's interests in El Salvador. The massive man had arranged a crew to help the mission.

At an airbase, the sergeant who had received the money got in a forklift and moved four green bombs onto a small red truck, with straw disguising the bombs. Accessories such as detonators were moved separately. The sergeant drove out of the compound with the bombs.

The truck travelled two miles and stopped at a busy restaurant, where Jorge was waiting with Nelson shadowing him at another table. The sergeant entered, and while walking past Jorge, he placed a key on his table. Jorge moved the key to the side of the table and left the restaurant. Nelson stood. While walking past Jorge's table, he grabbed the key. Outside, he got in the truck and left.

On the way to his hotel, Jorge stopped at a payphone. He told Miguel that they had possession of the articles. Miguel sent a plane to a landing strip on the border of El Salvador and Guatemala. Jorge told the pilot assigned to pick up the bombs that it had to be done in less than ten minutes to give the El Salvadoran authorities no time to respond to the breach of their airspace. They took note of the radio frequencies that they would use to guide the landing.

Anticipating military roadblocks, Nelson and his crew painted the bombs yellow to match the colour of the trucks and the Caterpillar equipment often seen in the area. For extra camouflage, straw and four pigs were added. The mess made by the pigs would hopefully deter any thorough searches.

It was night when Jorge boarded a canoe on the Zapote River, which took him to Nelson's house. Although pleased to learn that the bombs had been transported without any setbacks, he was disheartened to discover that Nelson had broken a leg, making him useless for bomb loading. The pilot radioed Jorge that he was thirty minutes away. On a motorbike, he headed for the landing strip, followed by Nelson's men in the truck with the bombs. Jorge arrived at a dirt runway barely visible in the darkness.

The men hushed to listen for the plane. A call came on the radio that the plane was minutes away. A light from the plane on the runway exposed a variety of farm animals. On a motorbike, Jorge sped to the runway to scare them away to prevent them from damaging the plane and destroying the mission. As he revved the engine, pigs and chickens scattered.

The plane was much smaller than he had expected. Was it big enough to transport the bombs? It landed and the passenger door opened. To make space, the pilot threw out empty fuel cans. The plane was so small that the crates holding the bombs wouldn't go inside. The men extracted the bombs from the crates. It took twenty minutes to pack three bombs. Attracted by the commotion, local people started gathering.

The third bomb had been placed so precariously that it slipped. Not wanting to risk taking any more bombs, the co-pilot insisted that they take off. Extracting a fourth bomb from a crate, Jorge told them to wait, but the door was slammed shut. The pilot pledged to return the next day. Jorge handed the bomb accessories to the pilot, while warning him to be careful with them.

Jorge was left with a bomb, farm animals and local witnesses gazing at him, while empty fuel cans littered the runway with MADE IN COLOMBIA written on them. Fearful of getting caught, he told Nelson to sink the bomb in the river.

Detecting a small plane invading their airspace, Colombian air traffic control alerted the military. Two fighter planes were dispatched to intercept the plane with the three bombs. When the cartel pilot noticed the fighter planes homing in, he hid in the clouds over mountain peaks and radioed for assistance. The cartel dispatched a second small plane. While the fighter pilots forced the decoy to land, the plane with the bombs escaped.

Jorge called Miguel from a payphone. To ensure that the

landing strip had not been compromised, they decided to wait a few days before sending a plane for the fourth bomb. Feeling unsafe, Jorge flew to Panama and called El Salvador. Distressed, Nelson's sister said that everybody had been arrested because the authorities had discovered the fourth bomb. She asked him where he was. Assuming that her phone had been tapped, he said that he was in Costa Rica.

While he sought sanctuary in a friend's house in Panama, the international news reported the discovery of a 500-pound bomb intended to kill Pablo Escobar. The news in Panama and Colombia described Jorge as a Colombian Army reserve captain involved in the plot and revealed his real name. Instantly, he went from operating invisibly to landing on El Patrón's most wanted list. Not only Jorge, but also his family were now targets for Pablo and the authorities he controlled.

The bomb plot ended the party atmosphere at the Cathedral. The prisoners evacuated the main building and moved to wooden cabins hidden in the forest beyond the soccer field at the limits of the perimeter fence. Pablo hid in a cabin in a mountain cleft, where his location was disguised from above and from the forest. It was so cold due to a spring below that he moved to another well-concealed cabin. He instructed his men to watch the sky and to shoot down anything that violated their airspace. He ordered anti-aircraft artillery and he commissioned an architect to sketch anti-bombing designs. The architect drew a building with individual pods, with bombproof insulation consisting of concrete and steel. Camouflaged by earth, the building would be undetectable by spy planes or satellites. Preferring to be disguised by nature, Pablo rejected the plan.

A dozen servings of seafood stew arrived at the prison, which nobody could recall ordering. "Give a couple to the dogs, so that we can see if they are poisoned," Pablo said. After the dogs survived, the remaining food was served to the soldiers.

A week later, Hermilda arrived. "How did you enjoy the seafood stew?" Pablo thanked his mother for such delicious food.

Media attention had ruined the plot, so the godfathers hid the bombs in a storage facility and tried to keep a low profile. A US Embassy cable in March 1992 stated, "The Cali Cartel is very concerned about the capabilities of the US government to interfere with their operations. They appear to be paranoid." The cable added that they were living less luxuriously, including driving Colombian cars. With Pablo protected by the Cathedral, the godfathers drew up plans to kidnap his son.

Juan Pablo was due to enter a car race organised by the Antioquia Motorcycle League. After practising, he went to register at the event, where spectators admired his cars and asked questions. Two men appeared, who started watching him and his bodyguards. Sensing something was wrong, he told his bodyguards to approach the men. While they did, he sped off in a car. Driving away, he noticed an ambulance outside the event headquarters – the same ambulance he had seen earlier on the way to school in a remote area at 7 AM. To avoid it, he had made a U-turn, and now here it was again.

His father had warned that Cali was trying to kidnap him. They intended to hold him hostage, get millions from Pablo and murder him anyway. He had told his son that if either of his kids were attacked, it would constitute a violation of the old-school Mafia agreement of not going after each other's family members. Pablo knew the locations and routines of all the family members of the Cali godfathers, and up until now he had honoured the agreement. If Juan Pablo were kidnapped, he would go after the godfathers' family members.

Juan Pablo was keen to participate in the race, but Pablo sent him an urgent message to come to the Cathedral. In the prison, he found his father sitting at a table with paperwork and cassette tapes. His dad had good and bad news. Cali had intended to kidnap him at the race, but, as usual, Pablo was on top of the situation. He had identified the kidnappers and needed Juan Pablo to remain at the Cathedral until the plot was destroyed. The plot had two phases. The first involved soldiers, and the second, the police, who had joined forces with Cali. Once more intelligence had been gathered, Pablo would contact the kidnappers. In the meantime, Juan Pablo needed to get clothes for at least ten days.

Later, in a room with two bodyguards, Pablo had his son sit next to him on a bed. He picked up a phone and began calling the kidnappers, one by one. After addressing each by name and ID number, he said he knew they were going to kidnap his son at the race, assisted by the army. The plan was to attack and immobilise the bodyguards, and to drag Juan Pablo by the hair. He knew where every single one of their family members lived, including their mothers. If any harm came to his son, they and their families would have to answer to him. They had better go ahead and evacuate their own houses, because his men were under orders to act if their family members were spotted. They had attempted to mess with Pablo's family, so now all bets were off. They had twenty-four hours to leave Medellín. If they didn't, their homes would become military targets. They should be glad that their lives had been spared. Did they think that because they were with the police and the military, and that Pablo was in prison, that he was afraid of them? Juan Pablo stayed at the Cathedral for three weeks, while Pablo ensured that the kidnappers lost their jobs.

CHAPTER 12
SLAUGHTERING FRIENDS

With his cash flow damaged by the war, Pablo considered kidnapping the billionaire Julio Mario Santo Domingo, one of the wealthiest people in the world.

"That might be hard," Popeye said. "That man spends his time in New York, boss."

"That's no problem," Pablo said. "We pick him up, put him in a cocaine hideaway in Queens and make them send the money here to a town on the outskirts of Medellín." Although he had thought through every detail, Pablo was distracted by a dispute among his men outside of the prison.

A friend of Pablo and senior figure in the Medellín Cartel, Fernando Galeano, had paid Big Gun to assassinate Jorge Mico. Although Pablo had once got along with Mico, most people now despised him. Every year, he had won the competition of the Horsemen's Association by telling the director, "Either my horse wins or you die." After he brought a horse with testicular implants, the director refused his entry and was killed. After Mico attempted to extort money from the Galeanos, Big Gun arrived at his farm and requested to see his horses. While Mico approached a feeding lot, a bullet entered his skull, all done with Pablo's consent.

Big Gun's paranoia led him to kill several men in El Mugre's gang. "They are giving me away in the Brigade, boss," he told Pablo, who, fearing an internal war, started an investigation. From El Mugre, he learned that Big Gun's wife had been denouncing him, and Big Gun had not killed her because she was the mother of his children.

Pablo's one-year anniversary of incarceration happened on June 19, 1992. Some writers have claimed that he went to watch a soccer game at Envigado Fútbol Club, but that's untrue. "Of course he could leave," Popeye said years later. "Not only did he not leave, but he forbade everyone to do so: 'If you got caught in a checkpoint, then you would leave me hanging by the balls,' Pablo used to say."

Bomb plots from Cali were Pablo's main concern; secondly, he worried about the loyalty of the other bosses, including the Ochoas, Moncadas and Galeanos. He claimed that his imprisonment was a sacrifice for the good of them all – for had he not single-handedly got rid of extradition? Due to the benefits they were receiving, his associates were expected to compensate him by paying a monthly tax of $250,000. In prison, he was tuned into everything going on outside thanks to his extensive communications network. Those who tried to cheat him out of the tax or were perceived to have swindled him in any way were dealt with harshly.

Fernando Galeano and Kiko Moncada ran two of the biggest Medellín Cartel trafficking groups that Pablo taxed. They were smuggling cocaine into America via a route that Pablo had established through Mexico. In early 1992, Fernando had been told at the Cathedral: "The successful routes are owed to me."

Pablo's relationship with Kiko had begun with him building secret compartments in cars for El Patrón. Tall, thin Kiko was a workaholic who owned his own factory and stayed off the police's radar by spending his money wisely, instead of showing off with zoos and fancy houses and cars. Over time, Pablo had begun to value him as a sincere friend. While on the run, he had used cars and hideouts that Kiko had provided. At critical points for the Medellín Cartel, Kiko had always offered help without being asked. After learning that Pablo wanted to build a house on Choncho Hill, but did not have enough cash, Kiko had given him $3 million. When Pablo had engaged in war, Kiko had enthusiastically pledged $100 million, repayable anytime interest free.

The money had been available at his downtown office whenever needed.

In the Cathedral, Pablo gave Kiko an update on the war with Cali. Having used some of the money that had been offered by Kiko, he asked him what was outstanding. Kiko summoned his bookkeeper, who extracted paperwork from a briefcase. Pablo stopped the bookkeeper and said there was no need for such formal accounting. He just wanted to know the total, so that it could be repaid.

Kiko said it was $23.5 million. He had not expected it to be paid back so soon. In fact, he had $76 million more available. After thanking Kiko, Pablo said that he hoped he would not need it, and that he was looking forward to paying back the $23.5 million using the profits from a large cocaine shipment through Mexico. They laughed about cocaine solving all their problems.

Their relationship became strained over the increase in monthly payments to $500,000. Pablo said it was justified because of the millions being made by Kiko and his partners from using his routes and infrastructure. The Moncadas and the Galeanos wrote him a letter where they promised to pay but asked for more independence and autonomy. They were opposed to his decision to finance the war through kidnapping.

One month, only $75,000 arrived in a cardboard box with a note from Kiko claiming that they were short of cash. Pablo returned the money with a note that said he was not starving. The withdrawal of financial assistance was aggravated by Pablo being told that Kiko had begun to make alliances with Pablo's enemies, hoping to avoid their attacks.

After hosting a meeting with his associates, Kiko sent a note asking Pablo not to be mad at them. He pointed out that they had invested their cash into the reconstruction of Fany's Route, which would soon be ready and would solve all their problems. Pablo responded that he understood and that his partner should not worry.

On Fany's Route, cocaine travelled by ship to Mexico from

Buenaventura, a coastal seaport city in the department of Valle del Cauca, Colombia. From Mexico, it was smuggled into America, often by speedboat to California. Facilitating approximately 10,000 kilos a month, Fany's route was generating a quarter billion dollars a year, from which Pablo expected his monthly $500,000.

Under interrogation by Pablo's men, a worker for the Moncadas revealed that a meeting had taken place with people from Cali at the Mi Rey Hotel in La Pintada, a town in Antioquia. Intercepting calls, they overhead the Cali contact being told, "We are blocking them financially."

When Pablo found out, he could not believe that his friends had betrayed him. He changed his mind after listening to a recorded telephone call of one of the Cali godfathers chastising Kiko for giving him money. To test Kiko's loyalty, he summoned him to the Cathedral. He gave him information that he had gathered on the Cali Cartel and disclosed some plans he had made to attack the godfathers. When the plans were foiled twice by Cali hit men and police working for Cali, he believed that Kiko had told the godfathers. Yes, Kiko had acted out of fear, but that was no excuse. Kiko should have approached him immediately about Cali.

At the same time, Fernando Galeano told Pablo that he had lost his fortune and could no longer pay for the war, but one of Pablo's men learned that Fernando had stashed approximately $23 million under the floor of a house occupied by the parents of a 16-year-old girl. Galeano's accountants visited the house often to make deposits, withdrawals and to adjust the stash so that it received enough air.

Due to the responsibility of guarding the cash, restrictions had been placed on the social life of the teenager, who had rebelled against her parents. After getting beaten by her father, she started to date a local hit man, of which there were many in that neighbourhood in Itagüí, the land of the Galeanos. She also began to steal a few hundred dollars every so often, which she flashed around at parties and gave to her boyfriend, who bought a motorbike. Eventually, she revealed the source of the money to her boyfriend. When she should have been in school, she was with him. After learning about her truancy, her father beat her. She offered her boyfriend money to kill him, which was carried out by two hooded men on a motorbike.

After learning about the murder, Galeano and his accountants arrived at the house. Hoping to relocate the money, he pledged to investigate the murder of the father and agreed to allow the mother and daughter to continue supervising the cash until he found another hideout.

At the father's funeral, the girl's boyfriend told a senior assassin about the source of his cash and motorbike, while withholding his role in the father's murder. Knowing that the boyfriend was eager to impress them because he wanted to work for the Medellín Cartel, the assassin and his associates insisted on going to the stash house with the boyfriend.

After tricking the mother into opening the front door, the men entered with their guns drawn and demanded to see the money. The terrified daughter watched her mother open the access door slowly. Transported to the outskirts of Medellín in a truck, the women were executed and thrown in the Cauca River. The boyfriend helped the men transport the money to another house. Some of the bills were rotting, so they applied talcum powder to detach them. After counting over $23 million, they went to a farm, where the boyfriend was shot.

At the farm, the band of assassins discussed their next move. Assuming that the owner of the money would retaliate against them and their families, they needed to make a powerful alliance, ideally with Pablo. If they found out that the money was Pablo's, they would return it. They informed Tití, their immediate boss, who told Big Gun.

After finding a new home for the money, Galeano arrived at the house, where no one answered. After forcing open the door, he saw it had gone. Kiko and Fernando Galeano went to the Cathedral, where Popeye answered the phone, and said they had urgent business to discuss with Pablo. In a truck, Limón transported them to Pablo. Without mentioning the $75,000 he had returned or Fany's Route, Pablo listened to their story and promised to launch an investigation into the missing money.

Pablo summoned the leaders of the band of assassins to the Cathedral. In his cell, he and Roberto listened to their story. After he heard that the stash consisted mostly of bills up to $20, he concluded that the money was only the small change from Fany's Route, which would have brought in mostly $50 and $100 bills. He told them that the money belonged to Kiko and the Galeanos, who had just left the Cathedral and would soon find out who had their money. They would be attacked until the money was recovered. The assassins were told that they had to stay the night because it was too late to leave the Cathedral.

After they had left his cell, Pablo discussed the numbers with Roberto. They concluded that when Kiko and his associates had sent $75,000 with the note explaining that they had been short of cash, they had lied. They calculated the cash flow of the Moncadas and Galeanos as approximately $400 million, plus they owned multiple properties. By eliminating the Moncadas and Galeanos, Pablo would receive the lion's share of the profits from Fany's Route.

Pablo gathered his top men and had the assassins repeat the story. After they had finished, he offered them a deal: he would keep $18 million and they could have the rest. They agreed. He announced that starting the next day, his people were going to seize the economic infrastructure of the Moncadas and Galeanos, including their accountants and workers involved in Fany's Route.

He intended to tell Kiko that he knew who had his money, which would lure him to the Cathedral, where he would be killed in Roberto's cabin with whomever he brought. With the cabin far away from the National Guard and army headquarters, the shots would go unnoticed. He requested a power saw and gallons of acid. Wood sourced from three unbuilt cabins was enough to incinerate body parts. Otto, El Mugre and Popeye would perform the executions: a single shot to each head. Roberto assigned tasks to various men: sawing body parts, transporting them in plastic buckets, burning them, tending the bonfire … Roberto would grill meat by the bonfire to disguise the stench. Although murder was routine, the prospect of killing such powerful Mafia leaders generated excitement among the men, who retired to their beds anticipating the events.

The Castaño brothers, friends of the Moncadas and Galeanos, suspected that Pablo wanted to kill them. To liquidate their assets, El Patrón had indeed decided to summon them to the Cathedral for a terrible fate. The older Castaño brother, Fidel, had grown so rich that he owned 50,000 cattle and he controlled an area in the northern province of Córdoba, where he expanded his landholding. He had made millions in the late 1980s, when Pablo sent him to Bolivia to source more coca base, which the Medellín Cartel had desperately needed. During that time, Carlos had stayed in Medellín, where he had earned money as a hit man for Fidel and Pablo. Fidel had sent his brother, Vicente, to Los Angeles to run cocaine distribution. While the other traffickers had splurged on luxury goods, zoos and social projects, Fidel had invested in a military apparatus that brutalised the guerrillas and anyone associated with them or who defended human rights.

The deceased included Senator Pedro Nel Valencia, Deputy Gabriel Jaime Santamaría – murdered in the Departmental Assembly – and Luis Felipe Vélez, the president of the teachers' union. Héctor Abad Gómez and Leonardo Betancur were murdered at the union leader's funeral. Dozens of peasants had been buried in mass graves on Fidel's farm, Las Tangas. Raiding villages near Segovia, the death place of their father, their army had grabbed babies from their mothers and shot them. A baby had been nailed to a plank, a man impaled on a bamboo pole and men and women hacked to pieces with machetes. Every man, woman and child living on the river had died.

Through bribery, Fidel had developed strong ties with the army, the police and the DAS. Generals provided him with information and protection, and his men did exterminations for the government. He was known as an alert military leader with an extraordinary perception of avoiding traps. If he sensed something was wrong, he would immediately leave any situation and disappear on foot until he found a bus or a taxi. Upon capturing a guerrilla or a collaborator, he was known to use one of his favourite quotes, "The best thing to do is to break his legs with a bat."

Prior to the dispute with the Galeanos and Moncadas, Fidel had claimed that he needed a place to hide at, so Pablo had given him a room next to his own at the Cathedral. They had eaten together and shared the same bathroom. Pablo had trusted his friend until his men had reported that they had caught Fidel gathering intelligence on the Cathedral. With Pablo growing suspicious, Fidel had left after a few weeks.

Now fearing for his life and that of his associates, Fidel told his brother to hide at their headquarters in Córdoba: the Las Tangas cattle ranch. After growing bored in the countryside, Carlos went to Caracas, Venezuela, where he contemplated how to deal with the situation. As Pablo's former friend and business associate, he knew the intricacies of the Medellín Cartel and knew that the drug lord's main weakness was his wife and children.

At Montecasino, Fidel greeted Fernando Galeano and said, "Pablo is planning to kill us all. Something must be done. I have spoken with several people who are willing to confront him, including the Ochoas."

"This is a dangerous and delicate situation," Fernando said. "I am very concerned. None of us agree with Pablo's terrorist acts and excesses. I'm not just talking about myself, but also my workers. Now that Pablo's in the Cathedral, he's stronger than ever, despite everything he's facing."

"I've visited the Cathedral several times," Fidel said. "Even in such a fortress, he's still vulnerable. If we have everybody's support and we are all in the union, we can come up with a good military operation to finish him. I'm going to station myself in Las Tangas, where I'll wait to see what develops. I advise you to seek sanctuary, too. We should leave the city together. If you accompany me, I assure you that no one will be able to touch us at Las Tangas."

"Due to all of the constant demands from Pablo for cash," Fernando said, "and all of the abuse, Kiko Moncada has gone to live in Bogotá. Look, Fidel, I know you're right, but I need to wait this one out because of possible reprisals from Pablo."

"OK, Fernando, take your time to think things through. My offer to protect you at our ranch in Córdoba stands."

Fernando requested a meeting with Don Berna, who was one of his senior security staff and a trusted ally of the Castaños. Don Berna had first encountered Pablo when he had helped the Castaños in the search for Pablo's kidnapped father. As a young man, Don Berna had joined the Popular Liberation Army (EPL). After his guerrilla group had kidnapped a trafficker from Medellín, its entire membership had been wiped out by hit men except for Don Berna. In Bogotá, he had earned a living washing cars for Fernando Galeano.

Don Berna arrived at the meeting. Present were Fernando's cousin, Jose Chicken, and Don Berna's brother, Seed. "The situation is serious," Fernando said. "I want to hear your views."

"It's best to leave things be," Jose Chicken said. "You need to leave Medellín as soon as possible."

"I agree," Don Berna said. "The time has come for us to band together with our allies and to confront Pablo. I'm convinced that he has sent men, including Earring, to spy on us, and eventually kill us. Nothing has happened against us so far because of our security precautions. We must not give them any opportunities."

Unsettled by Don Berna's advice, Fernando said, "I thank you all for the suggestions, but fleeing from Medellín is fraught with danger because Pablo is still so strong. I'm going to call Pablo to arrange to meet him in the Cathedral to resolve things."

On Thursday, July 2, 1992, Pablo agreed to receive Fernando at the Cathedral early on a Monday morning. Accompanied by Don Berna, Fernando visited his deeply religious mother Rosario. After a warm welcome and blessings, there was an unusual quiet as if something bad was imminent. Over dinner, during small talk, Fernando seemed to be distracted.

"Is everything OK?" Rosario asked.

"Don't worry," Fernando said reassuringly. "Everything's fine."

When it was time to leave, Rosario accompanied them to the door, kissed her son's cheek and blessed him. Walking to the vehicle, Don Berna looked over his shoulder and saw her crying. Don Berna went to a safe house near to a property where Fernando had spent the night. There he found Jose Chicken.

"Earring called me," Fernando said. "An appointment has been made for today."

"Everything seems very strange," Don Berna said. "I advise you not to go to the Cathedral. Make up an excuse and send someone else."

Fernando stood. "I need to tell you something. I completely agree with you. Something's not right. The previous time I spoke to Pablo about the theft of the money at my hiding place, he couldn't look me in the eyes. He avoided my gaze. But you know very well that saying no to Pablo is tantamount to a death sentence."

"I urge you not to go," Don Berna said. "Hide in Córdoba under the protection of Fidel Castaño. Pablo has become the biggest kidnapper in Colombia. Running out of cash has made him more dangerous than ever."

A call on satellite radio announced that Earring had arrived and was waiting for Fernando. "I'm coming." Turning to Don Berna, Fernando said, "Do you wish to join me?"

"I regret being unable to accompany you, but I do not trust Pablo. It's better for me to wait for your return. I prefer for Capi to accompany you," Don Berna said, referring to a Galeano bodyguard, who was a retired policeman.

"When I return from the Cathedral, I shall contact you immediately." They hugged goodbye. Transported to Envigado Park, Fernando, his accountant, Capi and other bodyguards ended up in a hardware store, where Limón's truck – designed to smuggle people into the Cathedral – was waiting.

On July 3, 1992, the men at the Cathedral went about their tasks supervised by Roberto because Pablo was asleep. At 6:30 AM, Fernando Galeano arrived with six bodyguards and an accountant. On the phone, he was greeted by Popeye, who agreed to wake up Pablo. After speaking to Fernando, the boss told his men that the operation was progressing ahead of schedule. He had someone contact Kiko to get him to come to the Cathedral. Separated from his bodyguards, Fernando and his accountant were escorted by Popeye along internal stairs to Roberto's cabin, where they were met by Pablo's brother, Otto and El Mugre.

"Can I see Pablo?" Fernando asked.

"He'll be right up," Roberto said. Fernando said that he knew where the money was because the neighbours had spotted the trucks taking it from the stash house. "Sit down," Roberto said. "We have the money and we are keeping it. You are being held for having denied Pablo $500,000, for attempting to steal Fany's Route in Los Angeles and for betraying Pablo to Cali."

Fernando covered his face with his hands. "Can I speak to Pablo?"

"No. Take them to the basement."

Speaking face-to-face with Fernando had softened Roberto's heart. He tried to convince Pablo to spare their lives. "Nothing can be done because we have no cash," Pablo said. "There are people who are sometimes like turkeys. You need to let them get fat and kill them."

"They have been your loyal friends," Roberto said. "They have stuck with you in good times and bad times. The money that you owe them, I'm sure they will not ask for it back."

After authorising their execution, Pablo ordered that he be left alone. He locked himself in a room, smoked cannabis and after years of prolonged abstinence, he drank some liquor.

In the basement, Fernando went from wishing that the matter would soon be resolved to remembering how Pablo had eliminated his friends in the past. Realising he was going to die, he offered to hand over property, to leave the country or to even remain in the prison with Pablo, who still refused to speak to him. In the afternoon, he and the accountant requested water and a bible, which was granted by Roberto. Handing over a bible, Popeye refused another request to speak to Pablo. Wood began to arrive near the cabin. At night, the bonfire and grill were lit. A stereo played loud. Pablo ordered the municipal guards to look out for anything suspicious, such as the National Guard sergeant on patrol, and told Popeye and Otto to perform the hit. Holding their guns, Popeye and Otto descended the basement stairs, their way guided by a flashlight.

"Relatives of the Galeanos are outside," said one of Pablo's men, "accompanied by officials from the Attorney General's Office."

"No, boss, this job is a bad idea. Do not kill those guys," said a bodyguard.

For a few seconds, Pablo contemplated silently. "Run, tell those guys to stop!"

In the basement, Fernando yelled, "They're gonna kill us!"

Before the accountant could react, Popeye shot him in the head. Otto grabbed Fernando's neck, fired into his head and started the power saw.

The man on his way to stop the murders arrived too late. He returned to Pablo, who issued an order: "Tell the people from the Attorney General's Office that if they come in, we'll feed them lead." Pablo told Big Gun, "Let none remain alive," which started the hunt for the senior traffickers in both families.

Outside of the Cathedral, Kiko was lured to a house and killed with his bodyguards. The same happened to his brother, William. Before they died, a phone was used to force them to transfer their properties into the names of Pablo's men. Their families and employees were killed, except for anyone deemed useful to Pablo. It was the beginning of a purge within the Medellín Cartel that ended with approximately fifty dead.

Held at gunpoint, Fernando's bodyguard, Capi, was hand-cuffed, transported to a farm in Envigado and tortured into revealing the names of Fernando's employees. After 10 PM, Don Berna placed a radio call to Capi: "How is our boss?"

Big Gun and other hit men forced Capi to answer: "Everything is under control. The boss is unable to leave the building because there is an INPEC [The National Penitentiary and Prison Institute] operative present, so it's more prudent to wait."

Don Berna grew suspicious due to the tension in Capi's voice and because Fernando had said that he would not stay long in the Cathedral. After the call, Don Berna ordered his men to tighten security and asked one of them to keep calling Capi every hour. Eventually, Capi claimed that he was running out of battery power, and after that, the phone remained unanswered. On a call to Fernando's cousin, Jose Chicken, Don Berna said, "I advise you not to go out alone."

Popeye found Pablo next to the bonfire, sat cross-legged, wearing his Russian hat, gazing silently at the flames. Otto's brother arrived with a bucket holding a bloodstained arm and a leg that had been sawn at the kneecap, complete with a sock and shoe. Fire devoured the limbs. The next bucket was placed down. Fernando's head was produced and tossed onto the fire. Due to its thick coating of slippery blood, it escaped from the fire and landed at El Patrón's feet, next to a log. More pieces of Pablo's friends added to the stench.

"Wash the basement and saw with strong soap and disinfectant," Roberto said.

After Otto had washed and changed his clothes, he arrived at the bonfire. "I've got a strong appetite for some barbecue." By 2 AM, the flames were shrinking. The remaining bones were hammered into dust and dissolved in acid. Roberto checked that there was no evidence, and the men left the cabin for the main building.

The next day, Pablo seemed more relaxed as he received visitors. Having seen the flames from the city, one visitor asked what Pablo had burned that night. He responded that they had been burning the Medellín Cartel.

Resting at an apartment, Don Berna couldn't sleep. He learned that men had kidnapped Jose Chicken, who had ignored his advice to leave his house to go cycling. With Capi still not answering and no one explaining why Fernando was still missing, Don Berna feared the worst and ordered the highest security measures for the entire Galeano family.

"I need you to be available," he told his brother on a call. "Get as many men as you can in the barracks." The kidnappers of Jose Chicken demanded a huge ransom and said that they would call his apartment in two hours. With his men, Don Berna arrived at the apartment.

After one hour, he received a call from one of his men: "Commander Berna, ten vehicles are approaching the apartment with about fifty men."

"Prepare for battle," Don Berna told his men. The vehicles surrounded the apartment and both sides opened fire. A bullet wounded Don Berna's left hand. Surprised by the resistance, the kidnappers eventually fled, leaving one behind known as Death, who was captured and transported to a house. Under torture, Death detailed what had happened at the Cathedral. Hearing the details of his boss's demise, Don Berna felt intense pain. He had considered Fernando an honourable man, a best friend and a father figure, whose honest nature had proven to be his downfall when dealing with a cutthroat such as El Patrón.

"Following orders from Pablo Escobar, they kidnapped Jose Chicken," Death said. "They killed Capi and left his body on a hill in the upper part of the village in La Cola de Zorro. Before he died, he managed to grab a small .22 calibre pistol he had hidden in a boot and kill one of Pablo's men."

Don Berna instructed the Galeano family to flee from Medellín. Fidel Castaño was waiting for him in Montería, the capital of Córdoba, situated by the northern Colombian coast east of Panama. In a recreational vehicle with two of his men alternating driving, Don Berna travelled along a rough road, overwhelmed by sadness and convinced that Pablo had to die. For the mission, he hoped to enlist the paramilitary forces controlled by Fidel.

In the centre of Córdoba, he arrived at an office, where Fidel greeted him, holding a glass of whiskey, even though he had a reputation for abstinence. "Tell me everything that has happened." After hearing the details, Fidel smashed the glass against the wall and slammed his fist on a desk. "By God, I told Fernando not to trust Pablo. He wants to kill all of us."

The room fell silent until Don Berna said, "Fidel, you're our commander. I am at your service to face Pablo."

"We are all suffering a lot of pain and sadness," Fidel said. "Recently, I dismissed most of the Self Defence Forces and I delivered a shipment of weapons as part of an agreement between the government and political leaders in Córdoba in response to the demobilisation of the EPL [Popular Liberation Army]. Presently, I don't even have twenty men. Put together with you, Don Berna, the most you would have to command is perhaps forty or fifty. We lack the resources and money that Pablo has, which includes more than 5,000 bandits in the communes [of Medellín]. We are between a rock and a hard place. We should wait because it is madness to face Pablo presently! If you desire, stay here in Córdoba, where it's safe. I'll get you a good house and nothing shall happen to you. What's happened is sad, but we need to be smart. When a train approaches at high speed, you must wait for it to decelerate to deal with it, because if you get in front of it, it will crush you into shit."

Don Berna stood and gazed into Fidel's eyes. "Commander, if you don't join me in this war, I'll fight it alone even if it costs my life."

"I wish you good luck. Las Tangas is at your disposal. It's a good shelter. Nobody can get you there. Take care of yourself, Don Berna."

"Thank you for your kind offer and recommendations." Departing, Don Berna's sadness returned, accompanied by frustration because so many were intimidated by Pablo. Both mentally and physically exhausted, he fell asleep in the vehicle on the way to Bello, a suburb of Medellín.

The Castaños distanced themselves from Pablo, while secretly working against him. They organised some of his terrorism and notified the authorities. This happened with an attack they arranged at the Medellín airport, whereby a suicide hit man would indiscriminately shoot executives travelling to Bogotá. The Castaños organised it and then told the DAS about it. The hit man was killed before the Ingram 380 could release any gunfire.

Pablo invited the Castaños to the Cathedral to sort out their differences. Big Gun was instructed to kill them on the narrow road back to Envigado. Sensing the danger, they avoided the trap and took measures to rebuild their paramilitary army.

At a friend's house, Don Berna's brother arrived. "Pablo's people are everywhere," Seed said. "They've kidnapped the accountants and secretaries and have stolen various properties and ranches. You need to leave Medellín because Pablo has complete control. It's impossible to even move a leaf without him knowing about it. To top it all off, several of our friends have switched sides and are working for Pablo."

"Brother, it's you who needs to leave Medellín for a few days. Someone has to take care of the family, and it's best that the two of us are not exposed." Although reluctant to go, Seed eventually agreed to leave the city.

Key people including accountants for the Moncadas and Galeanos were smuggled into the Cathedral, many of them expecting to die. Pablo said he wanted all the property belonging to their organisations. If they wanted to live, they now worked for him.

"I'm declaring an emergency," he said. "Your bosses are already dead. Now, you'll turn over all their resources to me. If you lie, you'll die painfully." He reminded them that he was the boss. They would all be safe provided they paid him his dues.

The DEA recorded a version of events based on an informant's statement: "Escobar argued that while he and his close associates were in jail and needed money for their expensive war with the Cali Cartel, Galeano and Moncada preferred to store money until it became mouldy rather than use it to help their friends ... Escobar convinced cartel members who genuinely liked Moncada and Galeano that if the two men were not killed, the Medellín Cartel would be in a war with itself, and they would all perish."

In the Cathedral, Pablo received a visit from Miki, a Galeano associate. "There's a lot of concern over everything that has happened," Miki said.

"It was necessary for the purpose of preventing an economic coup d'état," Pablo said.

"I understand the situation," Miki said, terrified. "I support you. For humanitarian reasons, is it possible to return Fernando's corpse, so that he can have a Christian burial?"

"It's impossible because whatever ashes remained were thrown into the river."

"Is it possible to have the body of Jose Chicken?"

"Yes. I will grant you that."

"You should talk to Don Berna to see if he will put himself at your disposal."

"That's a good idea."

Miki called Don Berna. "You should submit to El Patrón's military command, follow his orders, and deliver all of your goods and those of the Moncadas and Galeanos to his men. El Patrón wants to speak to you."

Don Berna gulped. "OK."

"I send you greetings," Pablo said. "I don't want scandals or media attention. I'll respect your life if you work for me."

"I have no problem with that," Don Berna said, contemplating how to stall Pablo. "You can count on me, but I'm presently far from the city. I assure you, I'll soon be in contact."

"To get Jose Chicken delivered, communicate with Earring. He'll leave him in the trunk of a grey vehicle on the Las Palmas Road." As the reality of his friends' deaths sunk in again, Don Berna felt a pain as if he had been stabbed in the heart. He struggled to muster the strength to sound and remain strong. "Call me when you arrive in Medellín. We need to speak in person."

Earring got on the phone. "And don't forget that here we rule." He cackled and hung up.

Resting the phone down, Don Berna noticed that his hands were trembling. Contemplating the conversation, his mind roamed over scenarios, but what frightened him the most was feeling alone in his struggle against Pablo.

A medical examination of Jose Chicken's corpse revealed that he had bled to death from drill holes, with his torturers concentrating on his knees and hands. The information sickened Don Berna on top of the news that dozens more had been murdered in the last few days as Pablo's purge of the Medellín Cartel continued. Hiding in an apartment, Don Berna stopped taking calls from Earring, so Pablo put a $5 million bounty on him and made him a military target. Alone, he was unable to contact anybody, including his family. One mistake could be fatal.

He was approached by Rodolfo Ospina Baraya, a.k.a. the Cricket, a Medellín Cartel defector who was also the grandson of the former president, Mariano Ospina Pérez. After getting involved in trafficking, Pablo had attempted to kill him twice. Accompanied by members of the Search Bloc, the Cricket showed up at a Galeano property, and left a note and his phone number with the butler, stating that he had a strategy to help Don Berna combat Pablo.

Don Berna called his brother for advice. "I've seen the Cricket sporadically. Despite the risk, I'm willing to meet him about this serious matter."

"I'll take care of you at the meeting. Stay alert," Seed said.

Surrounded by 100 policemen with their weapons drawn, they met in the Cricket's armoured Mercedes 500 at a car park at a cattle fair in Medellín. "I'm truly sorry about what happened with Fernando Galeano and your other friends," the Cricket said. "For a long time, I've been giving information to the authorities about Pablo. I've concluded that there is only one group with the capacity, contacts, power, money and resources to eliminate Pablo: the leaders of the Cali Cartel." He held out a note. "Here are some numbers, including Miguel Rodríguez's trusted secretary. Call him. He's on the inside. You guys can cooperate."

"That's no problem. I'm going to move to Cali. While I'm there, I'll call him."

To avoid Pablo's men, Don Berna and two bodyguards left during darkness and arrived at Cali in the morning. Using a public phone, he called the secretary of Miguel Rodríguez and described his location and vehicle. After several minutes, the police arrived on Sixth Street in vehicles, which circled Don Berna's location. After they had secured the area, a blue Mazda 626 pulled over. A well-dressed man got out and introduced himself as Miguel's private secretary. He told Don Berna to get in the back of the car alone; his two bodyguards would have to wait.

"Sir, for security reasons you must wear this hood," came Jorge Salcedo's voice from the back seat. Don Berna saw a tall man with a military bearing, the Cali Cartel's head of security. "I hope you understand."

After nodding, Don Berna's world went dark. Listening to the song "Party Cali" on the radio, he questioned whether he had pursued the correct strategy. Realising he had put himself in the lion's den, just like his boss had done, he started to pray and touch the crucifix his mother had given him. Under the hood grew so hot and stuffy that he felt as if he were drowning.

Eventually, the car stopped and an electronic door opened. "I've arrived with the guest," the secretary said by radio.

"You can remove your hood," Jorge said.

Snatching off the hood enabled him to breathe easier and to enjoy the view of a ranch with lakes, a soccer field and a fountain spurting water ten feet high in the middle of a meadow. Almost 200 armed men were protecting the property.

"Give me your gun."

Handing over his pistol, he felt completely helpless. He followed a bodyguard into a room with marble floors, where the four heads of the Cali Cartel were seated, the three eldest dressed like executives – the youngest, Pacho, in sports clothes.

One stood. "I'm Miguel Rodríguez, and this is my brother, Gilberto, Don Chepe Santacruz and Don Pacho Herrera. Why don't you sit down? Would you like something to eat or drink?"

"Just a glass of water," he said, his throat dry.

"Tell us everything that happened in Medellín and the Cathedral," Miguel said.

After he had detailed the massacre, Don Berna said, "Gentlemen, Pablo has killed more than 200 people in the past few days. He stole money, property and profits, which has enabled him to strengthen by gaining resources."

After the godfathers contemplated in silence, Miguel said, "I told you that if we did not confront Pablo, he would kill us all!"

"I begged my compadre not to go to Medellín," Chepe said. "He didn't listen and Pablo killed him."

"We've got to act fast," Miguel said. "He must be dragged out of his cave. Firstly, we need to publicly denounce everything that is happening in the Cathedral and Medellín, and then have our friendly journalists give it enough coverage. In addition to informing on Pablo, we need to pressure the president into getting him out of the Cathedral. Gaviria is frightened of Pablo, but through our senator friends and those at the top of the government, we can put pressure on him."

"Outside of prison, Pablo would be much more vulnerable," Gilberto said.

Miguel read the draft of a statement he wanted to issue to the public: "Pablo Escobar has murdered, tortured and disappeared hundreds of citizens. The government needs to take measures to prevent the shedding of more blood."

"And who is going to sign it?" Don Berna asked.

"Let's put, 'Citizens for the peace of Colombia.'" Miguel summoned an assistant. "Immediately make 10,000 copies of this statement. Using one of our small planes, drop them tonight over Medellín." He turned towards Don Berna. "You must be exhausted by what has happened. You can stay at a hotel of a friend of ours. Don't worry about the expense. Tomorrow afternoon, we'll talk again. On behalf of the Cali Cartel, we thank you for coming and for the information."

Back in the car, Don Berna was instructed to wear the hood, but after several minutes, he was allowed to remove it. The private secretary gave him a tour of the historical sites of Cali. When it was time to get dropped off, his two bodyguards smiled with relief when he arrived.

At the hotel recommended by the Cali Cartel, Don Berna called Seed. "Everything is going well. I'll tell you all the details in person." In the safety of the hotel, he fell into a deep sleep for the first time in days.

The next day, the private secretary collected Don Berna, who was not required to wear a hood or submit his weapon, which increased his faith in his new allies. Transported to the Cali Cartel's headquarters, he met the four godfathers in a luxury apartment.

After small talk, Miguel said, "Our conflict with Pablo has been going for a long time. He's crazy. He wants to end Colombia as we know it and we won't allow it. We'll help you with everything that you need. There's no need to worry about money or resources. We welcome all those harmed by Pablo who wish to speak to us. We commend your courage against your mortal enemy. In Medellín, for a long time, we've had a senior policeman who has our absolute confidence on our payroll. When you get there, contact him immediately. He is looking forward to your call. Do not hesitate to call our personal phones at any time. All of us combining our help will be the beginning of the end of Pablo. The public announcement that we dropped on Medellín was successful. Our friends in Congress and our journalists were already putting pressure on Gaviria about the Cathedral. The president was hesitant, but we've obtained reliable info that Pablo is going to be moved to a military barracks."

After getting wished good luck in his mission, Don Berna returned to the hotel. With his two men, he travelled north to meet Seed in Pereira, a mountainous city, halfway from Cali to

Medellín. He updated his brother and continued to Medellín, leaving Seed in Pereira for his own safety. Approaching the city in heavy rain, he encountered men drinking liquor, who were celebrating and praising the Medellín Cartel. Fortunately, the weather obscured Don Berna, who was in no mood to play the hero with them.

In Medellín, he used a payphone to call the high-ranking policeman, who told him to go to a restaurant near the Carlos Holguín Police School. Entering it, he noticed the presence of many police on high alert, including some in plain clothes. After sitting at a table, he was approached by a handsome man dressed as a civilian.

"I'm Dario González, Major of the Police, but for security my pseudonym is Manuel." While Don Berna detailed everything he knew about Pablo, Major González took notes. "Pablo's great power makes it difficult to gather intelligence on him. That's why our data is so poor. I'm delighted with the volume of information you've given me. For your safety, you should live within the security ring of the Carlos Holguín Police School. As Pablo has threatened to blow up the school using a suicide bomber in a car full of explosives, we have extreme security measures in place."

The media reported the Cathedral murders. Investigators sent to the Cathedral by the attorney general's office were denied entry. The minister of defence, Rafael Pardo, received an anonymous letter from someone claiming to be a Medellín Cartel associate:

"Respected Minister,

I wish to inform you of the real comforts and privileges being enjoyed by Mr Pablo Escobar Gaviria in his country retreat the Cathedral, disproving completely the affirmations by high-placed members of the government that he is 'just like any other prisoner in Colombia.'

1 – VISITS – There is absolutely no control; as well as the visitors fulfilling all the requirements demanded by the government,

there is a permanent queue of personalities: lawyers, journalists, footballers of Deportivo Independiente de Medellín, Nacional and Envigado Futbol Club, doctors, drug dealers, assassins, bosses of the popular militias etc. as well as more recently forced visits from kidnap victims that were later murdered.

2 – COMFORTS – Football pitch, gymnasium, go-kart track for his son, playhouse for his daughter, everything is structured with money provided by the government. Three apartments embedded in the mountain, between the trees, where helicopters cannot land. This is where they carry out their drug business, now he's sending more drugs than ever abroad. This is where he meets with the leaders of his murderous gangs. IN THESE APART-MENTS HE HAS POWERFUL COMMUNICATIONS EQUIPMENT, not even the authorities of the Brigade of Antio-quia have equipment as powerful as PABLO ESCOBAR.

3 – COMMUNICATIONS – Pablo has THREE MOBILE TELEPHONES FROM EMPRESAS PÚBLICAS DE MEDELLÍN, two for Pablo and one for his brother Roberto. THREE BEEPERS operated by his boss of assassins, who accompanies him and looks after his security.

4 – WEAPONS – Don Pablo and his brother Roberto keep a 9 mm PISTOL in their room and his companions or bodyguards have SHOTGUNS, GRENADES, PISTOLS and REVOLVERS.

5 – CRIMINAL ACTIVITIES – KIDNAPPINGS – It is not true what the international magazines say that Don PABLO ESCOBAR possesses millions of dollars. The truth according to him is that HE HAS BEEN LEFT WITHOUT ANY MONEY. HE IS BROKE, he was left without any money by his war against the STATE. For this reason … he decided to KIDNAP and MURDER to keep the money and property is not just [from] HIS FRIENDS AND COMPANIONS FROM THE CARTEL but also members of the ECHAVARRIA OLÓZAGA family, FABIO ECHEVERRI CORREA and THE DIRECTORS OF SURAMERICANA DE SEGUROS.

He has given orders that his assassins, EL CHOPO, ALEJO, PIÑA, TITI, ARETE, TYSON ETC. follow these people. He took a decision TO ESCAPE FROM THE CATHEDRAL, when he saw that his plan 'AFTER SEVEN YEARS I WILL BE RID OF THIS PROBLEM,' was failing owing to the proof that the government had received from abroad. For this reason, he said, 'I AM GOING TO GO BACK TO WAR.' He is thinking of escaping the same way the special visitors, narcos, guerrillas, assassins, etc. leave the prison in the WHITE CHEVROLET 3.5 TRUCK with the canvas cover or the RED TURBO DIESEL 3.5 TRUCK, that also moves visitors with the help of the prison authorities of the Cathedral."

Pablo told the widows of the Moncada and Galeano families that he was confiscating all their belongings, leaving them with an apartment and a car each. If they didn't like it, he wanted to know immediately because he was going to kill them and their children. They complained to a friend of the Moncada family, the Cricket, who brokered a deal with attorney general de Greiff, whereby he was granted immunity from prosecution in exchange for information about Pablo. The same deal was granted to eleven more witnesses, and together they became known as 'the dirty dozen.'

"We suspect that Pablo Escobar is ordering murders," de Greiff told the president, "and continuing to run his illegal business from prison. You do not have to be Sherlock Holmes to work out that Mr Escobar is aware that we know he is committing crimes from inside the prison, and consequently there is a danger that he will escape. For this reason, I ask that you change his place of detention."

CHAPTER 13
PRISON ESCAPE

The murders of Galeano and Moncada made the president look weak for not taking any action. More pressure came from the media publishing photos of the luxuries in the Cathedral. Two of Pablo's biggest enemies – George HW Bush and the Cali Cartel – were urging the government to eliminate him once and for all by moving him to another prison, where he could be assassinated, or by extraditing him to the US, where he would never be freed. Knowing that replacing the prison staff made no difference, Gaviria authorised moving El Patrón to a new prison. The attorney general ordered a prison inspection.

Roberto told Pablo that he felt something bad was imminent and urged him to investigate. Government and army people on Pablo's payroll confirmed that he needed to abandon the Cathedral. He heard that George HW Bush was threatening to invade Colombia because the government was incapable of extraditing Pablo. Military trucks were spotted heading for the Cathedral. Pablo received a message saying that officials were coming to speak to him.

Victoria received a call. "I don't know what's going on," Juan Pablo said, agitated, "but I just spoke to him and he told us to be on alert because of unusual movements of troops near the prison. I think something bad is about to happen." Victoria agreed to relocate with Manuela to her mother's house. On the next call, her son was even more upset. "They are going to take Pablo, Roberto and twenty of their men to army headquarters in Medellín." Fearing that Pablo would swiftly be put on a flight to America, Victoria sobbed.

Aiming to transfer Pablo to Bogotá, the president told the deputy justice minister, Eduardo Mendoza – a thin young man with a boyish face – to go to the Cathedral and liaise with an army general, whose troops were already raiding the Cathedral. "Shall I bring Pablo back to Bogotá?" Mendoza asked.

"Yes," the defence minister said. "We're moving him to a military base in Bogotá. Now run!"

On the way to the airport, Mendoza picked up Colonel Navas, the military director of prisons. "This is totally crazy," Navas said. "You cannot do this to Escobar and get away with it." Navas viewed the action as a violation of the government's agreement and a resumption of war. "Lots of people will die."

"Colonel, this isn't my decision," Mendoza said. "We've been ordered to go and we're going to put him on a plane and bring him back." At the airport, they were told that their military plane had no fuel. Waiting, Mendoza decided to seek further clarification from his boss. "I don't understand what's going on. Tell me again, what am I supposed to do?"

"Look, if the prisoners give you any trouble, tell them it's because of the construction. Tell them we're having problems because they've been bullying the workers, so we have to move them temporarily out of the way."

The sun was setting over snowy mountain crests when they landed. It was getting cold. Ascending a dirt road, Mendoza was expecting to hear gunfire from the raid. He translated the silence to mean that the raid was over and Pablo had been captured. Bringing him back would be easy now.

When the jeep pulled up at the prison, a general in green battle garb approached Mendoza. "What are your orders?"

"General, my orders are to take Escobar back to Bogotá."

"I have different orders." Mendoza was dismayed to learn that the general hadn't raided the prison. The troops were still outside. "If they want Escobar," the general said, "I'll go in there myself and get that bandit and tie him up and bring him out! But until my orders change …" Mendoza explained that he had been told that the raid was underway. A press release had been issued stating that Pablo was at another prison. "This is very confusing," the general said. "Do you think we should do this tonight or shall we wait until tomorrow morning?"

"General, I have no idea. I was sent to do this immediately. I thought it was done. I don't have the authority to tell you to wait until tomorrow. If it would be easier for you to do it in daylight, maybe we should wait, but I'm not a military officer. I don't know. Let's call Bogotá."

The general got on a radio phone. "I'm here with the vice minister. He wants me to do this thing tomorrow." The general hung up and invited the dumbfounded Mendoza to dinner.

A presidential military aide called Mendoza and chewed him out for interfering with a military operation by postponing it until the next day – which hadn't been Mendoza's idea. Troops gathering around the Cathedral was a hot media story. Pablo might be escaping. Mendoza turned towards the general. "You must do it tonight. Immediately." After getting off the phone, the general said that the new plan was to send Colonel Navas into the prison to assess the situation. "I should be the one to go in, not you," Mendoza told the colonel.

"No, don't worry about it." The colonel marched to the prison gate. "Open up!" Almost an hour later, he returned. "Well, the situation is under control, but these people are very scared. They told me that they'll start blowing up the place if the army tries to come in and take Escobar, which is what they hear on the radio is about to happen. If you were to go in there and explain what is going on and calm them down, we may be able to save lots of lives."

Exasperated and cold, Mendoza decided to go in. The gate opened. The guards lined up in formation. "Señor Vice Minister, welcome to the Cathedral!" After declaring the numbers of prisoners and guards, the captain said, "All is quiet."

In jeans, a dark jacket and sneakers – with the laces untied – Pablo emerged with Roberto to discuss the situation. "Good evening," he said to Mendoza. Despite being protected by fifteen armed prison guards, Mendoza trembled as he said that the army had been ordered to search the rooms. "I'm sorry, but I've made a deal with the government," Pablo said. "The police and the army are not permitted inside. If you want, you can bring the regular prison officials to do this search, but I will not allow the army and even less the police. Please remember, gentlemen, I fought a war with the police and this policy is the result." Watching Mendoza turn pale, he said, "I'll allow some soldiers inside, but without their weapons." Mendoza made a call. Refusing to accept Pablo's offer, the president demanded that the army enter with weapons. "They can't come inside with weapons," Pablo said. "No one's coming here armed to kill us. We don't know what their intentions are. I don't trust them with my life."

An army general called Pablo, and stated that the president intended to kill, capture or extradite him. Pablo told Roberto that he was going to keep Mendoza and the colonel hostage. Wearing jackets with concealed weapons, a dozen bodyguards arrived and formed a semicircle around Pablo. "You've betrayed me, Señor Vice Minister," Pablo said. "The president has betrayed me. You're going to pay for this and this country is going to pay for this, because I have an agreement and you're breaking it."

"You have nothing to fear for your life. You're only being transferred."

"You're doing this to deliver me to the Americans."

"No, we—"

"Kill them!" Popeye yelled with a cruel expression on his round face. "Sons of bitches."

Mendoza steered his eyes towards the prison guards and gazed, as if requesting help. They looked away.

"You're going to deliver me to Bush, so that he can parade me before the election, just like he did with Manuel Noriega. I'm not going to allow that."

"We should have killed this one during the campaign!" Popeye said. "It would have been easy."

"Look," Mendoza said. "It would be unconstitutional for us to send you to the United States."

"Then you're going to kill me. You're going to take me out of here and have me killed. Before I allow that to happen, many people will die."

"Let us kill them, boss!"

"Do you really think they're going to send someone like me to kill you?" Mendoza said. "There are hundreds of soldiers outside and other officials. Do you think we would send for this many witnesses if we were going to kill you? This is just not reasonable. I'll stay with you, if you want, all night. Wherever you go, you're a prisoner and we're obliged to guarantee your safety. So, you don't have anything to worry about." Pablo glowered. "All we have to do is finish the prison," Mendoza said, "and we can't do that with you here."

"No," Pablo said. "That problem we had with the workers was just a misunderstanding."

"Look, I'm going to walk out of here. I'll be right out there." Mendoza pointed at the dirt road. "We're going to deliver the prison to the army. I'll be out there and I'll stay with you guys wherever you're going."

As if planning, Pablo scanned the area beyond the fence.

"I'll talk to you later." Mendoza, the colonel and the prison guards advanced towards the gate.

"Boss, that son of a bitch is going to betray us. We should kill them all! Are you going to let them walk out?"

The officials were almost at the gate, when Pablo's bodyguards rushed after them with their guns drawn. Mendoza expected the prison guards to defend him. Instead, they pulled out their weapons and pointed them at him. Wondering what to do, Mendoza glanced at the colonel, who appeared nauseated.

"Boss, look, look! They are sending messages to each other. Kill him! Kill him, the son of a bitch!" Popeye said, stamping his feet. Bodyguards shoved the officials towards the prison.

"I'm sorry," Pablo said, "but you can't leave right now. We need you to ensure our own safety while we figure out what to do."

At the warden's house, Popeye threw Mendoza through the doorway and aimed a gun at the side of his head. "I'm going to kill the guy! I've always wanted to kill a vice minister." With his face right up to Mendoza's, he yelled, "You son of a bitch! You motherfucker! You've been trying to get us for years; now, I'll get you!"

"Popeye, not now," Roberto said. "Maybe later. Relax. He's worth more alive." Mendoza was instructed to sit on a sofa in the warden's room.

"Señor Vice Minister," Pablo said, brandishing a gun. "From this moment, you're my prisoner. If the army comes, you'll be the first to die."

"Don't think by holding me you'll stop them," Mendoza said. "If you take us hostage, you can forget about everything. They have heavy machine guns, lots of them. They'll kill everybody here! You can't escape!"

Pablo smiled. "You still don't understand. These people all work for me." He called his wife. "We're having a little problem here. We're trying to solve it. You know what to do if it doesn't work." He gave Mendoza the phone. "Call the president."

"The president won't take the call," Mendoza said.

"Get somebody to take the call, because you're about to die."

Mendoza got through to a staff member at the president's office. "Are you being held hostage?"

"Yes." The staff member hung up. Trembling, Mendoza imagined himself dying in the raid.

"Let me kill him, boss," Popeye said.

Pablo left the room to call his legal team, who had been summoned to Guido Parra's house. The lawyer's wife was in the Cathedral to beg for her husband's life, because Pablo had sentenced him to death for disloyalty. Guido Parra hoped that the crisis had presented an opportunity for him to redeem himself. "Make as much noise as possible," Pablo said. Immediately, the lawyers contacted journalists with the news that strange things were happening at the Cathedral, including a raid. Guido Parra's wife escaped through the fence, which is why the media initially reported that Pablo had fled disguised as a woman.

Juan Pablo called the radio stations: "My dad is in a tunnel under the prison and wants to negotiate."

With a gun tucked into his trousers, Pablo returned to the hostages. "You're detained, but you're not going to be killed. If anyone touches you, he'll have to answer to me."

"You can't escape from here," Mendoza said. "The army has the prison surrounded."

"You had an agreement with me and you're breaking it. I know you guys are bothered about those killings," he said, referring to Galeano and Moncada. "Don't worry. They were problems among Mafioso. They don't concern you."

Mendoza and the colonel were escorted to Pablo's lavishly furnished cell, where Popeye and a bodyguard kept watch. To stay warm, they were given ponchos. Popeye kept pumping his shotgun near Mendoza, who was still ruminating on the prospect of his death at the hands of the troops.

The colonel picked up a bottle. "This could be the last whiskey I'll drink in my life." After swigging some, he reached for a bible and read Psalm 91:

Whoever dwells in the shelter of the Most High will rest in the shadow of the Almighty.

I will say of the Lord, "He is my refuge and my fortress, my God, in whom I trust."

Surely, he will save you from the fowler's snare and from the deadly pestilence.

He will cover you with his feathers, and under his wings you will find refuge; his faithfulness will be your shield and rampart.

You will not fear the terror of night, nor the arrow that flies by day,

nor the pestilence that stalks in the darkness, nor the plague that destroys at midday.

A thousand may fall at your side, ten thousand at your right hand, but it will not come near you.

You will only observe with your eyes and see the punishment of the wicked.

If you say, "The Lord is my refuge," and you make the Most High your dwelling,

no harm will overtake you, no disaster will come near your tent.

For he will command his angels concerning you to guard you in all your ways;

they will lift you up in their hands, so that you will not strike your foot against a stone.

You will tread on the lion and the cobra; you will trample the great lion and the serpent ...

To say goodbye to his family, the colonel asked for and was granted a phone.

"How do you stay so thin?" a bodyguard asked Mendoza.

"I'm a vegetarian."

"What should I eat to lose weight?"

"More fruit and vegetables."

The bodyguard fetched a plate of apple slices. "Now I'm going to start a healthy diet."

Popeye shook his head. "What are you going to do that for? We're all going to be dead by seven o'clock."

While preparing to escape, Pablo kept trying to contact the president. His lawyers and Father Garcia were rebuffed by the president's office. The weapons buried by Roberto and Pablo – prior to their arrival at the Cathedral – were unearthed. In addition to the pistol in his pants, Pablo slung an Uzi over his shoulder. Approaching the perimeter, they relied on the fog for cover. With soldiers nearby, Roberto used wire cutters on the electrified fence, making a gap big enough for a person to slip through.

On July 22, 1992, Pablo told his men, "Either we flee or we all die." He and Roberto entered a hidden room and grabbed cash. To thwart the spy planes, Roberto used his emergency remote control to plunge the prison into darkness, which terrified everybody, including the hostages.

Pablo listened to radio stations report different stories. One claimed he had been captured and was on a plane to America. Another said the military had taken over the Cathedral and lives had been lost. Concerned about his family hearing the reports, he called them. "Don't worry. Don't listen to the news. The situation is being resolved directly with the president." After hanging up, he called and reassured his mother. He crouched, grabbed his shoelaces and finally tied them. "Roberto, let's put our radios on the same frequency." He returned to his room to check on the hostages. "Try to remain calm. The situation will be resolved without anyone getting killed. I'm going to sleep. I'll see you in the morning."

With darkness, fog and rain providing cover, he told his men to simply walk out through the hole that Roberto had cut, one after the other, five minutes apart. Hoping to blend in with the military units surrounding the prison, most of the men had put on army fatigues. Pablo went first. He positioned himself to watch the others emerging and everything going on around them. Due to the poor visibility, Roberto got lost. After wandering around afraid, he found the hole in the fence at around 2 AM.

Risking injury, the group set off down a wet slippery surface. Confronted by a rock face, the brawniest went first and allowed the others to stand on their shoulders. Prickled by thorny vegetation, they held hands going down another slope. After two hours, visibility improved as the fog thinned. Realising they had gone in a circle and hadn't achieved much distance from the prison, they were shocked and frustrated. They needed to keep moving because they could easily be shot. Pablo estimated that they had two hours left to evacuate the area.

The sun was up when they reached a neighbourhood called El Salado. People were going to work and children to school. In filthy ripped clothes, they emerged like vagrants and headed for a farm belonging to Memo, a trusted friend. They knocked and the groundskeeper answered, but didn't recognise them. Once it dawned on him, he let them in. The soaked clothes compressed to their weary bodies were peeled off and washed, while they finally rested. Almost an hour later, there was frantic banging on the door. Bracing for a gunfight, they grabbed their weapons and took aim. The door opened. In came friendly neighbours with a hot breakfast for the visitors. Resting their guns, they rejoiced. Other neighbours patrolled the streets to watch for the army. Pablo and his men cleaned themselves, shaved and put on fresh clothes.

After the general outside the Cathedral had refused to launch an assault, the president had ordered in special forces. A press release was prepared, stating that Mendoza and the colonel had died in a shootout. At first, the plane carrying the troops couldn't land due to fog. In the morning, the troops travelled up the slope in trucks. The army units there gave the truck drivers the wrong directions and they ended up back at the airport.

In Pablo's room, the captives and the guards watched the news report the setbacks with the raid. Through a shortwave radio, they listened to the preparations outside as units prepared to launch an assault. One of the units – trained by the Americans – was infamous for having killed everybody in a building on behalf of an emerald dealer. Knowing this, the kidnapped colonel resumed praying.

"Can I go outside for a look?" Mendoza asked.

Bodyguards allowed him onto the porch. The rising sun was illuminating the fog. Due to the poor visibility, Mendoza imagined his executioners closing in. Hoping that they would recognise his business suit and not shoot him, he dropped his poncho and surrendered to the chilly air.

Gunfire. Explosions. Screams.

The commander of the prison guards was opening a door as special forces launched their assault. A hailstorm of bullets dropped him. Of course, it was later reported that the deceased had opened fire on them.

Pablo's men dragged Mendoza back inside. "Please! They're going to kill us! Help us!"

"I've been telling you that all night! Now it's too late!"

Mendoza crawled to the bathroom and coiled his body behind the toilet, hoping it would shield him. Realising that the glass would shatter and injure him, he crawled back to the living room and joined the colonel, who was crouched next to a prison guard. The commotion grew louder. Mendoza attempted to leave the room.

"Get on the floor unless you want to be killed!" a prison guard yelled.

Mendoza and a guard tried to raise Pablo's mattress to hide under, but it was too heavy to move. Mendoza got on the floor and braced to die. A grenade detonated nearby. As he twisted away from the explosion, his forehead met the barrel of a gun held by a black, muscular man. With gunfire and blasts erupting all around, the special forces sergeant holding the gun threw Mendoza against a wall and sat on him.

"We're going to try to get out of here," the sergeant said. "Just look at my boots. Don't think of anything. Just look at my boots." They crawled onto the porch and behind a wall. "When I tell you to run, run."

With the raid raging and smoke stinging his eyes, the deputy justice minister sprinted uphill towards the gate with the sergeant behind him yelling, "Run! Run! Run!" He had never moved so fast in his life. Although he accidentally hit a wall and broke two ribs, the pain didn't register as his adrenaline propelled him forward. He bolted out of the main gate, where the general was waiting.

After catching his breath, Mendoza said, "General, is Escobar dead?" The general's expression said it all. "Oh my God!" Mendoza said. "He got away! How could he get away?"

Drinking coffee at Memo's house, Pablo listened to the radio, while helicopters buzzed by. The raid had netted five of his men. Twenty-seven guards had been charged with suspicion of cooperating with him.

Roberto's son called a radio station and claimed that the escapees were hiding in a tunnel under the prison with weapons and food. He told a reporter that Pablo would surrender and return to the Cathedral if the original terms were reinstated. Hoping to unearth the tunnel, the government sent construction equipment to the prison, so that the troops could start digging. Explosives were detonated in the fields.

Through a window, Pablo gazed at the activity. "The only thing they'll find is the money in the barrels," he said, referring to $10 million underground. The radio claimed that Pablo had ordered the assassination of all the top government officials. Hoax bomb threats and evacuation drills at schools were widespread.

Besieged by journalists, Hermilda told them, "To Pablo they had already sent the plane for him to be tortured in the United States."

On the evening news, the president called for calm and promised to protect the escapees' lives if they surrendered, but he never mentioned reinstating Pablo's original deal. The US news reported that Pablo and his men had stormed out of the prison in a hail of gunfire, with their weapons blazing. These stories increased support for George HW Bush to send soldiers to Colombia to capture the narco-terrorist and to incarcerate him in America.

When darkness came, the men left Memo's and trekked through the woods. Explosions at the Cathedral rocked the countryside as the troops searched for the tunnel.

After joining his mother, Juan Pablo said, "Before the power went out at the prison, I spoke to him several times on a radio." Hearing nothing from Pablo had created a sleepless night for his family. The news reported that he had tricked the authorities into believing that he had been in a tunnel, which had given the escapees a twelve-hour advantage. His family learned that the deputy justice minister and the director of prisons had been held hostage for hours.

At another farm, Pablo called his family and urged them to ignore the news. The escapees ate and set off again. Outside a farm, five German shepherds launched at them. They couldn't shoot the dogs because the noise would have alerted the authorities. One bit El Mugre on the leg, drawing blood. Pablo threw them some snacks, which distracted them. He stayed with the dogs while the others moved on and then followed everyone.

At 3:30 AM, they arrived at a friendly farm. A driver took Roberto to see his mother, so that he could explain the situation. He didn't want to stay long, but she insisted on making food for him and Pablo. Unable to say no, he positioned himself at a window and watched for the police.

When Roberto returned to the farm, some of the group had moved on, because Pablo felt they would be harder to find if they split up. More soldiers were arriving in the area around the Cathedral, hoping to flush them out. For two days, they stayed at the farm, watching TV reports and listening to the radio. Pablo released his men who wanted to quit the war. Earring and El Mugre hid by the sea. Those who decided to stay pledged their loyalty until death and followed El Patrón through the mountains.

As usual during a crisis, Pablo remained calm. He decided to conceal his whereabouts from everyone, including his family. If he met someone, he immediately moved. "The army could catch that person by the balls and lead them to me," he said.

Years later, Roberto said, "On Saturday, after we fled from the Cathedral, we were in a hiding place by Cama Suelta in El Poblado. Pablo had spoken to a radio station for one hour. He told them: 'Look, do not look for me, because I am already out on the street, so do not waste gunpowder on hens. I escaped from there because they let me go. I did not want to leave.' Then they detected the call. Helicopters began to fly over that area. On Sunday, around four o'clock in the afternoon, we had to go to the mountain. Pablo heard the football game between Nacional and Medellín via a small radio. 'Boss, the helicopters are there!' Popeye shouted. 'Be quiet, man, Medellín is going to score a goal.' 'Boss, it's just that they are already on top.' 'Wait, wait, wait … goal, goal, goal!' And he began to shout for the goal. This was the way he was."

On July 24, 1992, Pablo recorded a statement, offering to surrender if he could go back to the Cathedral. He said the arrival of the troops had taken them by surprise. He called Mendoza a liar as he had never been kidnapped or threatened. "As for the aggression carried out against us, we won't take violent actions of any nature and yet we are willing to continue with the peace process and our surrender to justice if we can be guaranteed to stay at the Cathedral, as well as handing control of the prison to special forces of the United Nations." At the end, he said he was in the jungles of Colombia, which prompted the government to send soldiers and helicopters there.

They had been at the farm for twenty days when 5,000 soldiers were dispatched to the area. With helicopters arriving, they ran into the forest and escaped into the jungle. Unable to find them, the army randomly dropped bombs. For twelve days, they slept on hammocks, with explosions disrupting their rest.

Popeye took the family to Pablo's hideout in Envigado. Reunited with Victoria and the kids, he boasted about the escape. "But one thing has been bothering me: the army announced that I had escaped in women's clothing. I need to set this straight tonight. I'm going to contact the director of RCN radio. Popeye, call the station and get him on the line." After rectifying the situation with the director, he stated his conditions of surrender. "I want a guarantee that I shall be housed in a prison in Antioquia. The police must not be involved in any trial." Until 4 AM, Pablo stayed on the phone with journalists, but nothing was achieved.

Pablo called Alberto in the Netherlands: "Please tell the president that I am going to surrender again. I thought the government was trying to extradite me, but I can surrender again."

Alberto called Gaviria: "Look, he wants to surrender."

"No, no, no! Not this time! We're going to kill him."

CHAPTER 14
DECEPTIVE HIDING TACTICS

"The Cathedral is a grotesque monument to corruption," announced the minister of defence after visiting the prison.

"This was not a prison but a recreational ranch," announced Attorney General Gustavo de Greiff. "Photographs of parties were seen showing guards serving food and drinks to inmates and their guests. There was an inmate disguised as a woman – there was women's underwear present and graphic porn videos. It was as easy to get out as to get in. It is incredible what we saw: fake inmate cells that were actually apartments with all the possible comforts. Mr Escobar actually had three apartments: one in the main part of the prison, another in the upper part and another in the famous cabins built among a pine forest, where there were houses annexed to the headquarters and other cabins outside the perimeter of the prison where the inmates could go at any time. Radio transmitters and different weapons from those inventoried for the guards were found."

The spotlight on the conditions embarrassed the president, who was appearing on TV daily, trying to restore confidence. He told the American ambassador that he didn't have a problem with US troops on Colombian soil. He wanted all the help he could get to quickly fix the situation.

Grateful to have miraculously survived the raid, Mendoza flew back to Bogotá, where the president told him, "We must hide nothing. Don't take time to prepare a response. Just get out there and tell people exactly what happened."

Mendoza updated the Americans, who were pleased that they could resume the hunt. It was an opportunity for George HW

Bush to distract the public from domestic issues and to increase his popularity. Catching the supervillain whom he had labelled the biggest cocaine trafficker in the world would surely increase his chances of re-election. The DEA in Bogotá sent a cable to Washington:

"The BCO [the local US Embassy] feels that Escobar may finally have overstepped his self-perceived illegitimate boundaries and has placed himself in a very precarious position. Escobar's gall and bravado may lead to his ultimate downfall. But then again, the GOC [government of Colombia] has always bowed to Escobar's demands in the past. This current situation again provides the GOC with an opportunity to demonstrate its dedication to bring all narco-traffickers to justice, including the most notorious and dangerous cocaine trafficker in history, Pablo Escobar."

Amid hyped-up threats that Pablo might assassinate him and explode bombs in America, George HW Bush dispatched Delta Force, Centra Spike, the DEA, the FBI, the ATF, the CIA, the Bureau of Alcohol, Tobacco and Firearms, the army, navy and the air force after El Patrón. Out of all the agencies, Centra Spike quickly obtained results by flying planes over Medellín with technology that picked up Pablo's calls.

Pablo responded to America's involvement with a fax:

"We, the Extraditables declare: that if anything happens to Mr Pablo Escobar, we will hold President Gaviria responsible and will again mount attacks on the entire country. We will target the United States Embassy in the country, where we will plant the largest quantity of dynamite ever. We hereby declare: the blame for this whole mess lies with President Gaviria. If Pablo Escobar or any of the others turn up dead, we will immediately mount attacks throughout the entire country. Thank you very much."

George HW Bush approved a $2 million reward for information leading to Pablo. The US Embassy in Colombia offered $200,000 and relocation to America for any useful information. Advertised on TV, the reward programme included pictures of Pablo and his henchmen.

The Centra Spike eavesdropping enabled the authorities to determine that Pablo was using at least eight phones. He viewed himself as a victim of a violation of his agreement with the government and wanted to return to the Cathedral.

Centra Spike overheard him tell a lawyer that he feared the raid on the Cathedral was a US-sponsored assassination attempt: "The situation arose because they went in there shooting and all, and we were defending our lives, but our intention was to comply with the government until the end … It is possible that one or two persons were smuggled into the jail. I won't deny it … that happens in jails all over the country and the world, and, in reality, I am not to blame. The person to blame is the person who lets them in … So that if people entered shooting and all, and we had information that Americans were participating in the operation, we must put our lives first. We have families!" He said that incarceration outside the Cathedral was unsafe.

"Yes," the lawyer said. "That was the first issue that I explained to the president."

Pablo criticised Mendoza's attempt to construct a new prison at the Cathedral. "There was a delineation of the jail. It had been arranged. We made the design. We reworked the map, so the only thing that we didn't bargain for was a jail different from that one. And we need a public guarantee from the president that he will not take us out of the country … The problem is, I have some information … that there were some gringos [Americans] looking for Bush's re-election, so we need their [the Colombian government's] guarantee in this respect … Do me a favour. Tell Señor President that I know he's misinformed. Now, they say that I am perpetrating crimes from jail." Even if he were found guilty of committing a crime while in jail, Pablo said that they could have extended his stay up to a maximum of a life sentence, but they had no legal right to move him from the Cathedral.

"Perfect," the lawyer said. "We'll see that all this works out."

"Anyway, accept my apologies," Pablo said. "There'll be no more acts of violence of any nature, although some resentful people have been making some phone calls. People want to create chaos. But anyway, we are well disposed and we want to get this thing resolved … Tell the president that we were very uneasy because the gringos were going to be a part of the operation."

Another lawyer told Pablo, "We saw the tapes of the grey uniforms [CIA] and all that."

"Of the gringos?" Pablo said, wanting to make CIA and American involvement into trouble for the Colombian president. "And how many were there?"

"Well, we could see some uniforms on TV. This afternoon we asked for tapes from the evening news programme."

"There are two things that are very important," Pablo said to another lawyer. "When you have a chance of making a statement, say that what caused the biggest concern to us was the presence of the gringos. The fact that the army would be going along with the gringos. What explanation can be given for that?"

"Yes. The press is already after that. We're on top of that."

"OK. And another thing. The president has to say it officially and make an official commitment. Everything is a contract. Now it's going to be a contract signed by the minister who makes the commitment that if tomorrow or the day after tomorrow I kill the warden and get thirty more years, they don't transfer me from here. This is a commitment."

The escape concerned Don Berna, who believed that on the run Pablo would become more dangerous than ever. Accompanied by Major Gonzalez, he went to the Cathedral, which the police had converted into its headquarters, with the commander based in Pablo's room. Delta Force members used Pablo's observation tower at the prison. They were fed map coordinates from Centra

Spike when Pablo got on a phone. They started to home in on a neighbourhood called the Three Corners. The next time he made a call, his location was detected and photographed. Upon receiving the information from Delta Force, a Colombian commander dismissed it. The Americans contacted the president and suggested he send a small covert unit. Instead, he ordered a full assault by Search Bloc special forces.

From the Cathedral, Delta Force watched the headlights of the special forces convoy ascending a hill towards the Three Corners, while another set of headlights descended on the other side, which they assumed was the traffickers escaping. Troops spent four hours searching the empty ranch.

No matter what information the Americans provided, the response was always inept, which allowed Pablo to always escape. With General Maza gone, the Americans needed someone gung-ho to liaise with. That was Colonel Martínez, the head of the Search Bloc. Surely the man whose troops had killed Pablo's beloved cousin, Gustavo, could be trusted? Prior to the Cathedral, Martínez had hunted Pablo for two years. Lacking success, he had been passed over for the promotion he wanted. Just like with Maza, Pablo had made many attempts on his life.

In 1991, he had been on a flight to Spain with his family when a bomb had been found on board. The plane had to make an emergency landing otherwise the bomb would have exploded at a certain altitude. In 1992, a car bomb had been found by the Colombian Embassy on the route Martínez took to work. Afterwards, the embassy had asked Martínez to avoid their building.

With Pablo free, Martínez jumped at the chance to finish the job. Soon Martínez and Pablo were probing each other like chess players. Trying to shut down Pablo's ability to communicate and run his organisation, Martínez oversaw a blackout of cellphone use in Medellín. Pablo switched to radio and couriers. Knowing that Martínez was listening to his calls, Pablo displayed a remarkable ability to use code words and numbers. Nothing fazed him. Every time Martínez tried something new, he shifted his strategy with the indifference of a grandmaster.

On a wall in the Carlos Holguín Police School, Martínez had set up a massive photo map of Medellín. Images from the heavily militarised city were examined for illegal activity and any signs of Pablo. Every day, pieces were added to the map from photos provided by Centra Spike. By picking up phone frequencies, houses and farms were targeted for surveillance. By analysing the photos, raids were launched in the hope of finding weapons, bomb-making material and incriminating documents.

With so many agencies after him, including foreign merce-naries wanting the reward offered by the Americans, Pablo was slowly getting backed into a corner. A Colombian judge had ruled against his claim that his escape from prison had been legitimately taken out of fear for his life. The president was resolutely against him returning to the Cathedral. Even though the forces against him were increasing, he felt confident enough to give a radio interview in mid-1992.

"Do you regret having surrendered a year ago?"

Pablo said that he did, but it had been necessary to stay alive. "Does one seek escape alternatives when you have arrived at a jail to which you have voluntarily surrendered?"

"Were you the man in charge in the prison?"

"I wasn't in charge ... I wasn't just any prisoner. I was the prod-uct of a peace plan, whose cost wasn't high for the government ... They simply gave me a dignified prison and special conditions previously agreed to by the government with the lawyers and me."

About his extravagant living quarters, he said, "Even if it is the most beautiful mansion in the world, if you're limited in your movements and watched by tower guards with weapons and soldiers, then that is a prison. But I'm not going to evade responsibility in the sense that I permitted some curtains and some special furniture, and I'm willing to pay for that error in accepting the most humble cell in any jail in Antioquia as long as my rights are respected and I'm guaranteed that I'll not be moved for any reason."

"Is your head worth more than the one billion pesos offered

by the government and more than the two and a half billion pesos offered by the government of the United States?"

"It seems my problem has become political and could be important for the re-election of the president of the United States."

"At this moment, you've become once again the most sought-after man in the world. The Colombian authorities, other secret services, DEA agents, the Cali Cartel, former accomplices of your activities, deserters from your organisation, indirect or direct victims of terrorist acts. Whom do you fear the most? How do you defend yourself from them?"

"I don't fear my enemies because they are more powerful. It has been my lot to face difficult circumstances, but I always do it with dignity."

"For you, what is life?"

"It's a space of time full of agreeable and disagreeable surprises."

"Have you ever felt afraid of dying?"

"I never think about death."

"When you escaped, did you think about death?"

"When I escaped, I thought about my wife, my children, my family and all the people who depend upon me."

"Do you believe in God and the hereafter? In heaven and hell?"

"I don't like to speak publicly about God. God, to me, is absolutely personal and private. I think all the saints help me, but my mother prays a lot for me to the child Jesus of Atocha, that is why I built him a chapel in Barrio Pablo Escobar. The largest painting in the prison was of the child Jesus of Atocha."

"Why have you been willing to risk having yourself killed?"

"For my family and for the truth."

"Do you accept that you have ever committed a crime or had someone killed?"

"That answer I can only give in confession to a priest."

"How do you think everything will end for you?"

"You can never foretell that, although I wish the best."

"If it depended on you, how would you like to end your life?"

"I would like to die standing in the year 2047."

"Under what circumstances would you commit suicide?"

"I have never thought about those types of solutions."

"Of all the things that you have done, which ones are you most proud of and of which are you ashamed?"

"I am proud of my family and my people. I'm not ashamed of anything."

"Whom do you hate and why?"

"In my conflicts, I try not to end up hating anybody."

"What advice have you given your children? What would you do if either of them dedicated themselves to illegal or criminal activities?"

"I know that my children love me and understand my fight. I always want the best for them."

"What do your wife and children mean to you?"

"They are my best treasure."

"Do you accept that you are Mafioso? Does it bother you that someone says that about you?"

"The communications media has called me that thousands of times. If it bothered me, I would be in an insane asylum."

"What is it that most angers you and gets you out of control?"

"You can get angry, but you cannot lose your control. I get angry at hypocrisy and lies."

"Do you accept that they say you are a drug dealer or a criminal or don't you really care?"

"My conscience is clear, but I would respond as a Mexican comedian once said, 'It's completely inconclusive.'"

"People say that you always get what you want."

"I have not said that I have always gotten what I wanted. If I had always gotten what I wanted, everything would be rosy, and I would calmly be drinking some coffee in the Rionegro Plaza or the park at Envigado. I fight tirelessly, but I have suffered too much."

"What is the key to your immense power?"

"I don't have any special powers. The only thing that gives me strength to keep on fighting is the energy of the people who love and support me."

"Corruption. To what extent has it taken hold in the government?"

"Corruption exists in all the countries of the world. The important thing would be to know the causes of corruption in order to avoid it and stop it."

"Of what do you repent?"

"All human beings make mistakes, but I don't repent of anything because I take everything as an experience and channel it into something positive."

"If you were born again, what would you do? What would you repeat and what would you dedicate yourself to?"

"I would not do those things that I thought would turn out right, but which came out wrong. I would repeat everything that has been good and nice."

"What did your wife and children say when you were in prison and what did they think of your activities?"

"They have loved and supported me always. And they accept my cause because they know it and understand it."

"Do you consider yourself an ordinary man or someone of exceptional intelligence?"

"I am a simple citizen, born in the village of El Tablazo of the municipality of Rionegro."

"Have you personally ever taken drugs?"

"I am an absolutely healthy man. I don't smoke and I don't consume liquor. Although, with respect to cannabis, I'd have the same reply that the president of Spain gave when he was asked about it."

"Do you consider it a mistake on your part to have entered politics?"

"No, I do not accept it as a mistake. I am sure that if I had participated in other elections, I would have defeated everyone in Antioquia by an overwhelming majority."

"Why so much money? What do you do with it? Is your fortune as large as the international magazines say?"

"My money obeys a social function. That is clear and everyone knows about it."

"If you had to make a profile of yourself, what would you say about you, Pablo Escobar?"

"It's very difficult to portray oneself. I prefer that others analyse me and that others judge me."

"Why did you enter drug trafficking?"

"In Colombia, people enter this type of activity as a form of protest. Others enter it because of ambition."

"Do you feel bigger than Al Capone?"

"I'm not that tall, but I think Al Capone was a few centimetres shorter than I am."

"Do you consider yourself to be the most powerful man in Colombia? The richest? One of the most powerful?"

"Neither one nor the other."

"Did you feel complimented when the magazine *Semana* presented you as Robin Hood?"

"It was interesting and it gave me peace of mind."

"By temperament, are you violent and proud?"

"Those who know me know that I have a good sense of humour and I always have a smile on my face, even in very difficult moments. And I'll say something else: I always sing in the shower."

With his enemies assuming that he travelled everywhere with a convoy of bullet-proof vehicles and a small army of men holding rocket launchers, he did the opposite to fool them. While the war raged, he wandered on foot through the centre of Medellín, his thick beard disguising his features, accompanied only by Popeye, with them both enjoying the Christmas lights.

Walking by a car park, Popeye spotted six policemen, three on each side of an avenue, and reached for the gun tucked into the back of his trousers. Pablo grabbed his arm, told him to relax and not to look at the police, because if he gazed at them like an angry dog, they would be shot. With the police heading directly for them, Popeye felt his heartbeat jump. Calmly, Pablo walked up to the car park attendant and started small talk. Upon observing that everything seemed normal, the police walked by them. Smiling, Pablo told Popeye to spit. Reaching over, he felt Popeye's heart beating ferociously. Pablo spat and told Popeye to feel his heart. Detecting a normal heartbeat reinforced Popeye's belief that his boss was supernatural.

Instead of hiding in buildings full of bodyguards and technology, he used deception. One night he would hide in a house with a family and a child. The front door would be open, and the child would be riding around on a tricycle. Inviting the neighbours over reduced suspicion. To fool the neighbourhood porter, the family would ask him to help with a task such as a leaking tap. Walking through the house, the porter would see that everything was normal.

To move outside of Medellín, he employed more deception. One method included a friend who raised dogs. The man would show up in a van with his most dangerous dogs. Pablo would hide in a compartment at the back of the van. At checkpoints, the barking dogs deterred the police from performing an inspection.

Pablo, in his new refuge, a house in the rural area of Envigado, summoned his closest men. He was annoyed, angry and indignant because the government had breached the agreement, was refusing to negotiate his surrender, and, with the help of the Americans, was planning to extradite him. He decided to send the government a chilling message: he ordered his men to place the largest ever number of car bombs in Bogotá. He told his family members to leave the country for their own safety.

Due to the deaths and the destabilisation of the country, the president ordered the Search Bloc to redouble its efforts to kill him by any means necessary and to form any alliances required. He advertised a reward of $5 million and ordered several telephone lines at the headquarters of the Search Bloc in Medellín to receive information. The messages called in were mostly from people close to Pablo, and their objective was to misdirect any clues that could lead to the boss.

CHAPTER 15
LOS PEPES DEATH SQUAD

Pablo warned his son to watch out for the Castaños because they were working with Cali and spreading rumours that he was killing his friends, so that he could steal their money. In his book, *My Confession*, Carlos Castaño documented his meetings with Gilberto. He wrote that he had loaned Gilberto helicopters, and that the Cali godfathers were the big bosses, which was a normal thing in Colombia. Through Don Berna, the Castaños cemented their relationship with Cali.

As well as the Castaños, numerous other traffickers abandoned Pablo. According to the DEA, "As soon as Escobar killed the Galeanos and Moncadas, their people saw themselves as vulnerable and they ran to the Cali Cartel and said, 'We want to change sides.' The Cali people said, 'OK, if you want to change sides, you need to pay us.' A lot of money changed hands."

Hunting El Patrón, Don Berna, his troops and police associates only managed to capture and kill some of Pablo's men. Torture extracted valuable information. During raids, Don Berna was surprised to see altars with candles lit not just for Antioquia's most popular saint, Maria the Helper, but also lit for Pablo Escobar. In Cali, he reported his progress. The godfathers were surprised that candles were heralding Pablo as a saint, because they had underestimated the extent of the poor's admiration.

"We cannot ignore the great effort you have made," Miguel said to Don Berna, "but as long as Pablo is still alive, the country will never rest. We are offering a reward of $10 million for his head. We need you to transmit that message to everyone. Please talk to the communications expert we sent to Medellín, Chapulin."

Leaving the meeting, Don Berna hoped to have better news for the godfathers next time. When he returned to the Carlos Holguín Police School, he learned about the record number of police killed by Pablo's assassins who were claiming rewards. Fear had spread throughout the academy, causing many cadets to quit, and the family members of others to arrive and demand that they come home with them out of harm's way. As other branches of the police in Medellín disintegrated, members of the DIJIN, a.k.a. the Reds, pledged to redouble their efforts to eliminate Pablo.

The $10 million reward motivated an associate of Don Berna's called La Chiva to dupe Pablo into meeting him. At the Carlos Holguín Police School, La Chiva strategised with Don Berna, Major Gonzalez, two DEA agents and a communications expert from the US Navy.

"We're going to give you a special pen," said the communications expert, "which looks just like any other pen but has a tracking system, which will give away its location to a US spy plane 20,000 feet above you."

Don Berna, his men and members of the Reds disguised themselves as hikers and positioned themselves in El Peñol's main park in the Antioquia region. After parking in a recreational vehicle, La Chiva was escorted by one of Pablo's men to the edge of a massive dam with a small boat waiting. A DEA agent told the spy plane that La Chiva was on his way to Pablo.

"Due to the mountain range and thick cloud cover, we've been unable to detect any type of signal so far," reported the spy plane.

After twenty minutes on the water, La Chiva arrived at an island and was escorted to a house named after Pablo's daughter: La Manuela. During a thorough search, the bodyguards ignored the pen, much to La Chiva's relief.

Sporting a thick beard and having gained weight, Pablo was relaxed despite his predicament. "I need you to help me find Berna. My information says he is with the Search Bloc. Due to his cooperation, several of my men have died."

La Chiva gulped. "That's no problem at all. You have my full support." Believing that his location had been pinpointed by the pen, La Chiva expected the police to raid the house at any moment. When nothing happened, he struggled to appear calm and kept talking to buy time before the authorities arrived.

Hours later, the plane contacted the men on the ground. "Despite all our efforts, obtaining the signal has been impossible. We're so low on fuel, we have to return to the base, so this mission is over." With sad faces, the men on the mission returned. La Chiva appeared in Medellín unscathed, glad he was alive but disappointed about not getting the reward.

Despite Pablo managing to evade capture, many of his men started to fall at the hands of Los Pepes and the Search Bloc, including Tyson. The Americans provided information they had received through their reward programme. An informant had located Tyson. To trigger the raid, "The party has begun" was whispered over a radio to Search Bloc troops. An explosive charge blew a steel door off its hinges and blasted it through a wall. The door flew into the air and dropped nine storeys. Twenty-six troops charged inside. Due to the iron bars on the windows, Tyson couldn't escape. He was executed with a bullet between the eyes. His death was recorded as due to a gun battle with the National Police.

Pablo responded the same day. His hit men shot four police. Over the next two days, five more died. Pablo paid $2,000 per killing. Over six months, sixty-five police were killed in Medellín, including many of the men working for Martínez. Even though their identities were supposed to have been a state secret, many of them were executed at home or travelling to work.

With Gaviria still refusing to negotiate, and Pablo's legend deflating, El Patrón decided to demonstrate his strength. At a nightclub in El Poblado called Loose Bed, he gathered 200 men in sixty cars loaded with weapons and dynamite. After touring around Medellín, they established a checkpoint on the Las Palmas route, which connects Medellín with the Rionegro airport, and situated two car bombs nearby. As cars stopped at the roadblock, their passengers were asked to identify themselves and whether they were armed. All guns were confiscated. Despite his beard, many of the passengers recognised Pablo, who was toting a machine gun, a pistol and a communications radio.

Seeing people surprised and afraid by his presence, he said, "Don't worry about the situation. My war is only against the government." Growing suspicious about a car, he approached it. With the man and woman inside failing to recognise him, he said, "I'm a DAS officer. Can you show me your ID?"

The driver displayed a police-major's badge. Pablo gave his men the nod. Two of them dragged the major from the car and beat him ferociously. They forced him to kneel and shot him in the head. The woman was executed.

Pablo noticed his men confiscating weapons from a car containing a woman and two men. "Can we have our weapons back, Pablo?" asked Maria Lia, Jorge Ochoa's wife.

Greeting her, Pablo told his men, "Return everything to them!"

Don Berna received calls about the roadblock. The authorities and the communications expert from the Cali Cartel eavesdropping on calls originating from the checkpoint confirmed that it was Pablo issuing commands. At a meeting hosted with great urgency, Major Gonzales asked for suggestions:

"Sending men by land is too dangerous and risky, because there are probably car bombs in the area to counter such attacks."

"The only way is by air. We need to send a helicopter."

When the helicopter arrived at the checkpoint, dozens of Pablo's men aimed their weapons at the sky. The helicopter returned fire, but due to all the civilians below, it withdrew.

While Pablo congratulated his men, members of the Search Bloc attempted to approach the checkpoint on foot until an abandoned Renault drew their attention. Examining the car, technicians discovered over 300 kilos of dynamite, which they deactivated. After three hours, Pablo and his men abandoned the checkpoint, satisfied that the show of strength had been a PR victory.

The vehicles headed west of the city, through the Bulerías sector, in search of the house of Captain Posada, commander of the DIPOL (Directorate of Police Intelligence in Medellín), who had led operations against the cartel. Stoking fury in the hearts of his men, Pablo told them that Posada detained young people from the communes and tortured them with a device to pluck chickens and killed them. Their vehicles surrounded the house. A dynamite blast reduced the building to rubble. They found Posada alive, so they executed him.

In the Bethlehem neighbourhood, they dynamited the house where Tyson had died a few days earlier. Tyson's family attempted to bury him discreetly. In the Villanueva Chapel, they closed the doors to the public. At 6 PM, the San Pedro cemetery was closed. At 8 PM, the funeral procession arrived. The family had suffered from the war: two dead and three arrested. In prison in America, Tyson's brother, La Kika, had converted to evangelism and requested a pardon for his acts, which didn't save him from getting multiple life sentences.

The authorities tried to pin Captain Posada's murder on Juan Pablo. A witness claimed that Pablo and his son had been seen together on the night of the murder in a bar in Envigado. In juvenile court, Juan Pablo pointed out that on the night of the murder he had been in a building that had been raided by the Search Bloc. Eventually, the witness recanted his testimony and stated that he had been tortured into making the allegation.

Invited to dinner in August 1992 by the Castaño brothers, Don Berna arrived at Montecasino with Major Gonzalez. Carlos, Fidel and Vicente Castaño said that they were in Medellín to challenge Pablo. Having rebuilt militarily, the Castaño brothers were ready to take on El Patrón. After the deaths of Gacha and Henry Perez, Fidel had become the national paramilitary leader. Although wanted for massacres in peasant communities, his ties with important sectors of the army kept him free.

They discussed the latest developments, including the death of Captain Posada. Pablo's displays of strength had intimidated the government into lashing out at the Search Bloc. Attorney General de Greiff had criticised the Search Bloc for being cowardly and inept.

"We need to form an organisation," Fidel said, "that will unite everybody who Pablo has terrorised, all those who disagree with his methods and desire peace and harmony to be restored to Colombia."

"I propose the organisation be called Los Pepes [People Persecuted by Pablo Escobar]," Carlos said. Everyone agreed.

"Later on, Los Pepes," Vicente said, "will become the continuation of our counterinsurgency project and we'll only have to change their name to AUC [United Self-Defense Forces of Colombia]."

Fidel would be the commander of the organisation, Carlos the head of operations and Don Berna would gather information, organise the other collaborators and maintain relations with Cali.

"I recently met the president and the minister of defence," Major Gonzalez said. "They've authorised me to use any methods necessary to eliminate Pablo. They also agreed to hide and divert any investigations into our activity."

"Let's issue a communiqué to influence public opinion," Carlos said. "It should announce the formation of Los Pepes and invite citizens to collaborate and join our cause. We need to carry out a forceful operation to draw attention to its launch."

They planned to kill everybody who worked for Pablo and to destroy his properties. Wiping out his hit men would deplete his army. Murdering his lawyers would destroy his legal power. Assassinating his accountants and money launderers would sap the lifeblood from his business. Then the noose would be tightened around his family. By killing the household staff, the servants, the children's nanny and teacher, Los Pepes would bring the terror of death into the family's home. Knowing how much Pablo loved his wife and children, Carlos calculated that the threat would force the drug lord to reveal himself. At that point, Pablo would have to decide whether he wanted to be taken dead or face the consequences of getting tortured by Los Pepes if he were captured alive.

By the end of 1992, the government was escalating the raids on traffickers. Fearing for their lives, Popeye, Otto and Roberto handed themselves in and were incarcerated. Pablo told Victoria that he would have to relocate after his 43rd birthday and that they would be apart. In an atmosphere tainted with tension, his birthday was celebrated with a modest amount of food and cake. Around midnight, Victoria approached Pablo. "If I must take the kids to Medellín, it'll be after December 7, the Day of the Little Candles, as we have always celebrated it together."

On December 7, 1992, the family joined a statue of the Virgin Mary in a courtyard at the rear of the safe house. While Manuela played, Pablo and his son bowed their heads and Victoria prayed to the Virgin Mary. A candle was lit for each of them. Before leaving the next day, he warned his wife to urge her siblings to flee overseas as the situation was getting increasingly dangerous.

During Christmas 1992, Pablo wrote to two senators, offering to surrender if he could be housed at a police academy in Medellín, under military supervision. He wanted the Search Bloc to be disbanded and claimed that Martínez was torturing people to get information. He said he was going to respond to the war in kind with more kidnappings and bombings: "What would the government do if a 10,000 kg bomb were placed at the Colombian prosecutor general's office?"

With multiple agencies still unable to catch him, the US proposed a two-pronged strategy. As he had targeted the family members of his enemies, the CIA suggested doing the same: "Escobar does seem to have genuine paternal feelings for his children, and the young daughter Manuela is described as his favorite. His parents were once kidnapped by a rival group and Escobar apparently spared no effort or expense rescuing them. Whether his concern for his parents or his children would overcome his stringent security consciousness is not clear." The other prong was to employ a method that the CIA had used for decades in South

America: arming and training a death squad, for which Los Pepes was ideal.

In December 1992, Juan Pablo was in a building saying Christmas prayers with thirty other children and almost 200 adults. A bodyguard charged into the room. "There's a raid!" Juan Pablo tried to escape through the back, but men with rifles blocked his path. Troops searched the congregation and requested to see their ID papers. The plucky teenager, who was big for his age, identified himself as Pablo's son. He said that he lived in the building and his papers were upstairs. A police colonel arrived, and ordered two troops to guard Juan Pablo, with instructions to shoot him if he so much as blinked. The colonel called the Search Bloc's headquarters to report that he had Pablo's son and was going to bring him in.

A former governor of Antioquia, who lived in the building, came downstairs. Dressed in pyjamas, he asked the colonel whether the raid had been conducted lawfully. Emboldened by the governor's presence, the parents started demanding food for their children. The colonel ordered Juan Pablo to follow him. Pablo's wife watched the guards prod her son. Separating Juan Pablo from everybody, they took him into a foyer and ordered him to stay still. Dozens of men with black hoods – including the Castaño brothers – surrounded Juan Pablo and aimed guns at him. They ordered him to yell his name. The other male guests and Pablo's wife and daughter were brought in and told to yell their names. The colonel ordered his troops to take Juan Pablo away. He protested that he hadn't done anything illegal. The colonel said that they were going to have a little fun with Pablo's son at the Search Bloc's headquarters.

At 3 AM, troops escorted Juan Pablo out. An official from the inspector general's office arrived. He ordered the troops to remove Juan Pablo's handcuffs because they had no authority to arrest a minor. The official and the colonel yelled at each other. Eventually, the troops departed without Juan Pablo.

Even though they did not know that the Castaño brothers had

been present, Pablo's family were in shock at the close call. They realised that they had been targeted in violation of the agreement with Cali to not go after each other's family members. Now they would not be safe anywhere.

During Pablo's final Christmas, an explosion on San Juan Street in western Medellín killed four police and injured forty-six people. At night, with a long beard and with his daughter on his shoulders, he walked along the crowded La Playa Avenue in the city centre, enjoying the festive lights.

In a letter to Attorney General de Greiff, Pablo announced the formation of a group called Rebel Antioquia. He wanted to gain political status with a new negotiation by removing the stain of the Extraditables:

"Reporting the perpetrators of kidnappings, torture and massacres does not make sense, because everyone already knows about it. No criminals are being sought or sanctioned by the criminal police because they work for the government, and the government, eager for medals in its fight against drug trafficking, only considers medals rewarded from Medellín to be useful. So, these are obtained using methods of barbarism. My lawyers have been raided and looted, imprisoned, threatened and charged with carrying weapons, drugs and dynamite to be shown as delinquents and terrorists. Faced with these circumstances, I have no alternative but to rule out the legal struggle and undertake an organised armed struggle, so I would like to inform you of my determination to found and lead a group that will be called Rebel Antioquia. As on previous occasions, I will always be attentive to dialogue and the search for peace, but from now on, the conditions of that dialogue will be the same as those used for all rebel groups called subversives or guerrillas."

He aimed to revive the regionalist memory of the Antioquia sector and fight for a separatist project. He once said that he wanted to blow up the bridge over the Magdalena River to definitively separate Antioquia from Bogotá, citing a political motive as the goal of his struggle had become stale and he lacked the power to be treated as a political figurehead.

Colonel Naranjo later stated: "Pablo never had a preconceived superlative goal around the whole struggle he gave. He never intended that the terrorist campaign be aimed, for example, to legalise drug trafficking. It was simply for challenging the state. For what? It is not known, which places him in an anarchist profile. If you study his profile well, you can conclude that it was terror for terror without a specific goal. He was a social revenge-specialist, and drug trafficking was his instrument to charge society and the establishment for what he felt was unfair. He wanted to claim a sense of class struggle ... but that is not expressed, it is not elaborated, and it is only speculation to try to elaborate on it today ... He was typically an anarchist."

Pablo spent New Year with his family, but they quickly separated again for safety reasons. He notified the attorney general that due to the raids on his lawyers, he had no choice but to concentrate on war, because the legal channels for negotiating his surrender had been cut off. He criticised the violence, murder and torture by the authorities.

In early 1993, his sister-in-law, Luz, was shopping at a mall. Trucks arrived with armed men led by Carlos Castaño. Intending to kidnap her, they approached Luz, but they backtracked when they saw she was in the company of the wife of a powerful trafficker. Seeing smoke in the distance, Luz fled. Carlos Castaño and his men had set fire to her house, including art worth millions. The only piece Carlos had salvaged was Salvador Dalí's *Rock 'n' Roll*. Luz reported the incident to Pablo's family, and warned that Carlos was capable of anything.

Going into 1993, the war escalated. Several of Pablo's key men were killed in battle. He ordered car bombs in Bogotá, which killed dozens of civilians and outraged the public.

To Los Pepes, the Cali godfathers contributed $50 million for weapons, informants and assassins, in the hope of eliminating their competitor, while in America, the godfather Chepe invested in an expensive computer system that Cali used to collect information and analyse data on the Medellín Cartel. The former Colombian president, Ernesto Samper, credited Cali's intelligence network for being the key element in toppling El Patrón.

Many members of Los Pepes were off-duty police and troops who had lost colleagues and family members to Pablo. They could now torture and murder with impunity. Colombian and US government agencies – including the DEA, CIA and State Department – provided them intelligence.

When asked who was in Los Pepes, Carlos Castaño responded, "From the president down we are all Los Pepes." The president pardoned fifty traffickers who agreed to cooperate with the prosecutor general's office, which meant joining the fight against Pablo.

On January 30, 1993, Pablo arranged a car bomb in Bogotá by a bookstore. It destroyed part of the building and sent human limbs flying. Twenty-one died and seventy were injured. Over the next few days, his family's dwellings were burned or bombed, injuring his mother and aunt. A DEA cable described a vigilante group – ideal raw material for a CIA-backed death squad:

"The CNP [Colombian National Police] believe these bombings were committed by a new group of individuals known as 'Los Pepes' (Perseguidos por Pablo Escobar). This group ... has vowed to retaliate against Escobar, his family, and his associates, each and every time Escobar commits a terrorist act which injures innocent people ... Obviously the CNP and the GOC [Government of Colombia] cannot condone the actions of 'Los Pepes,' even though they may secretly applaud these retaliatory acts."

The government's response to Pablo's bookstore bomb was to make him "public enemy number one" and to offer over $6 million for information leading to his capture. The Search Bloc and Los Pepes started to execute any of Pablo's underlings whom they could locate. Murders were reported as "Killed in a gun battle with the Colombian police."

On the run from El Patrón for years, Mauricio Restrepo had been waiting for Pablo's enemies to form an alliance. After the disappearance of his friend Valencia, the trafficker had warned the Ochoas, Moncadas and Galeanos that Pablo would canni-balise his friends. After the murders at the Cathedral, Restrepo had paid a pilot to repeatedly fly over the prison's restricted air to spook Pablo and his men into believing that they were about to be bombed. One flight had dropped leaflets over Medellín, which had stated that Pablo was murdering his friends. For days, he had observed the prison with a telescope and had documented the routines of the inmates. After studying the characteristics of different helicopters and explosives, he had a new detailed plan to bomb the Cathedral, which had ended with the escape.

Restrepo later stated: "Escobar had many enemies, the mourn-ers of his thousands of victims. Let's not forget that in Medellín alone he killed about a thousand policemen. When Los Pepes began to act, many of those anonymous enemies took that fight as their own. Of course, there was a singular group that we could call the elite that was connected with the authorities and with people from Cali, and that gave him the toughest blows. But primarily what Escobar faced was a great social resistance."

The CIA didn't want to get caught training and arming a death squad that was getting financed by the Cali Cartel, which wanted to expand its cocaine business at Pablo's expense. To circumvent the law, the CIA trained the Los Pepes members who were police and special forces. With $2,000 bounties on their heads, many of the police had become frustrated by the limits of the law that prevented them from responding with the same deadly force that Pablo used on them. In their official capacity, these police were trained by the CIA in torture and assassination techniques.

The Cricket gave the Americans some advice, which the DEA relayed in a cable:

"[Ospina] states that Pablo Escobar's apprehension should be planned by accomplishing five goals. First ... key Escobar orga-nization members ... should be arrested or killed, if there are no charges pending against them in Colombia. [Second], [Ospina] then named attorneys who handle Escobar's criminal problems and whose deaths would create havoc for Escobar. Third, the informant named properties and important assets belonging to Escobar which should be destroyed ...

"Ospina stated that the five lead attorneys who handled Pablo's criminal and financial activities were worse than Pablo and should be killed. 'These attorneys negotiate with the Colombian government on [his] behalf and are fully aware of the scope of [his] activities since [he] consults them before he carries out any action.' Step five was the destruction of Pablo's property and possessions to make Pablo angry.

"[Ospina] claimed that in order to bring Escobar out of hiding, he needs to be provoked or angered and made desperate so that he wants to strike back. The informant claimed that Escobar may then make mistakes."

The Cricket suggested using the media as a weapon. "He [Pablo] controls the media through fear and payments and has confused the Colombian public by having himself portrayed as a wronged Colombian citizen, not really as dangerous as he appears to be in the foreign press." To obtain invaluable information about Pablo, he recommended cutting deals with incarcerated traffickers.

The Americans employed the Cricket's strategy on Carlos Lehder, who was claiming that Pablo had played a role in his capture and extradition. Lehder detailed Pablo's habits:

"Escobar is strictly a ghetto person, not a farm or jungle person. He fears more the communist and nationalist guerrillas than the army, so he remains in the Magdalena Medio Valley, a non-guerrilla region. Since the guerrillas remain in the high mountains one could disregard the mountains as Escobar's hiding place ... Escobar always tries to keep within distance range for his cellular phone to reach Medellín's phone base. That's approximately 100 miles, so he can call any time.

"Generally, P. Escobar occupies the main house with some of

his hit men, radio operator (Big High Frequency radio receiver), cooks, whores and messengers. For transportation they have jeeps, motorcycles and sometimes a boat. I have never seen him riding a horse. Escobar gets up at 1 or 2 PM and goes to sleep at 1 or 2 AM.

"Fugitive Escobar uses from 15 to 30 security guards, with arms and WT (walkie-talkies). Two shifts of 12 hours each. Two at the main road entrance, some along the road, the rest around the perimeter of the main house (one mile) and one at his door … The main house always has two or three gateway paths which run to the forest and thus towards a second hideout near a river where a boat is located, or a tent with supplies and radios. Escobar is an obese man, certainly not a muscle man or athlete. He could not run 15 minutes without respiratory trouble. Unfortunately, the military-police has never used hunting dogs against him.

"The only realistic de facto solution, as I analysed it, is a new military government or, at the very minimum, a freedom fighters brigade, controlled by the DEA, and independent of the Colombian politicians, police or army … There are a great number of Colombian people from all walks of life that are genuinely willing to assist, support, finance and even participate in the effective forming of a civilian militia … The rich, the poor, the peasant, the political left, center and right are willing to cooperate. Every day Escobar remains at large, he becomes more powerful and dangerous."

In January 1993, Los Pepes went public by announcing they were engaged in a war to the death against Pablo. The group used dynamite to blow up Hermilda's country house in El Peñol, Antioquia. It also exploded car bombs in El Poblado near other family properties. The media coverage was so large that Pablo quickly became aware. From his safe house, he had his men call the news and state that he was going to cover Colombia with blood and death.

He told his wife to send the kids to America, where she should join them later after obtaining a new visa. She agreed to send them with her sister-in-law, her sister-in-law's two children and Juan Pablo's girlfriend Andrea. With Manuela refusing to abandon her two pet poodles, it was agreed that they could go.

Victoria's sister Astado and her three kids hid from Los Pepes in a tiny city in Central America, surviving with a meagre amount of furniture, bedding and cutlery. Tuning into Colombian radio stations, hoping to hear any news, they were distraught to learn that Los Pepes had executed three of their friends and left signs around their necks, which stated that they had collaborated with Pablo.

Trapped in a safe house, Victoria learned that her mother had suffered a debilitating stroke, which had rendered her mute, bed-ridden and depressed. A sister emerged from hiding in Medellín to collect something by car, only to be tailed by Carlos Castaño, until she managed to lose him, which saved her life.

In the Tequendama residences in Bogotá, owned by the army, Fidel Castaño interrogated people with a question: "Are you with Pablo or against him?" The faithful were tied and tortured. The compliant received properties and benefits.

To find out whose side the Ochoas were on, Los Pepes burned one of their houses. When they were about to destroy another property, Mauricio Restrepo stood in front of the men. "To do something against the Ochoas, you'll have to kill me first." After preventing the operation, he went to Fidel Castaño. "If you're going to attempt this against my friends, kill me at once, because I will not allow it."

To defuse the situation, Restrepo arranged a meeting between Cali and some of the Ochoa women. After finding out, Pablo wrote: "I know that there is a call from Fidel pressing Jorge Ochoa to turn against me. You know that Jorge is a serious and loyal man and does not switch sides, because he knows that I have acted with just reason." Without Restrepo's intervention, the Ochoas might not have survived the war.

Information received by Los Pepes indicated that Pablo was

scheduled to hide at a farm in Venecia, south-west Antioquia. After coordinating an operation with the Search Bloc, the troops enlisted a fisherman to help them cross the Cauca River. His fragile canoe made multiple trips across turbulent water. On the last trip, a high-ranking officer had so much equipment that he drowned. The men exerted all their effort trying to rescue him but failed. For three days, they searched until his corpse was found floating on another river. In his safe house, Pablo celebrated the officer's death.

In Medellín, Carlos Castaño led Los Pepes. They dynamited more properties, including luxury homes, farms and the famous Cama Suelta nightclub in Envigado. People associated with Pablo were detained, tortured, thrown on the roads, disappeared or dropped from helicopters into the jungles of Chocó – known as Operation Ruana Verde.

South of Medellín, in a warehouse in the industrial zone of Guayabal, Pablo stored his classic cars, including a 1930s Ford worth over $1 million. Using rockets, Los Pepes obliterated the vehicles. An American antique car collector who had spent years trying to acquire the 1930s Ford arrived at the scene. Observing the remains of the vehicle, he yelled that an infamy had been committed against history and sobbed.

For the purpose of tracking Pablo, Hugo Martínez Junior, a.k.a. Frequency, and a communications expert from Los Pepes, received equipment provided by the US. Due to Antioquia's unique topography, the equipment was failing to detect signal locations. The two men began to refine the equipment.

Pablo set off car bombs in Cartagena and Bogotá. Big Gun's men detonated a truck by an Elite Force checkpoint on the road to Las Palmas near the Intercontinental Hotel. The media blamed suicide hit men. The truck driver had belonged to a group called the Disposables, mostly consisting of street beggars. For about a month, those desperate souls would be cleaned, fed and, if necessary, taught how to drive. With the authorities providing security at a soccer game, a car bomb exploded which killed some police, three passers-by and injured twenty. After hearing the news, Gaviria intensified pressure on the Search Bloc to get Pablo.

Years later, General Maza commented on how and why Pablo's power had collapsed by now: "Escobar was weakened by having killed his friends, more than from the casualties we committed against him. Because by having confronted his friends, Los Pepes were formed, who acted outside the law and knew all his ways. Having fought against them was the worst of his mistakes, as he received a response from new enemies who were, at the end, more powerful than him. When Pablo Escobar murdered his lieutenants, some traffickers like Ospina Baraya-Chapulín, Guillo Ángel and Molina Yepes testified before the prosecution and helped to dislodge the organization. Those of Cali and Gacha's former enemies played a crucial role. Escobar, with the decision to kill his lieutenants, re-united what he had divided. The only true thing is that Los Pepes, with Fidel Castaño at the helm, finished not only Escobar, but the entire organization."

Pablo wrote a letter to one of his lawyers: "If it sounds like bombs, it's not my fault. People are incensed about tortures, and people do not see a way to fix this, and people disappear every day in the neighbourhoods, but to finish us, they will have to throw an atomic bomb on Medellín, and there would still be a danger of us coming out of the ashes. They better not believe anymore in the fictitious victories claimed by the police, since the police do not have time to do intelligence because they are staying up late robbing and burning farms. Several of the properties that have been burned are not mine, the one in El Tablazo in Rionegro was burned only because it was called Manuela, but it's just that the owner's daughter also has that name. I did not collect farms. The Manuela farm from El Peñol was burned by the government because they wanted to confiscate it; the same as the car warehouses."

Patrolling a street near the Atanasio Girardot Sports Complex, Don Berna learned that one of Pablo's men, the Cat, was running a business there. His men and Search Bloc troops surrounded the building and captured the Cat. Under torture, he revealed the location of 5,000 kilos of dynamite, two vehicles customised for car bombs and the name of the person who had purchased the dynamite in Ecuador. The buyer died in a shootout with the Search Bloc, who also killed one of Pablo's finance managers.

With Los Pepes closing in, Pablo hid in an apartment in the Conquistadores neighbourhood and stopped all telecommunications. For two months, Los Pepes made no progress, as he had effectively disappeared.

A call to his mother was intercepted: "The painter Botero invites you to his exhibition, in the usual place." Surveillance was established at her El Poblado residence, which Hermilda left to get a taxi, which circled and looped all over the place to avoid detection. By using twenty cars in rotation, she was successfully tailed to a restaurant on Colombia Street. After she went inside, Major Gonzalez ordered officers to follow her. Unable to locate her after a few minutes, they radioed that she wasn't there. A raid revealed that the restaurant had another exit, which she had escaped through.

Thanks to their insider knowledge, Los Pepes went on the rampage: kidnapping, bombing, torturing and murdering anyone associated with Pablo, regardless of whether they had committed a crime. Prime targets were family members, his workforce and especially his lawyers and accountants. Many of his employees defected to Cali, which was flourishing and tightening its grip on the Colombian government through bribery. The Americans claimed to be in Colombia waging a War on Drugs, yet they were sharing intelligence with Los Pepes and Cali, who were increasing the cocaine supply to America.

In a note, Pablo blamed Colonel Martínez:

"Personnel under your supervision set car bombs at buildings in El Poblado, where some of my relatives live. I want to tell you that your terrorist actions will not stop my struggle under any circumstances. Your threats and your car bombs against my family have been added to the hundreds of young people that you have murdered in the city of Medellín in your headquarters of torture in the school Carlos Holguín. I hope that the Antioquian community becomes aware of what you do with the dynamite you seize, and of the criminal actions undertaken by men who cover their faces with ski masks. Knowing that you are part of the government, I wish to warn you that if another incident of this nature occurs, I will retaliate against relatives of government officials who tolerate and do not punish your crimes. Don't forget that you, too, have a family."

The warning from Pablo didn't deter Los Pepes, who were just getting started on annihilating his personnel. Using Medellín Cartel organisational charts provided by the CIA and Centra Spike, Los Pepes knew exactly who to target to maximise the damage. They offered rewards for information and caused a stir in the media by announcing what they were going to do to Pablo's associates.

In February 1993, a manager low down in the cartel hierarchy was found dead with a sign attached to his neck: "For working for the narco-terrorist and baby-killer Pablo Escobar. For Colombia. Los Pepes." They started to kill up to six of Pablo's employees and associates a day, including a director of the National Police of Colombia who was on Pablo's payroll. They shot the man in charge of financing operations multiple times in the head. Seven teenage friends of Juan Pablo were found shot dead.

In Itagüí prison, the Ochoa Brothers hired saddlery teachers and set up a workshop which hosted interns. In the dining room, they hung a picture of Father Garcia, whom the prisoners worshipped as a saint. Popeye's incarceration had been peaceful so far. Up at 5 AM, he exercised, ate breakfast, went to the workshop in the morning to carve leather, and in the afternoon, he played games with his classmates. After dinner, he retired to his room to read before falling asleep. Used to squandering millions of pesos, he now counted every peso and spent cautiously. When he thought about Pablo's warm smile and the security that he had felt, he wanted to be back at his side, but he reminded himself that the war could destroy everyone at any moment.

As Los Pepes knew the locations of Pablo's safe houses, he was forced to find new ones, a job assigned to his men, Limón and El Angelito, who had pledged to stay with him until the end. With each hideout costing Pablo up to $100,000 in hush money to the occupants, he was burning through cash, which was becoming increasingly difficult for him to obtain from his stashes.

On the run, Pablo's family moved from hideout to hideout. At one, they arrived to find Pablo there. He said they needed to leave the country as soon as possible. They decided to flee to America. They booked flights for Miami scheduled to depart on February 18, 1993, at 10 AM. Pablo told them to get to the airport by 5 AM, and if they were recognised, Cali and Los Pepes would be alerted. A car transported the luggage separately the day before.

Pablo told Victoria, "They must be vigilant on the way to the Rionegro airport because Los Pepes will seize any opportunity to snatch our kids."

Victoria visited Juan Pablo's girlfriend's house to get travel permission from her mother. After chatting for twenty minutes, Andrea's mother warned her daughter that she was now entering a life of suffering. At 4 AM on January 19, 1993, Victoria hugged her children, wondering whether she would ever see them again.

The family members took taxis and shuttles to the airport to avoid attracting Los Pepes on the road. Upon arrival at the airport, Juan Pablo and his girlfriend went straight to the car with the luggage. They remained inside for three hours, unable to sleep.

When it was time to enter the airport building, Juan Pablo exited the car and realised that something was amiss. Noticing airport police in a no-parking zone and a white pickup truck that Pablo had warned belonged to Los Pepes, he told his girlfriend they had been spotted. With his adrenaline surging, he insisted they quickly go through passport control to get to a safer area. The queue was so long that they bolted to the front with the other people in line yelling at them.

In a booth, a DAS agent studied Juan Pablo's passport, which had been signed by Pablo because his son was a minor. Eventually, he reluctantly stamped both passports. Beyond the booth, Juan Pablo noticed hooded figures lurking behind tinted windows, carrying machine guns and rifles. The airport staff were tense, as if bracing for the hooded men to act. No officials or police approached the men.

The rest of the family joined the line for the metal detector and drug-sniffing dogs. Young men appeared with their suitcases and started opening them for inspection by Elite Anti-terrorist Unit agents. With onlookers marvelling at the drama, Juan Pablo protested that the agents shouldn't be ripping open their luggage just as they were about to board a plane. Undaunted, the agents kept repeating the same searches to ensure that they missed their flight, so that Los Pepes could intercept them on the way out. Juan Pablo hand-signalled to a bodyguard who was shadowing the family. An agent noticed, but the bodyguard disappeared. Juan Pablo protested that he had only been itching his ear.

After the plane left without them, they were told to leave immediately. Pointing at the hooded men outside the windows, Juan Pablo said that the agents had delayed the family on purpose, so that Los Pepes could abduct and kill them. The agents were now responsible for their lives, and if anything bad happened, his dad would hold them accountable. The prospect of retribution from Pablo frightened the agents.

The media arrived with lights and cameras flashing. The hooded men disappeared. A 50-year-old airline worker approached Juan

Pablo and offered help. He took the teenager to an office with a phone and a copy of the *Yellow Pages*. They ordered a helicopter. When it arrived, agents blocked the family from boarding it. The bodyguard whom Juan Pablo had signalled had alerted an official from the inspector general's office, who finally arrived and ordered the agents to release the family. They had too much luggage for the helicopter, so they abandoned it.

A colonel from the Search Bloc told Juan Pablo that they were going to find and kill his bastard father. Juan Pablo wished him luck. The colonel clenched his fist, as if to throw it at Juan Pablo, but changed his mind upon noticing the cameras. The colonel said that Juan Pablo would not be so lucky next time, and that they would all be killed.

The helicopter took them to another airport, where a member of the inspector general's office was waiting to help them. The media arrived again. The family waited in an office, while Juan Pablo devised a plan to dodge Los Pepes, which he assumed was on its way. He announced to the reporters that the family had almost been killed in an ambush at the previous airport. He needed their help in exchange for an interview. They were going to leave the building, but they needed the media to follow them and to keep filming in case they were abducted.

At high speed, the family left in a taxi, followed by the media, and headed for the building that the Search Bloc had raided during the pre-Christmas celebrations. In the basement, Juan Pablo gave his first media interview. He discussed their situation and the prospect of Pablo surrendering to the authorities. After the interview, the family fled through an escape route by the swimming pool. They traversed a small creek to get in the backyard of the next property, where they owned an apartment and a getaway vehicle. After they had sped off in an SUV, five trucks arrived and hooded men emerged. Los Pepes searched everywhere for the family. At another property, they changed clothes and vehicles.

After learning that the American mission had failed, Victoria frantically paced in the safe house, expecting the news to report that they had been abducted by Los Pepes. Reporters started to claim that they had fled in a helicopter. Frustrated by developments, she packed clothing, while awaiting to be collected by one of Pablo's men.

Seven hours later, when she was on the verge of madness, her transport arrived. "Don't worry. I'm going to take you to meet your children." The driver blindfolded her. At the new location, the blindfold was removed, and she was relieved to see her family. Crying, she hugged and clung onto them. Juan Pablo described the day's ordeal.

Juan Pablo was warning that the new location was unsafe, when someone rang the doorbell. A bodyguard sent by Pablo confirmed that they had to leave immediately. The apartment had been compromised, so they needed to extract the cash hidden there. They tried to undo the screws for the wardrobe containing the money, but they were too tight. At first, they were afraid of breaking it open in case the neighbours reported the noise. Assuming that by the time the authorities arrived, they would be gone with the money, they took a hammer from the kitchen and smashed the wood. They packed the money into a briefcase and fled.

Driving away, they scoured the area for hooded men. Their car snaked across town on a convoluted route to shed any tails. Pablo had opened the garage door. As soon as the car was inside, he closed it. Relieved they had dodged Los Pepes, he hugged them. He told them that he had been watching everything on TV and listening on a radio. He praised Juan Pablo for his quick thinking and for evacuating them in a helicopter.

As part of a strategy to keep Pablo's family in constant danger from Los Pepes to draw him into making a mistake, the US government cancelled their visas, so that they couldn't flee to America. In late February, he assured them that arrangements would be made for them to go to another country, even if it meant getting fake documents and false visas. The alternative was that they could join him in the jungle, where he had the support of the

ELN guerrillas. Unable to bear the thought of their children in the jungle, his wife sobbed.

On February 27, 1993, Los Pepes destroyed more property. On March 2, the death squad assassinated the manager of Hacienda Nápoles, who unfortunately had the last name Henao, which the killers had assumed meant he was related to Victoria. On March 4, one of Pablo's lawyers died.

In late February and early March, Los Pepes went on a killing spree. The group wiped out the brother of a man who dealt real estate for Pablo. They bombed properties belonging to Pablo's bankers and lawyers. On March 4, 1993, the corpse of one of Pablo's lead lawyers was discovered with a note from Los Pepes threatening the rest of his lawyers, two of whom were swiftly executed. They killed Roberto Escobar's lawyer as he exited the prison he had been visiting. They tortured one of Pablo's lawyers and his 18-year-old son. Kidnapped by fifteen men with machine guns, the father and son were found in the trunk of a car, shot in the head, their hands taped together, with a note from Los Pepes: "Through their profession, they initiated abductions for Pablo Escobar. What do you think of the exchange for the bombs in Bogotá, Pablo?" Most of his lawyers quit. One thought he could outsmart Los Pepes by continuing to work undercover. In Medellín, he was strolling with his brother when Los Pepes shot him twenty-five times. Another fled the country.

Carlos Castaño sent one of his suicide attackers after Pablo's friend, the mayor of Envigado, Jorge Mesa. The attacker, Marcos, was terminally ill and wanted to buy a house for his family before he died. Carlos gave him a suit, a tie and an MP5 machine gun. Pretending to be a DAS agent, he entered Jorge Mesa's office, only to learn that his target was absent. After firing his machine gun at the furniture, he was surrounded by police, so he swallowed a cyanide capsule and died.

A caller claimed to have seen Pablo leave a building in the centre of Medellín. Major Gonzalez asked Don Berna whether the sighting was credible. "It's highly unlikely that El Patrón, the most wanted and recognisable man in Colombia, would expose himself like that, but there's no harm in going to the site to verify the information." Dressed like civilians, Don Berna and his men arrived at Maracaibo Street and established surveillance. With no suspicious activity apparent, the men grew frustrated and left after several hours.

Don Berna was wrong. The most wanted man in Medellín had walked calmly through the centre of the city on his way to the Metro Avenue cinema to watch a film starring Chuck Norris. Pablo's appointments were arranged in public places. He lived in a building in the heart of the city that only two or three of his men knew about, the same building where his nemesis, the newspaper *The Spectator*, worked clandestinely.

Big Gun oversaw eliminating the last traces of the newspaper. He murdered its managers and threatened its editors, so the newspaper abandoned its headquarters in the Prado neighbourhood. The traffickers took control of the building, and during a raid, the authorities found thirty kilos of coca base, chemicals and equipment. One of the survivors of the newspaper's staff, Carlos Mario Correa, installed himself clandestinely in a downtown building to maintain the presence of *The Spectator*.

Heading 500 assassins responsible for numerous police murders, Big Gun was crucial for Pablo. He served as a liaison between his boss and the military and financial wing of the organisation. He had played a lead role in the purge that had started at the Cathedral with the executions of the Galeanos and Moncadas. He was also coordinating the terrorist offensive. While Pablo had been in the Cathedral, Big Gun had boasted that he was the Pablo Escobar of the streets.

A chain reaction of events ended Big Gun. One of his men, Boliqueso, was a kidnapping specialist famous for his size. He was called the Strangler because he choked people with one hand. While he was attacking a woman on 70th Street, an army patrol captured him. Unaware who they had detained, they grew suspicious and decided to contact General Martínez: "We have a large, corpulent man, six foot one, and we want you to come and see if you recognise him." Identified, the Strangler broke down and revealed which actions each hit man performed.

One of Big Gun's men, Juan Caca, was scheduled to meet one of Pablo's messengers by the Soma Clinic, an extremely busy and congested area. Don Berna decided to capture him in an operation by recruiting one of Pablo's former employees. On March 19, 1993, Los Pepes and the Reds camouflaged themselves among the citizenry by the Soma Clinic. The ex-employee was visibly nervous. Shortly after arriving, Juan Caca sensed that he had fallen into a trap and tried to escape. Captured, he begged not to be tortured and agreed to cooperate. "Big Gun is nearby, but, if I don't show up in half an hour at the designated place, he'll leave."

"No problem," Don Berna said. "Take us there. The government is offering a massive reward for collaborating."

General Maza later stated: "All the terrorist wings fell, including those responsible for bombings, which involved sixteen guys who were not members of the Medellín Cartel, but contractors coordinated by Big Gun. They all pointed to each other. Among them, Titi and Juan Caca were detained, and they took them to the barracks of the Search Bloc, at which point they decided to speak. The one they called Juan Caca was convinced, as most of Pablo Escobar's men were, that if the police took them, they would get killed, and that's why they had the slogan that they had to resist, and this was why most of them killed themselves, because they believed that we were looking to kill them and not to capture them. So, on the way, this man said: 'Please don't kill me, I will help you.' 'Where is Chopo?' I asked. 'I'll take you to where he is.' He was on the top floor of a building, and the prosecutor and the Attorney General's deputy, who accompanied us, immediately issued the search warrant."

On March 19, 1993, at the twenty-one-storey Bancoquia building, a ten-man commando squad smashed down an apartment door. Hit by dozens of bullets, Big Gun died. Inside Big Gun's hideout was a hit list of over 200 police Pablo wanted executed.

General Maza later stated: "The men climbed to the top floor, and when they broke the door with an explosive, fire started to come from the inside, fire caused by a blast. We waited, then threw a grenade inside. Everything was silent. The men were prepared to enter and, again, fire came out. Big Gun then opened fire with his gun until his ammunition ran out. One man entered, then another entered, firing the whole time. The first one who entered gave Big Gun a burst of his machine gun across his entire chest."

Journalists went to the twentieth floor and found the walls painted with blood. Then they rushed to the first floor, where they photographed the corpse in a courtyard. In a crucifix position, Big Gun was wearing a sweatshirt and a single shoe. His naked torso revealed an eagle tattoo. Having previously believed that he had been a well-dressed rich gentleman, his neighbours were shocked.

"Pablo has visited this apartment on foot several times because he is living nearby," Juan Caca said.

"How could he walk so quietly through the centre of Medellín?" Don Berna asked.

"Callers have reported him doing so in recent days," Major Gonzalez said. Surveillance was established in the area, but Pablo was never seen.

While Los Pepes devastated his infrastructure, more of Pablo's associates defected and started to provide information, including Yellow, who told Don Berna that to get Pablo's brother-in-law Hernán Henao, a.k.a. HH, it was necessary to abduct El Grillo, HH's closest associate, who frequented a car repair shop.

The mechanics was surveyed for one week. After darkness on a Monday, El Grillo appeared and was captured. Under torture, he protested that he did not know HH's whereabouts, but he was willing to set him up. Major Gonzalez and the Castaños agreed to trust El Grillo. They sent him home with a radiophone. After a week with no results, Los Pepes felt betrayed, until finally El Grillo revealed that HH had organised a meeting at a house in the Laureles neighbourhood. Numerous troops surrounded it, and trying to escape, HH was shot dead.

The Castaños received information that Pablo was in the municipality of La Estrella, the home turf of many of his hit men. Don Berna and his men were unable to find him there. Leaving the area at 9 PM, they came under heavy machine-gun fire. While bullets strafed their vehicle, Don Berna's bodyguards returned fire. After fleeing from the scene, Don Berna took the vehicle to a repair shop, where over twenty bullet holes were counted. The mechanics assumed that someone had died in the vehicle. Relieved, Don Berna could not understand why he was still alive. For months, Pablo disappeared. With no calls to intercept, Los Pepes and the Search Bloc grew frustrated.

Most of Pablo's long-standing bodyguards had either died or surrendered. He had never been more isolated or had to depend on so few people. With the authorities conducting so many searches in Medellín, he left for a few days, and returned to take his family to a new hideout. Responding with bombs, he was losing his ability to retaliate as the violence spiralled out of control and eroded his organisation. No one dared to stand up to Los Pepes, including the authorities, who made up so many of their membership. On April 15, a car bomb exploded in Bogotá, causing multiple casualties in a shopping area. In response, Los Pepes increased their kidnapping and killing.

On April 29, 1993, Pablo wrote a letter to the attorney general:

"Los Pepes have their headquarters and their torture chambers in Fidel Castaño's house, located on El Poblado Avenue near the country club ... There they torture trade unionists and lawyers. No one has searched the house or confiscated their assets ... The government offers rewards for the leaders of the Medellín Cartel and for the leaders of the guerrillas, but doesn't offer rewards for the leaders of the paramilitary, nor for those of the Cali Cartel, authors of various car bombs in the city of Medellín.

The state security organisations have zero victories in the matter of the assassinations of the lawyers, zero victories in the El Poblado car bombs, zero victories in the investigation into the deaths of the trade unionists and zero victories in the investigations into the massacres in which thousands of young Antioquians have died. I remain disposed to turn myself in if given written and public guarantees ..."

Pablo had referred to Fidel Castaño's house because the Castaño brothers, including Carlos and Vicente, were leaders in Los Pepes. Carlos believed that Pablo wanted him dead because his army was taking over cocaine labs in the jungle. DEA cables documented Fidel Castaño's role in the hunt for Pablo:

"As a result of a disagreement with Escobar, Castaño contacted the ... [Search Bloc] and offered his help in attempting to locate Escobar. Castaño advised ... that his disagreement with Escobar stemmed from his (Castaño) telling Escobar that he (Castaño) was not in agreement with his (Escobar) terrorist campaign, i.e., bombs, police killings. Castaño was also concerned that Escobar could have him (Castaño) killed at any time as had been the case with the Galeano/Moncada brothers.
    Fidel Castaño had made telephonic contact with the incarcerated Ochoa clan (Jorge, Fabio and Juan David). Castaño asked the Ochoas to leave Escobar and join sides with him. Castaño explained that Escobar would have them killed just like the Moncadas and Galeanos. The Ochoas stated that they had recently given Escobar $500,000, however, they were thinking of abandoning him ... Castaño told the ... [Search Bloc] that the Ochoas would never abandon Escobar for reasons of fear and that they 'always lied in order to stay in neutral with everybody.'"

In May, Los Pepes kidnapped Roberto's son, Nicolas, but released him after three hours. Toying with Pablo's brother, they had demonstrated that they could get anyone associated with Pablo at any time. On May 25, Pablo organised a celebration for his daughter's 9th birthday by arranging horseback riding. Two men approached Juan Pablo's girlfriend, and asked if she was the wife of Fabio Ochoa. Spooked by the men, she notified Pablo, who ordered everybody to pack their things. With the horses loaded with luggage, guns, cash and a birthday cake, they traversed a mountain. The rain increased, as did the gradient of the slope. A horse fell over and slid backwards towards the family. The family members only just jumped out of the way in time to avoid it. On the other side of the mountain, they eventually arrived at a hideout, soaked from the rain.

In the house, insects and cold and damp kept them awake. They used hairdryers to heat up the beds. Pablo's inability to protect his family was apparent, so he offered encouraging words about joining the guerrillas. He claimed to have bought a position as a guerrilla commander for $1 million. In the jungle, he would be safe. It would allow him to rebuild his cocaine empire. It was his only option, as the government had refused to negotiate.

Rattled by Los Pepes, he needed to get his family out of the country. Knowing that they were his weakness, the US and Colombian authorities schemed to prevent them from leaving. After cancelling their visas, the US ambassador announced that they could reapply, which was the right of all Colombian citizens, but Pablo would have to be present for the embassy to issue a visa to Manuela because she was only 8. Following instructions from his father, Juan Pablo showed up at the US Embassy and demanded to see the ambassador because his family were looking for domicile.

The head of the DEA in Colombia told him, "There's no way the US is gonna issue you a visa."

"What will it take for you to issue us a visa?"

"Even if you gave me the entire Cali Cartel on a silver platter, I still couldn't get it for you."

Due to the uproar, the Colombian government pretended to clamp down on Los Pepes. In response, Los Pepes announced that they had disbanded, but the killings didn't stop. In June 1993, Pablo's brother-in-law Carlos arrived home from the

Caribbean and was kidnapped by twenty-five hooded men near an airport in Medellín. After torturing him, Los Pepes shot him multiple times in the head and ditched his body on the outskirts of Medellín. Watching the news on TV, Pablo's wife sobbed. In *Pablo Escobar: My Father*, Juan Pablo claimed that Carlos had never been involved in violence and had earned a living selling mops. After a psychic predicted that Pablo would die that year, Pablo located the psychic and provided his family's dates of birth and other information to get more predictions.

On July 14, 1993, Los Pepes targeted Earthquake, Roberto Escobar's championship horse, worth approximately $3 million. With the authorities looking to confiscate his assets, Roberto had hidden Earthquake at a farm in Manizales. The horse's trainer was at a restaurant with his family, when members of Los Pepes arrived. They took him outside, where a commando held a gun to his head.

"Where is Earthquake? If you don't tell us, we'll kill your entire family right here." After he told them, he was shot in the skull.

Earthquake was transported to a stable owned by a farmer who had suffered harm from Pablo. After getting castrated, the horse was abandoned on Las Vegas Street with a sign that read: THIS IS EARTHQUAKE, PROPERTY OF THE SINISTER PABLO ESCOBAR. SINCERELY: THE PEPES

With no bodyguards left to protect them, Pablo's sister, Luz Maria, and his brother, Argemiro, took their families to Costa Rica in July, but they were all promptly deported back to Colombia. Roberto's son Nicolas took his family to Chile, which attempted to expel them, so they fled to Germany and filed for asylum.

Carlos Castaño let it be known that he wanted to chop Pablo's kids into pieces and send them to him in a sack. He hoped to capture Pablo and have his arms and legs surgically removed. By keeping him conscious with the help of a doctor and drugs, he planned on throwing the limbless drug lord onto a city street and watching the former king of Medellín beg for his life. Reducing El Patrón to a torso would guarantee his legend. Rather than be taken alive by the Castaños, Pablo told his closest men that if nearly all his bullets were spent in a battle, he would rather shoot himself in the head to avoid the torture.

CHAPTER 16
FAMILY USED AS BAIT

"Colonel, I'm going to kill you. I'm going to kill all of your family up to the third generation, then I will dig up your grandparents and shoot them and bury them again," Pablo warned Martínez. Three police bodyguards were on the way to pick up one of the colonel's sons from school when hit men assassinated them. Despite the threat to his family and the stress they were under, Martínez refused to back down.

A year after Pablo's prison escape, there was a media backlash against the Search Bloc for failing to capture him. People were tired of the murders, which in Medellín were almost twenty a day. In July 1993, the Search Bloc responded to criticism by publishing a list of its successes: 13,122 searches, including over 11,000 in Medellín; 165 large-scale operations nationwide, including hundreds of troops; 1,879 roadblocks; 920 observation posts; 145 alleged members of the Medellín Cartel killed during raids, as well as three Search Bloc troops, seven sub-officials, 103 police agents and six support workers; 1,314 arrests; the seizure of 7,000 kilos of dynamite, 1,215 guns, 273 radios and $1.4 million in cash.

Martínez's son Hugo, nicknamed Frequency, was experimenting with new tracking technology. Martínez didn't want Hugo working on the case in Medellín, where police were constantly being murdered, but Frequency insisted that he wanted to end the threat to their family by locating Pablo.

Frequency's team went out in vans. Parked on hills with their antennae raised, the vans could triangulate a location. Once a signal had been received, Frequency would race off in an undercover vehicle with a monitor that made a noise as it picked up the signal's strength. As the technology was new, the team was having a hard time getting used to it. He ended up chasing signals that led nowhere.

Due to the threat from Los Pepes, Pablo was in sporadic contact with his family. His wife wrote him a letter:

"I miss you so very much I feel weak. Sometimes I feel an immense loneliness take over my heart. Why does life have to separate us like this? My heart is aching. How are you? How do you feel? I don't want to leave you my love. I need you so much, I want to cry with you … I don't want to pressure you. Nor do I want to make you commit mistakes, but if our leaving is not possible, I would feel more secure with you. We'll close ourselves in, suspend the mail, whatever we have to. This is getting too tense."

Despite the setback and fifteen months of searching, Martínez was convinced that Pablo would soon be found. The eavesdropping technology was accumulating more information and its location techniques were being refined. The intense focus of the hunt caused Martínez to dream about having conversations with Pablo, including asking how he had escaped from the Cathedral.

Not everybody supported the efforts of Martínez. The press attacked him for taking too long to find Pablo. The attorney general wanted Martínez removed and prosecuted with Los Pepes for the murder and mayhem of which Pablo was accusing them. The DEA – whose mission statement was to combat drug trafficking – heard that Martínez was on the payroll of the Cali Cartel.

The DEA noted: "[Gilberto José] Rodríguez Orejuela [a Cali Cartel leader] told [an informant] they had bandits working within the Search Bloc … The informant advised that Rodríguez Orejuela states they had made an arrangement with PNC [Colombian National Police] General Vargas and Colonel Martínez regarding a reward for Escobar's capture. According to Rodríguez Orejuela, the Cali Cartel will pay a total of $10 million immediately following Pablo's capture and/or death. Of this, $8 million has been promised to the Search Bloc and $2 million for the informants who provide the information that leads to a successful operation." The Americans knew that if this information leaked it would embarrass the DEA, but they decided it was worth the risk. They lobbied against the attorney general for trying to remove Martínez.

In August 1993, Pablo and his family were scheduled to arrive at the blue house in El Poblado. In the newly constructed home, he hired a handyman to paint the walls baby blue. Remaining mostly in a bedroom, Pablo trusted the handyman to work for two weeks to ensure that his family felt more at home. With his empire gone, he now only had a handful of people around him. El Gordo and his wife Gladys performed household tasks. The sicario, Angelito, protected him and coordinated messages.

Blindfolded, Victoria and the kids arrived at the blue house. A dark green gate slid open to allow their vehicle inside an area policed by a German Shepherd and a white goose that Pablo praised for being fiercer than a dog. The second gate was ten feet tall, dark blue and had the added protection of barbed wire at the top. Inside, the family was surprised that it had been painted in Pablo's favourite colour, the same blue that had adorned the walls of his childhood bedroom, but Victoria disliked the dark bedroom with a double bed flanked by nightstands.

The house had an empty car park with space for twelve cars. As hardly anybody visited, the family used it to play basketball and soccer. In their swimming clothes, they took advantage of the hot weather. Pablo enjoyed showering his family with a hose. His demeanour softened, as if the ever-present danger had been temporarily forgotten.

One evening after midnight, Victoria went to bed, only to have her sleep interrupted by nightmares about intruders raiding the house and guns getting pointed at her head – these night terrors would continue to haunt her until 2015, after over two decades of engaging in various therapies. In the small hours, Pablo and his daughter fried bologna, which they devoured with Coca-Cola and rice. After keeping watch all night, Pablo slept at dawn. Sometimes, Manuela joined them in bed, where she enjoyed gazing at the stars on the ceiling that her parents had glued there for her enjoyment. She said that when she could not see Pablo or when he was not with her, she hoped to find him in the sky by looking at the stars. After she fell asleep, they moved her to a large cot next to the bed.

At 7 AM, Victoria rose to cook breakfast for the kids. At 10 AM, she taught her 9-year-old daughter Spanish. For almost six years, her two children had not attended school upon Pablo's insistence, because he feared that they would be kidnapped, tortured and killed. Using notes taken by his former classmates, Juan Pablo maintained his studies and completed homework. Manuela pined for her schoolmates and other family members, including Grandmother Nora, and she missed horse riding. When the pressure on his daughter elevated, Pablo would allow her a weekend visit with one of her teachers.

At 11 AM, Victoria started to cook for Pablo, who preferred grilled beef, fried eggs, rice, sliced plantain, arepas, and salad of mostly beets topped with lemon, salt and tomato. Finally awake, he grabbed some string from a drawer and measured his waist, relieved that the knot he had made the previous day still contained his girth, indicating that he had not gained weight overnight. Arriving for brunch, he picked up a glass of milk. "This is essential for strengthening our bones," he told his kids.

After eating, he flicked through the three main newspapers, with the TV on, so that he would not miss the 12:30 PM news. Desperate to find any updates on his case, he aggressively channel-surfed, which annoyed his family. The news reported the possibility of him surrendering and the conditions that would have to be met, including a guarantee that his family could leave the country.

With his wife holding up a mirror, he shaved. Then she cut and buffed his nails. As it was too risky to go outside, he insisted on his wife cutting his hair, even though she offered to bring a barber to the house. The result was uneven, but he never complained. Occasionally, he used a comb and his fingers to display a tuft that needed trimming.

Much to his family's annoyance, his time on the toilet and in the bathroom still took up to two hours. They mocked his incessant flossing, during which he had to get in-between each tooth multiple times. Using a child's toothbrush, he cleaned his teeth. Victoria said that his two-hour preening session was excessive. He replied that due to the impossibility of going to the dentist, he had to take extra care to not even get so much as a toothache.

One morning, Victoria had a toothache. "I need to go to the dentist in the San Diego shopping centre in Medellín," she told Manuela and Juan Pablo's girlfriend. "It will get us out of the house, so let's put on sunglasses and scarves." During the outing, the prospect of getting abducted prevented Victoria from relaxing.

One night, the family was gazing at the sky and spotted a cobalt-blue star. For decades after Pablo's death, Manuela would search for the distinctive star in the hope of communing with her father. On nights that she couldn't sleep, it consoled her.

Having gone months without seeing his mother, Pablo prepared her a room and recruited two men to bring her to the house blindfolded. She arrived with home-cooked food, which they devoured. After chatting for hours, Pablo told her that they had spent the week arranging a special room for her. Gazing at Pablo, Hermilda said that she was unable to stay because she had promised to visit Roberto in prison on Sunday. Pablo protested that she saw Roberto often, and that now was the time to stay at the blue house, because their lives had become so complicated. She said that she understood the situation, but she had already pledged to visit Roberto. Afterwards, sensing his heartbreak, Victoria consoled her husband, who expressed his disappointment. She said that life was difficult and hugged him.

Pablo had almost been captured by Los Pepes at a previous

location, so the longer the family stayed at the blue house, the riskier it became. Victoria said that she was barely able to continue living under such intense pressure, and if they were all assassinated in the blue house together, at least they would be free. She said that the government was trying to trick Pablo into surrendering, so he could be killed. He told her to go overseas with the kids, marry quickly for residency and to get a new surname. At some point, he would get on a boat and find her. Agonising over what to do was destroying both of them mentally. It was becoming obvious that their chances of survival would be increased if they went separate ways. At the edge of the house, Pablo spent time alone, absorbing the view of Medellín. Down to his last few million in cash, his chances of winning the war were over.

Through letters, he sent messages to his lawyer and few remaining workers. Collected every four hours, the letters travelled through five locations in Medellín, with the routes and carriers constantly changed. After a night-time pickup at the final location, up to fifty letters daily were delivered to Pablo. The system acted as an alarm: collections previously falling out of sync had indicated an imminent threat, and the need to move to a new safe house.

One day around 4 PM, he sat at a desk and spent hours reading the latest news from his family, his men in prison and the kids' teachers. Detailing the negotiations with the government, letters from his lawyer were prioritised. While reading, he tore off page corners, rolled them into balls, mostly launched them through the window onto the grass and occasionally ate some. He told Victoria that after Attorney General De Greiff had honoured his promise to obtain her refugee status in another country, he would surrender. "If that fails, we can hide in the jungle. They are establishing electricity on my land there. Only Roberto knows the location. I can join the guerrillas in their struggle."

She protested that her and the kids were not suited to jungle combat life. His idea was madness and she would not consider it as an option. For days after the conversation, she fretted over suffering in the jungle for a prolonged period and wondered which guerrilla group he had made arrangements with.

On September 3, 1993, he arranged a surprise for Victoria's 33rd birthday: gifts, a cake made by a famous baker and half a dozen bottles of Dom Pérignon. "How did you get these things?" she asked, impressed. She was told that somebody who had gone to fetch the mail had collected them. On September 5, 1993, Pablo enjoyed watching Colombia beat Argentina by five goals in a World Cup qualification match. The game lifted his mood.

During a meeting at Montecasino, Major Gonzalez said, "We need a strategy that will enable us to hear Pablo on a phone or a radio. If he remains silent, we'll never locate him." Out of the ideas put forward, the men selected what they thought would be the best one: to convince the government, especially the prosecutor's office, to separate Pablo from his family by housing them in Bogotá.

The attorney general decided to put them in an apartment complex, where his office could guarantee their safety. Having identified Pablo's family as his weakness, the attorney general's informants – including former members of the Medellín Cartel – had suggested unbalancing Pablo emotionally by making him think that his family was safe one minute, only to have them thrown back into danger the next minute. His concern for his family would drive him to make phone calls, which could be traced.

On September 18, a legal letter prompted him to announce that everybody needed to pack their belongings because they were being moved to the Altos building, where the government would protect them. After protesting that she did not want to be separated from her husband, Victoria warned that it might be a trap. With his face pale and his breathing laboured, Pablo told her not to worry, because he had arranged it with the government. They needed to leave, otherwise they would all be killed if the present safe house were discovered.

Weeping, Victoria said she would prefer for them all to die

together. All their problems would end. His enemies would be unable to seek revenge. After his death, his enemies would try to kill his family. He insisted, for the sake of the children, that they go to the Altos building. They would be safe there until the government found them a country to go to. She needed to get married, so that she could get citizenship. He would travel to them by boat. There was no time left to debate. She needed to start packing immediately. "Tell Manuela that you're going on a trip to a beautiful place, but I'm unable to come. Juan Pablo will understand. In a few hours, we'll be able to travel under the cover of darkness."

While the sun set, Victoria felt her heart break. Imagining life without Pablo, she was saddened by thoughts of Manuela not having her father around to read bedtime stories. One last time, she insisted on staying and protested that she would rather they were all killed than separated. Watching her cry, Pablo's eyes misted over. He said that raising their children was now her priority. They needed to be educated and be in a place where they could rebuild their lives. As if it were their final moments together, he hugged her tightly.

At 11 PM, the family gathered by the car to say goodbye to Pablo. Holding Victoria, he touched her hair and cheek. With his voice betraying his emotion, he said how much he loved her and thanked her for protecting the children. He said that luck was on her side and everything would work out. After hugging his wife, he said goodbye to his son. He shook his hand and kissed him on the cheek. Saying goodbye to Manuela, he broke down and cried in front of his family for the first time. Gazing at Juan Pablo's girlfriend, he was too choked up to speak. Days later, she would receive a letter from him apologising for his lack of strength to say anything. He expressed his appreciation.

When he was finally able to talk, he told Victoria that people from the Technical Investigation Corps (CTI) would meet them at the Altos building. He handed her addresses for Los Pepes and promised that raids would ensue from the intelligence he had gathered. In a Chevrolet Sprint, Juan Pablo drove the family away. In a vehicle behind them, Pablo and Angelito watched over them and occasionally honked the horn. Nearing the Altos building, Pablo honked goodbye, turned away and returned to the blue house. Instinctively, Victoria felt that the final honk was goodbye forever.

In the Altos building's car park, Victoria emerged, sobbing. Four CTI cops welcomed them: Alfa (the boss), A1, Pantera and Imperio. Behind walls of sandbags, these men protected the building from the roof and the corners of the building at street level. They took their luggage to a furniture-less 5,000-square-foot apartment on the fourth floor. A neighbour provided a plastic table and four chairs. Using two mattresses found in the utility room, they set up makeshift beds. Sleeping uncomfortably, Victoria dreamt of an overseas freedom without bodyguards and journalists. The kids would be in school and she would be a normal housewife.

The next day, a neighbour brought food and cooking utensils. Victoria hired a woman to shop for provisions. Laundry was done in an apartment in the Altos building that Victoria's mother owned and had abandoned due to a car bomb attack in February. With no telephones, they listened to the radio for breaking news. If they wanted to sleep in the daytime, a blackout curtain enabled them to rest. The other amenities were off limits: a massive swimming pool and spa, a gym, a gazebo by lawns …

From Bogotá, more CTI cops arrived, until forty armed men were noisily patrolling around. With gunfire erupting throughout the day and night, triggering the alarm on the roof, the family hunkered down in the utility room, where they whispered and prayed for their lives.

Without his family, Pablo barely ate for two days and didn't shave. At night, he gazed at the stars while playing with his beard as if insane. After a few dark days, he decided to recruit 100 young men from Moravia, where he had built houses for the homeless, to perform kidnappings. The mission would commence on December 31, 1993. Each hostage would be hidden in the mountains near Medellín and released for 500 million pesos, which would provide him with enough cash to stay on the run.

One evening, as if inviting fate, Pablo told his worker, El Gordo, to put on a hat and a poncho because they were going out. He insisted on them walking through downtown Medellín. While El Gordo was terrified, Pablo acted oblivious to the danger.

When two helicopters started circling above the blue house, Pablo hid in a closet, while El Gordo and his wife pretended to work in the garden to deceive the authorities. After thirty minutes, they flew away. Mostly, he stayed in his room depressed; occasionally, writing letters at his desk.

He gave El Gordo a letter to take to a lawyer, but El Gordo returned with bad news: at the lawyer's office, he had dodged four men with guns and disappeared to a cafe and a church to ensure that he had not been followed. Pablo responded that it was all falling apart. It was time for him to move to a new safe house, where Limón would assist him. Shaking his hand goodbye, El Gordo felt that he would never see El Patrón again.

Distrustful of the CTI cops, Juan Pablo recruited one of his childhood friends, Nariz, to provide extra security. When he arrived with a shotgun and a permit, the cops ordered him to leave, but the family convinced them that he would help in an emergency. Due to the gunfire and death threats, the other residents fled, except for two females.

Los Pepes was relying on Pablo calling his family, so that Frequency could trace the calls. To avoid detection, Pablo used letters written in code to communicate with Juan Pablo. The strapping teenager was using binoculars to watch out for Los Pepes. He photographed suspects and jotted down licence-plate numbers. Pablo sent him instructions about dealing with officials. Pablo received a response from his son:

"Dear Father,

I send you a big hug and warm wishes.

I see that Corrales [from the attorney general's office] is in high spirits, fighting Los Pepes. He doesn't have a choice anyway … The prosecutor played the fool about us leaving the country … to test us, to check what we were going to say and how we were going to react. I have been firm about your conditions and I have persuaded them. I even told them that you had planned to deal with the Cali people after turning yourself in, because you were willing to have peace back in the country.

Corrales was very rude to me. We were talking and he started to tell me, 'I have to look for your father because that is my mission. I'm not from here or there [allied to any side], I am a righteous person and he (you) knows that I am serious about that.' So I told him that there was no need for him to tell me that to my face every time he came around here because he has been here three times and all three times he has said the same thing – that I knew that was his job, but that he had to respect me, because it was my father he was talking about, and I told him he should calm down because my father was also after all those who were looking for him, and that destiny will say who finds whom.

He answered, 'I'm afraid, because it's my job and no one has told me to stop looking for your father, because there are forty arrest warrants against him.' I answered: 'This is not for you to be afraid, but for you to show me some respect because I am with him [Pablo] and I support him,' so he'd better cut it out or else. Then I told him that the prosecutor was the most fake guy in this country, that how did he expect us to believe him regarding you turning yourself in if he wasn't a man who kept his word, and that he had protected us so far only to trick us with false promises. And he answered: 'I don't allow anyone to speak about my boss at my table,' and I told him, 'I, like a member of this family, cannot allow you either to say bad things about my boss, who is my father.'

It would be good to tease the TV people, so they won't make the building [housing Pablo's family] stand out so obviously,

235

because when they came here they told me they were going to erase the tape and they didn't do it.

Take care of yourself.

I love and remember you.

Your son."

The letter detailed where Juan Pablo suspected Martínez stayed in Medellín and described suspicious people lurking around their building.

Centra Spike and the Search Bloc heard Pablo call his son. Initially, the code words used and the alternation of radio frequencies presented problems. Frequency led his team on so many wild goose chases that they almost gave up on him and the technology.

Two of the bodyguards at Pablo's family's house, Diamond 1 and Diamond 2, reported to Los Pepes that Pablo had started to speak to his son daily, usually between 6 PM and 8 PM. When talking, they used a chart of codes and signals to thwart eavesdroppers. The first signal led the team to the Boston neighbourhood east of Medellín. Raiding a school and seminar building, Los Pepes found no sign of Pablo.

"The high mountains may have caused the signal to bounce, which sent us to the wrong place," Frequency said to the frustrated team.

"At least we know that Pablo is still somewhere in the city," Don Berna said. "For the moment, he is not abandoning Medellín."

By listening to calls, Frequency decoded the words used to indicate that it was time to switch frequencies. He was so convinced that he had located Pablo that raids were launched on the wrong buildings.

Juan Pablo caught Diamond 1 and Diamond 2 transmitting information by radio. Pablo declared that they were now military targets. Immediately, they were removed from the building and transferred to other cities.

Major Gonzalez and Search Bloc officers had a strategy meeting with Los Pepes. The goal was to find a plan that would force

Pablo to make a mistake that would reveal his location. Out of various suggestions, it was decided to fire a grenade at the empty apartment next to the one housing his family.

On a Thursday afternoon, the siren wailed, gunfire erupted and there was a huge thud against the wall. Nariz grabbed his shotgun. While the cops returned fire, the family hid in a dressing room and prayed. Through the door, Nariz whispered to Juan Pablo. The alarm stopped and a cop arrived. "Two cars arrived at the crossroads. Three Los Pepes got out. Two of them opened fire, and the other shot a grenade at the building, which hit the fifth floor, but failed to detonate."

Terrified by the grenade attack, the family members wrote urgent letters. Couriers were intercepted, but under interrogation, they were unable to reveal Pablo's location because they didn't know it.

The family complained to the government about the ease with which Los Pepes could move weapons through check-points. After contacting the attorney general, Hermilda blamed Martínez for the attack. "Martínez called me the mother of a monster," Hermilda said. "Martínez warned me, 'To prevent you from supporting what your son is doing, I'm going to put a bomb under your bed.' That same night, someone put a bomb in front of the house. He said the next one would be under my bed."

With the CTI cops, the family rehearsed different attack possibilities and agreed on hiding places. Bracing for Los Pepes to arrive at night, they often slept in the day. Manuela's insomnia posed a problem for Victoria, who tried to only weep when her daughter was asleep. Unable to eat, Juan Pablo's girlfriend fainted in the bathtub and was hospitalised, accompanied by bodyguards. Although diagnosed with life-threatening dehydration and asked to remain in a hospital bed, due to the risks involved, she returned to the Altos building. Unable to walk, she remained on a mattress for days. Juan Pablo gave her injections and medicine.

CTI cop Pantera brought Victoria a message from de Greiff: the attorney general apologised for the delay in finding them a country to go to, but it was a delicate matter that had to be handled discreetly. She should trust that he wanted Pablo to surrender.

Unannounced, Pablo's sister arrived with a letter from her brother. Pablo described the negotiations and urged them to increase their security, because he knew about the attacks on the Altos building. She responded with a letter describing their woes, including Manuela's constant crying and asking questions about the whereabouts of her father and grandmother. In another letter, he urged Manuela to be patient, because she would soon be in a safe country.

With more technology and intelligence coming in, Los Pepes and the Search Bloc were homing in on Pablo's whereabouts. While he was on a call with his son, they traced his location and launched a huge manhunt. He rushed from his hideout on a mountain. Fleeing, he dropped his light and radio. In complete darkness and lashed by torrential rain, he scrabbled across cliffs, convinced he would die. Barely holding on, he imagined that his corpse would never be found at the foot of a cliff. Caked in mud, he showed up in a neighbourhood and got in a taxi.

After receiving a lengthy letter detailing his escape, Victoria wondered what kind of conditions he was living in, because the paper had been taped together with Band-Aids. Reading it, his sister, Luz Maria, was devastated by the sad and bitter tone. Previously, he had always been upbeat and they had relied on his stoicism. "If this is my brother's letter, then his days are numbered." She felt like dying.

Armoured vehicles stopped in front of the Altos building and a dozen men charged inside. Victoria and the kids dashed for the hiding places that they had used during their security rehearsals. Bracing for gunfire, they learned that the arrival was the national director of the attorney general's office. In a menacing tone, she told Victoria that if Pablo did not surrender within three days, the government was going to remove the cops protecting them at the Altos building.

"We are totally separated from Pablo," Victoria said. "We have absolutely no influence over his decision to surrender." She assured the national director that if they were allowed to leave the country, he would surrender the following day. She emphasised that she knew that the government's goal was to assassinate him, not to have him surrender. Before leaving, the national director taunted Victoria with the threat of removing the men protecting the Altos building.

Realising that they needed an evacuation plan in case their protection was removed, Victoria had Nariz walk around the building to document the movement of the cops. Separate from the cops, the building had security guards who had worked there for years. She put them on standby to open a garage door, so that the family could escape in their Chevrolet Sprint. On two occasions, they were on the verge of fleeing, but the attorney general assured them that their plan to move overseas was proceeding.

Near the end of September, on the day of Love and Friendship, the arrival of bouquets of flowers from Pablo to the captive females in the Altos building did little to lift the gloom. Victoria viewed it as a security risk that could have given up his location.

In early October, Angelito – who had become Pablo's right-hand man – ignored El Patrón's advice and went to deliver cash to his brother. Both were killed. Upon hearing about his death, Pablo announced that it was over. He didn't have anyone left to work with. CTI cop Imperio delivered the news about Angelito to Juan Pablo, who struggled not to cry, as he knew his father's days were numbered. Playing dumb, Juan Pablo asked Imperio who Angelito was. After Imperio left, Juan Pablo told Victoria. Grabbing her head, she repeatedly yelled no. Paperwork found at Angelito's brother's included the addresses of newly purchased properties that could be used as safe houses. The authorities watched the properties and intercepted calls from Pablo.

That same month, with the government continuing to threaten to withdraw the guards from the Altos building, Victoria asked the attorney general to visit them and to give Pablo more time to surrender. Why should she and her children be getting punished when they were not criminals?

With nearly everyone associated with Pablo now dead or in prison, the main targets left were his immediate family, but they were worth more to Los Pepes alive, because they were the ultimate bait. US agencies such as the CIA were banking on Pablo finally exposing himself as the threat from Los Pepes intensified.

Worried that their government protectors could grant Los Pepes access to them at any time, the family slept on mattresses in a single room, with Juan Pablo guarding them with the shotgun. Unable to communicate with Pablo because the messengers were all dead, the family suffered some of its darkest days.

The Marroquin Castle in Bogotá was owned by trafficker Camilo Zapata, who was hiding in Medellín under the guidance of witches and fortune-tellers. Daily, his chief fortune-teller consulted the astral charts and issued recommendations, such as bathing with herbs and praying to a priest in Cuban Santeria, an Afro-Caribbean religion based on the beliefs and traditions of the Yoruba people, with a twist of Roman Catholicism. While he consulted his fortune-teller by telephone, Frequency listened in and tried to pinpoint the signal. With some members of his own team losing faith in his ability, Frequency was desperate to produce a result. He traced Zapata to a rural area north of Medellín. Due to the mountains, the signal was intermittent, but he stayed on the case. With Zapata placing regular calls at noon, it was just a matter of time before his location was exposed.

"With you being an Aries star sign, you're going to have an excellent day, because Jupiter and Mars are aligned, and the stars are in their best position for you."

The vehicle with the tracking equipment found the hideout.

"There are some strange movements outside," Zapata told the fortune-teller. Surrounded, he grabbed a gun and tried to flee, but was killed. Although no information could be obtained from the deceased, the success of the tracking equipment increased the troops' morale.

On November 7, 1993, Nariz asked to take the weekend off to

go to see his son. The family warned that their enemies would try to capture him outside of the building. Juan Pablo advised him to leave surreptitiously by going over a creek. Not wanting to get his shoes wet, he refused. Two CTI cops offered to drop him off, but he never arrived home. The cops claimed that he had insisted on leaving their vehicle halfway home to get a taxi.

Two days later, Los Pepes raided the house of the manager of the Altos building, a woman who daily had asked Victoria if she needed anything. She had brought the family walkie-talkies that they had managed to use a few times to communicate with Pablo. She had fetched groceries, supplies and had transported letters for Pablo to his delivery system. She had also carried Victoria's correspondence with her family members, friends and the kids' teachers. After her abduction, the woman was never seen again.

Within hours, another disappearance was reported. The teacher whom Victoria had hired to maintain the kids' studies, her own former high-school teacher, had been snatched from her home in Medellín by men dressed in utility-company uniforms. From her house, they seized fifty boxes of property, which they rifled through, hoping to find information about Pablo. The boxes contained Victoria's property, including books and encyclopaedias. Devastated, her two children arrived at the Altos building and begged Victoria to find their mother. Knowing that she was gone, she wept as she hugged the teenagers, who remained at the Altos building because they had nowhere to go. In the coming years, she would do everything she could to help raise those children, including paying for their education.

By the evening, Victoria realised that Manuela's nanny might be targeted next. In an empty apartment with a phone, Juan Pablo called her home, hoping to warn her to hide with her kids. Her son said that she had just left to get a taxi. Juan Pablo ordered him to drop the phone and chase her as fast as he could, because the taxi was a trap. When he got back on the phone, he was sobbing. She was gone.

Worried about a bodyguard, Juan Pablo sent a house cleaner

to warn him. Approaching the house, she saw several Los Pepes vehicles. The bodyguard fired at the hooded men, but there were too many of them. They shot him non-fatally and dragged him away to be tortured. After losing so many people in one day, the family huddled in the dressing room, bracing for anything to happen.

Juan Pablo sent the attorney general a letter stating how worried and desperate the family was getting. He tried to negotiate a deal for Pablo's surrender. The conditions were that Roberto Escobar would be moved out of lockdown and into a part of the Itagüí prison housing the Ochoa brothers and other Medellín traffickers. Upon surrendering, Pablo wanted to be housed with Roberto and to be allowed twenty-one family visits each year. The final requirement was for his wife and children to be flown out of the country. The attorney general promised to help them move to a safe country, but only after Pablo had surrendered. Pablo gave his word that he would surrender as soon as his family was flown overseas. Claiming to accept Pablo's word, the attorney general started to make arrangements for the family to leave the country.

With the Americans desperate to prevent Pablo from surrendering, he tried to distract them by starting a rumour that he was in Haiti, while arranging for his family to fly to either London or Frankfurt. The US asked the Spanish, British and German ambassadors to refuse entry to his family.

CHAPTER 17
DEATH

In late November, Pablo moved to building number 45D-94 on Street 79A, a two-storey home. He lived with Limón, and a cook, his mother's cousin, Luzmila. When he wanted to make calls, Limón drove him around in a yellow taxi, which had given him a false sense of security. With so many of his workforce dead, incarcerated or defected to his enemies, he had lost his military might. He spent his time reading newspapers and watching TV, mostly remaining quiet except for the occasional outburst about him getting blamed for every crime in Colombia. Although he hoped to find refuge in the jungle with the guerrillas, he didn't want to leave until he had guaranteed his family's safety.

The family considered fleeing to Germany, because Roberto's eldest son had stayed there for three years without any problems, and Pablo's sister had been there for three months. From a travel agent a neighbour had recommended, Victoria sent an anonymous person to buy four business-class tickets to fly to Frankfurt on November 27, 1993, which was less than a week away, so rapid preparations were required. She informed attorney general de Greiff that they were leaving and requested protection for the trip to the airport and at the connecting airport in Bogotá, before the transatlantic flight.

When they were all packed, they learned that the attorney general wanted Pablo to surrender before they would be allowed to fly. A female official arrived and announced that criminal charges had been filed against Juan Pablo, which would prevent him from leaving, including transporting illegal drugs and sexually assaulting young women. Summoned to the room by Victoria,

Juan Pablo angrily protested his innocence. He pointed out that he had a girlfriend and as Pablo's son he had never lacked female interest.

The official responded that Juan Pablo matched the description of a rapist, who had claimed to be Pablo Escobar's son. Even though she had no evidence for the sexual-assault charge, a witness had reported seeing him bring a box of guns into the building, so the weapons offence had proof. Juan Pablo granted her permission for the building to be searched. He said that the only thing they would find was the shotgun left by Nariz. The conviction in his voice convinced the official that he had told the truth, so she departed.

The attorney general's office dropped the charges but issued a death sentence by stating that the CTI cops were going to be removed from the Altos building in the next few days. Pablo's wife screamed at the officials for threatening to leave her children unprotected and at the mercy of Los Pepes. On November 27, the family were informed that ten SUVs with CTI bodyguards had arrived to escort them to the airport. In the living room, they hugged each other and prayed not to be intercepted on the way to the airport.

A decoy SUV led the convoy, with Victoria and Manuela in one vehicle, and Juan Pablo and Andrea in another. In helicopters, cops with machine guns escorted the speeding convoy as it roared along the road, with other cars screeching out of its way and keeping their distance. A few hours later, they arrived at Rionegro, where dozens of police assigned to protect them swarmed around.

Boarding the plane first, Victoria wondered about Pablo, whom she had not heard from in days. At least the absence of any new stories meant that he was still alive. Waiting for take-off, she braced for agents to storm inside and remove the family. Unable to take her eyes off the door, she was momentarily distracted by Juan Pablo and his girlfriend playing a game of spot the undercover cop posing as a passenger. Two men particularly stood out.

During the flight, her eyelids slid, but she forced them open, terrified that if she dozed, she would lose her children. Ten years of dodging raids, assassination plots and adrenaline spikes had taken their toll. After a few hours in the air, a reporter approached her, revealed that someone high up in Bogotá had tipped him off and requested an interview. Figuring that his presence would reduce the risk of anything bad happening to them, she agreed to speak to him in Frankfurt.

With his family airborne for Germany, Pablo learned that they were going to be denied entry. The attorney general had tricked him. Plans had been made to return his family, because their safety had been guaranteed by the Colombian government. Infuriated, he made a call: "This is Pablo Escobar. I need to talk to the president."

"OK. Hold on. Let me locate him," an operator said, and contacted the National Police.

A policeman got on the phone. "We can't get in touch with the president right now. Please call back at another time." He hung up.

Pablo called again. "This is Pablo Escobar. It is necessary that I talk to the president. My family is flying to Germany at this time. I need to talk to him right now."

"We get a lot of crank calls here. We need to somehow verify that it is really you. It's going to take me a few minutes to track down the president, so please wait a few more minutes and then call back."

The president refused to speak to Pablo. Gaviria wanted Pablo's family members back in Colombia because he believed that if they were safe overseas, El Patrón would be free to unleash unlimited terrorism. With them in the country, they would all be at risk, which meant that Pablo would have to be more careful.

After the phone rang, a policeman told Pablo, "I'm sorry, Mr Escobar, we have been unable to locate the president." Enraged, he threatened to bomb the presidential palace and the German Embassy if his family couldn't stay in Germany. Martínez and his team were listening to the calls. The longer the incident could be extended, the better chance they had of tracing him.

At 6 AM on November 28, the plane landed. The pilot announced that some people needed to be removed before it could dock at the terminal. The two obvious undercover cops sprung up and approached Victoria. After stating that they were from Interpol, they claimed that they wanted to protect the family. Outside of the window, police cars surrounded the plane.

When a cop grabbed Manuela's arm, Victoria rushed over. "Please don't take her. She's only 8 and still drinking from a bottle." While Juan Pablo and Andrea were escorted to police cars, Victoria started screaming. Speaking in Spanish, a cop explained that Pablo had threatened to bomb every German airport. Not knowing whether that was true, Victoria insisted on accompanying Manuela in the same car.

With the family classified as undesirables and detained in Germany, the attorney general announced, "If Escobar gives up, we will try to mediate to get protection for his family in Germany."

Pablo's desperate calls enabled the Search Bloc to narrow down an area with a radius of 1,500 metres. Out of five properties identified in the zone, two were believed to be owned by Pablo, one by Roberto, and two others were classified as hideouts. Martínez ordered the perimeter of the area to be secured. He didn't want to repeat previous mistakes such as sending in helicopters and hundreds of troops, which Pablo had always been able to dodge. This time, Martínez wanted to be certain of trapping his nemesis.

With everyone expecting a massive raid, only twenty-two men had been selected to launch a targeted attack. Stationed at Pueblito Paisa, the men had an excellent view of Medellín, including the Los Olivos district they had narrowed down as Pablo's area, a neighbourhood in Medellín near the football stadium, consisting mostly of two-storey homes. The men waited for information from surveillance units discreetly posted, including one led by Frequency – only ten blocks away from Pablo's hideout.

At Frankfurt airport, the family were searched, and interviews started in separate rooms. Pablo's emergency phone number remained concealed in one of Juan Pablo's shoes. For over thirty hours, with Manuela next to her on a sofa, Victoria was questioned about Pablo's whereabouts, finances and crime partners. Why had they come to Germany? Who were their local contacts? How much money had they brought? Holding her bottle, Manuela fell asleep, so Victoria extracted a blanket from her handbag and covered her daughter.

A sympathetic Spanish-speaking lawyer listened attentively to Victoria's pleas to stay in Germany, rather than risk death in Colombia. After Victoria broke down crying, the German lady confessed that she had been instructed not to help them. They had to go back. Before a harsh German voice ordered her to leave, she wished them luck. The typist departed. The lead interrogator said that Victoria needed to get her family ready for departure. They were leaving immediately. With the family in police cars heading for the plane, she protested that they were being condemned to die.

As soon as they were aboard the delayed flight, the door was closed. The passengers scowled at the family for stranding them on the runway for hours. After an hour, the pilot announced a further delay because France had denied access to its airspace because Pablo Escobar's family was on board. The tension rose. An attractive dark-haired woman approached Victoria, gave her a bible and said that Psalm 23 would help her situation. In case Victoria ever needed anything, she wrote down her contact details. Relieved by the act of kindness, Victoria thanked her and read Psalm 23:

"The Lord is my shepherd; I shall not want.

He maketh me to lie down in green pastures: he leadeth me beside the still waters.

He restoreth my soul: he leadeth me in the paths of righteousness for his name's sake.

Yea, though I walk through the valley of the shadow of death,

I will fear no evil: for thou art with me; thy rod and thy staff they comfort me ..."

As Victoria was a practicing Catholic, the words resonated. With so many forces operating against her, God was her only hope. (In the coming years, she would treasure that bible.) Approaching Colombia, she grew terrified about what might happen when the plane landed.

In Bogotá, Major Gonzalez lobbied the government to relocate Pablo's family to the Residencias Tequendama Hotel, where the Search Bloc had installed hidden microphones and had tapped the phone lines, which were monitored from an electronic-surveillance office.

At 8 PM, the flight landed in Bogotá. As if refusing to risk confronting danger, Victoria's legs froze and she remained seated with breathing difficulties. Hugging her kids, she said that their fate was in God's hands.

Three government agents boarded. "Everyone needs to remain seated while we remove some passengers." Promising to get them stamped, they took the family's passports. They emerged to a cold night and numerous cops with rifles. An agent stated that the government could only guarantee their protection if they stayed at a hotel owned by the Colombian Armed Forces Retirement Fund. Feeling uneasy, Victoria requested transport to a regular hotel with a high level of security, only to be told that she had no choice.

Travelling in an armoured SUV, they were escorted by over 100 cops in a procession of vehicles to the Residencias Tequendama Hotel, which included an apartment building. In an elevator with armed bodyguards, they got out on the unoccupied twenty-ninth floor, and were escorted to two mundane apartments at the end of the hall. Exhausted, they tried to sleep, but kept waking up terrified. Outside, over 100 cops patrolled with bomb-sniffing dogs. Using mirrors, they inspected the undercarriages of cars.

The following day, Victoria heard nothing from Pablo, but

received a call from her sister. Assuming that the phones had been tapped, she was unable to ask about her husband or even mention his name. With the building surrounded by guards, she fretted over the impossibility of him getting a message in to them. To let him know that they were OK, she asked Juan Pablo to give a radio interview, describing what had happened in Germany.

After hearing the radio interview, Pablo started to call his family using fake names. On the phone, he told them to stay at the hotel, to lobby the government to go to another country and to contact the United Nations. Pablo contacting his family raised the hopes of the authorities, but as the calls were short and sporadic, pinpointing their origin was difficult. For fifteen seconds, he stayed on the phone to his brother-in-law Alonso, but after that, the calls stopped for thirty-five hours, which tested the patience of the surveillance team, Colonel Martínez and Los Pepes. While waiting for them to resume, the men in the surveillance units, including Frequency, ate and slept in their vehicles.

To test the tracking equipment, Frequency sent a man to Medellín with instructions to call Don Berna. By sheer chance, and completely unknown to everybody involved, the man ended up near Pablo's hideout. The tracking system worked, and Pablo failed to notice the unusual activity in his area.

When the receptionist at the Residencias Tequendama Hotel received a call from a man identifying himself as Pablo, she was sceptical. The electronic-intelligence agents instructed her to delay him on the phone. The team in Medellín determined that the caller was in a moving vehicle.

Lonely and surrounded, Pablo's health deteriorated further. Weight gain reduced his mobility. Due to gastritis, he kept jars of Mylanta in every room of the safe house. Staying longer on the phone out of concern for his family, Pablo was dropping his guard. Slowly closing in after years of hunting El Patrón, the team in Medellín set up headquarters in a car park at the Atanasio Girardot Sports Complex. But a few setbacks occurred: several key members of the police had to leave for promotional courses, a new Search Bloc senior member arrived who was a desk worker, and pressure from the government to produce a result exacerbated the fatigue shared by the pursuers. In newspapers, the attorney general stated that the failure to capture Pablo was not just due to his talent at remaining invisible, but also because of the corruption of the Search Bloc. The government announced that Martínez would be replaced.

"An unusual noise is obstructing the clarity of the signals received," Frequency said.

"It sounds like water," Don Berna said, after listening to the call.

"Maybe a stream." The signal indicated that Pablo was moving between America Street and a sports complex. The only ravine in the area was the Bone.

Los Pepes announced that their cessation of operations – which had been initiated at the government's request – was over and they were resuming hostilities with Pablo. Fearing a bombing, the other guests checked out of the hotel housing his family. Walking around the hotel, Pablo's daughter, Manuela, sang about Los Pepes coming to kill her and her family.

On November 30, 1993, Pablo sent a letter to the suspected leaders of Los Pepes, including Colonel Martínez, the leaders of the Cali Cartel, the Castaño brothers and members of the Search Bloc. "I have been raided 10,000 times. You haven't been at all. Everything is confiscated from me. Nothing is taken away from you. The government will never offer a warrant for you. The government will never apply faceless justice to criminal and terrorist policemen."

On the same day, he met Milton Hernandez, one of the leaders of the National Liberation Army, and the second most powerful guerrilla in Colombia. Over the years, Pablo had remained close to the organisation, even recruiting its members to help fight Cali. Milton offered to protect him, provided that authorisation was granted by the guerrilla group. Pablo planned to leave on December 3 to eastern Antioquia, where he would be protected by the

Carlos Alirio Buitrago Front. He thanked Milton and gave him a gift: a SIG Sauer pistol.

The tracking signal indicated that Pablo's vehicle had just driven by the car park the team was using as headquarters. Immediately, Don Berna and his men took to the roads, but due to congestion, he escaped yet again. They returned confounded that the most wanted man in the world was driving around like an ordinary person.

Now they had him worried about his family's safety, the authorities relied on him calling the hotel. Returning early from a rest period, Frequency resumed the hunt. In a dangerous neighbourhood, Frequency's van was spotted. A child on roller-skates approached the van and gave Frequency a note: "We know what you're doing. We know you are looking for Pablo. Either you leave or we're going to kill you."

Roberto received a note from someone on his payroll to warn Pablo to stop talking on the phone or else he would be caught. Immediately, he sent a note to his brother urging him to stop using his phone, because it had been compromised. Other sources told Pablo that if he surrendered, he would be killed.

Aware that the end was near, Pablo left a recording for his daughter telling her to be a good girl and that he would protect her from heaven. He bought his brother a copy of *The Guinness Book of Sports Records*, wrote a personal note to Roberto – who he described as his soul brother – and put it in the book. In one of his final letters, he wrote: "Mother, Don't believe everything you read in the newspapers. I was good. They turned me bad."

With Los Pepes closing in, he spent his 44th birthday, December 1, 1993, at his hideout. Pouring champagne, Luzmila knocked a glass over which didn't break. "What good luck," she said.

"No," Limón said. "It means something bad is going to happen."

Breaking his usual abstinence, Pablo drank some champagne. He lit a cannabis joint. With Limón and Luzmila, he ate one of his favourite Antioquian meals, chicken sancocho, a hearty soup similar to a stew, including potatoes, yucca, corn, plantains and meat. Due to gastritis, he hardly ate any of his dessert: a chocolate cake sent by Victoria. With his mood low, he took Mylanta medicine.

With tunnel vision, he read the mail sent by his family, including drawings and a card from Manuela: "Daddy, I love you very much. I want to give you a big kiss on your birthday. You are my heaven. You are my dove. You are my heart. I wish you lots of luck on your birthday. I adore you. Your little girl." A card from a sibling read: "Even though you try to hide … You cannot escape another birthday."

A fly persistently attempting to land on Pablo upset Limón, who viewed it as an omen, because flies are attracted to corpses.

Birthday congratulations kept Pablo on the phone longer than usual with his family. Frequency picked up a signal and sped to the location, which brought him to a roundabout with nobody there. Convinced that he had just missed Pablo, he was disappointed. The next day, he returned to his apartment to rest.

Getting so close to El Patrón spread apprehension among the troops, some of whom were instructed to write letters to their families because of the likelihood of death. With Pablo determined not to be captured alive, the troops expected a heavy battle. They were awarded extra money to buy clothes and send presents to their families in case they never saw them again.

Pablo wanted to say goodbye to his mother first, so he risked going to her apartment in the early morning. He told her that it was the last time he would see her in Medellín. His plan now was to form a new group, establish an independent country and be its president. Without crying, his mother said goodbye.

On December 2, 1993, the cloudless sky and peaceful weather held a promise of good things to Don Berna, as his driver took him and his bodyguards to a wine cellar that had been converted into a Los Pepes headquarters. Afterwards, he moved to a car park by the Atanasio Girardot Sports Complex, where Major Hugo Aguilar was waiting with tracking equipment.

"I'm very worried," Aguilar said. "The government wants results, so they have increased pressure on the police. The president is close to finishing his term, and he doesn't want that to happen with Escobar still on the loose. He has given us one week to find him. If we don't achieve that objective, we're all going to be dismissed."

"You need to remain calm," Don Berna said. "His days are numbered, so don't be getting anxious. He is unable to detonate bombs. He is unable to set up police to be murdered. He is unable to kidnap people from the government. His power is totally reduced. As his brother and Popeye have surrendered, he can receive no support from them. On top of that, we've intercepted a letter from one of his men, Marlboro, in which he told Pablo that he had to sell his motorbike and gun to buy food. His men have run out of money and out of work, or else they are in jail. The message issued by Los Pepes – whoever helps El Patrón must die – has been extremely effective."

"I hope things get sorted out," Aguilar said, "because even though I'm happy to be assigned to the promotional course to acquire the degree of lieutenant colonel, I find it disappointing that after so much effort and time, we haven't been able to finish Escobar. In the entire history of Colombia, nobody has endured such a strong and relentless enemy, where forces so dissimilar have had to combine to be able to eliminate him." At 12:30 PM, Aguilar said, "I'm tired of eating chicken and potatoes, so for lunch, I'm heading to the Carlos Holguín School." He departed. In the car park, Don Berna ordered restaurant food and waited with twenty of his men, his brother Seed, Frequency and a sergeant called Toño.

"The teams are ready," Frequency said on a call to his father, "but Pablo hasn't used his phone."

Pablo woke up around noon. He dressed in jeans, a polo shirt and flip-flops instead of sneakers. He learned that the police had raided and killed Gustavo's son at 11 AM. After eating Italian food, he sent his cousin to buy the supplies he would need in the jungle: stationery and toiletries.

News broadcasts of his family's ongoing suffering at the hotel disturbed him. In a taxi, he called them while they were in a meeting with some generals, but upon recognising his voice, Juan Pablo kept referring to him as 'Grandma,' stating that the family was OK, and hanging up out of concern that the calls would be traced. Noticing the strain in her son's voice, Victoria knew that 'Grandma' was her husband. The generals said that the hotel had authorised them to bring an additional 100 soldiers to protect the building and that they were going to completely lockdown the twenty-ninth floor. After Pablo called a third time, Juan Pablo told 'Grandma' that they were doing fine, but instead of hanging up, he handed the phone to his mother. While he said goodbye to the generals, she rushed into another room.

Excitedly, Victoria spoke, but was quickly interrupted by Juan Pablo, who insisted that she needed to hang up, because the call was being traced. She told Pablo to take care of himself because they all needed him. He said his only motivation in life was to fight for his family, and that he was safely hiding out in a cave and that the hardest part of their struggle was over. Despite the warnings, he called two more times, and Juan Pablo hung up on him. A call to Manuela and Victoria was interrupted by Juan Pablo yelling that Pablo would be found and killed if they didn't hang up.

While putting on a brave face to his family, he was adjusting mentally to the reality of death. He wrote a prayer, which he put in his wallet:

"Pray for us
O Lady Saint Marta
To the mountain work you entered
With the serpent that you found
With your great symbol
You tamed it, defeated it and dominated it
I ask you Queen and Lady
That you defeat, calm and dominate all the enemies that challenge me

Be they men or women, tigers or lions
I have to defeat all of them and make them tremble with fear
in front of me
The Lord played the seven horos
Being horo and game
They are the seven arts that killed him with poison
And now they are my companions
There are seven of them, eight including me
I call on all of them to defend me from fist, bullets, force and
every type of firearm that could come against me
Christ gives me courage and gives me faith
The Holy cross travels with me
In front and behind"

By adding himself to the seven horos or evils, he appeared to be taking responsibility for his crimes in the face of his mortality.

Martínez notified his son that Pablo was talking. Frequency rushed back to his team. After 1 PM, pretending to be a radio journalist, Pablo called his family. The house receptionist unsuccessfully attempted to delay the call. The noise of the creek convinced Don Berna that Pablo was nearby. His wife, Victoria, was crying. Numerous of their family members and associates had been killed by Los Pepes. The family was distraught.

"So, what are you going to do?" Pablo asked.

"I don't know," she said, still crying.

"What does your mother say?"

"It was as if my mother fainted," she said, referring to a few days earlier at the airport, when the family had unsuccessfully tried to flee to Germany. "I did not call her. She told me bye, and then—"

"And you haven't spoken to her?"

"No. My mother is so nervous ..." Victoria said the murders committed by Los Pepes had traumatised her mother.

"What are you going to do?" Pablo asked softly.

"I don't know. I mean, wait and see where we are going to go, and I believe that will be the end of us."

"No!"

"So?"

"Don't you give me this coldness! Holy Mary!" Pablo said.

"And you?"

"Ahhh."

"And you?"

"What about me?" Pablo asked.

"What are you going to do?"

"Nothing … What do you need?"

"Nothing," Victoria said.

"What do you want?"

"What would I want?"

"If you need something, call me, OK?"

"OK."

"You call me now, quickly," Pablo said. "There is nothing more I can tell you. What else can I say? I have remained right on track, right?"

"But, how are you? Oh my God, I don't know!"

"We must go on. Think about it. Now that I am so close, right?" Pablo said, referring to his proposal to surrender.

"Yes," Victoria said. "Think about your boy, too, and everything else, and don't make any decisions too quickly. OK?"

"Yes."

"Call your mother again and ask her if she wants you to go there or what …" she said. "Ciao."

"So long."

Concerned about his family due to the death of Gustavo's son, Limón called his wife, who had been registering their children for school. "Take care, because you know things are going to get very hot." Upon learning that one of his daughters had slept at his sister-in-law's house, he said, "Get her back to the house. Things are going to get ugly."

"Are you OK?" his wife asked.

"I'm fine. Give my love to the kids."

At 2:52 PM, Pablo called his son.

"We have narrowed down the location," Frequency told Don Berna. "Let's go with all of your men." With the Search Bloc attempting to find the precise location, Juan Pablo asked his dad to help him formulate answers to questions from a journalist. Pablo got out of the taxi and returned to the apartment, making the mistake of speaking for longer than five minutes.

"Look, this is very important in Bogotá," Pablo said, hoping to present his case favourably through the media. He wanted to hear the questions first. "This is also publicity. Explaining the reasons and other matters to them. Do you understand? Well done and well organised."

"Yes, yes." Juan Pablo began with the first question from the magazine *Semana*: "'Whatever the country, refuge is conditioned on the immediate surrender of your father. Would your father be willing to turn himself in if you are settled somewhere?'"

"Go on," Pablo said.

"The next one is, 'Would he be willing to turn himself in before you take refuge abroad?'"

"Go on."

"I spoke with the man and he told me that if there were some questions I did not want to answer, there was no problem, and if I wanted to add some questions, he would include them."

"OK. The next one?"

"'Why do you think that several countries have refused to receive your family?' OK?"

"Yes."

"'From which embassies have you requested help for them to take you in?'"

"OK."

"'Don't you think your father's situation, accused of X number of crimes, assassination of public figures, considered one of the most powerful drug traffickers in the world …?'" Juan Pablo stopped reading.

"Go on."

"But there are many. Around forty questions."

Pablo said he would call back later in the day. "I may find a way to communicate by fax."

"No," Juan Pablo said, concerned about a fax being traced.

"No, huh? OK. OK. So, good luck."

Frequency traced the call to the Los Olivos neighbourhood. They waited for him to make another call.

At 2:57 PM, Pablo called his son for the last time. Juan Pablo said that the journalist wanted to know what conditions Pablo would be satisfied with in order to surrender. Members of the Search Bloc started to go street to street, hoping to detect his location. Frequency's scanner led him to an office building. Convinced Pablo was inside, the troops stormed in, but Pablo was still conversing as if nothing had happened.

"Tell him, 'My father cannot turn himself in unless he has guarantees for his security.'"

"OK."

"'And we totally support him in that,'" Pablo said.

"OK."

"'Above any considerations.'"

"Yep."

"'My father is not going to turn himself in before we are placed in a foreign country, and while the police in Antioquia—'"

"The police and DAS is better," Juan Pablo said. "Because the DAS are also searching."

"It's only the police," Pablo said.

"Oh, OK."

"'While the police—'"

"Yeah."

"OK," Pablo said. "Let's change it to, 'While the security organisations in Antioquia …'"

"Yeah."

"'—continue to kidnap—'"

"Yeah."

"'—torture—'"

"Yeah."

"'—and commit massacres in Medellín.'"

"Yes, all right."

"OK," Pablo said. "The next one."

Due to the amount of time Pablo had spent on the phone, Frequency's scanning equipment had narrowed down the location to a street in the América sector, on the right beyond La Hueso Creek. He led Don Berna's men to a stream by Pablo's house.

Juan Pablo asked why so many countries had refused to allow their family in.

"'The countries have denied entry because they don't know the real truth,'" Pablo said.

"Yes."

"'We're going to knock on the doors of every embassy from all around the world, because we're willing to fight incessantly. Because we want to live and study in another country without bodyguards and hopefully with a new name.'"

"Just so you know, I got a phone call from a reporter who told me that President Alfredo Cristiani from Ecuador, no, I think it is El Salvador—"

"Yes?" Pablo went to a second-floor window and scanned the street, checking for cars.

"Well, he has offered to receive us. I heard the statement. Well, he gave it to me by phone," Juan Pablo said.

"Yes?"

"And he said if this contributed in some way to the peace of the country, he would be willing to receive us."

"Well," Pablo said, "let's wait and see, because that country is a bit hidden away."

"Well, but at least there's a possibility, and it has come from a president."

"Look, with respect to El Salvador …"

"Yeah?"

"In case they ask anything, tell them, 'The family is very grateful and obliged to the words of the president, that it is known he is the president of peace in El Salvador.'"

"Yeah."

The length of the call had exceeded his safety limits. When asked about how the family had felt about living with government protection, he said, "You respond to that one."

"'Who paid for maintenance and accommodation? You or the attorney general?'" Juan Pablo asked.

"Who did pay this?" Pablo asked.

"Us. Well, there were some people from Bogotá who got their expenses paid ... but they never spent all of it, because we supplied the groceries, mattresses, deodorants, toothbrushes and pretty much everything."

After two more questions, Pablo said, "OK, let's leave it at that."

"Yeah, OK," Juan Pablo said. "Good luck."

"Good luck."

The call had lasted for so long that Frequency and Los Pepes were on Pablo's street, driving up and down. Frequency stopped studying his equipment and started observing the houses. He noticed a bearded man behind a second-storey window, phone in hand, watching the traffic. After a few seconds, the man disappeared into the house.

Frequency leaned out of the window. "This is the house!" he yelled at the vehicle behind him. Suspecting that Pablo had noticed his white van, Frequency told the driver to keep going. He radioed his father: "I've got him located. He's in this house." Assuming that Pablo's hit men were on their way, Frequency wanted to leave.

"Stay exactly where you are!" Colonel Martínez yelled. "Station yourself in front and back of the house. Don't let him come out!"

"Are you sure Pablo is there?" Aguilar asked.

"I'm absolutely sure of it."

"Do not make any movement. We're on our way with backup."

With the roads congested with holiday traffic, the journey would take approximately forty-five minutes. To Don Berna, waiting was eternal and too agonising.

With all units of the Search Bloc on their way, Frequency parked in a back alley and got his gun ready.

At 3:15 PM, Frequency asked Don Berna, "Do your men have the area completely secured?"

"Yes. It's impossible for El Patrón to escape."

"Let's go in. I assume responsibility."

Seed put on a bulletproof vest, grabbed an M16 rifle loaded with ammunition provided by the Americans and approached the residence accompanied by two of Don Berna's men and the policeman, Toño. A sledgehammer demolished the door.

"Boss, they found us!" Limón yelled.

"Limón, run, because you still have time," Pablo said. "It's easier for you to run. I know what I have to do."

Limón dashed out of the back door. Charging up the stairs, one man fell as if shot, startling the rest, but he had only slipped. Limón went through a window onto an orange-tile roof. As he fled, Los Pepes members behind the house sprayed gunfire. Shot multiple times, he careened off the roof onto the grass. Limón's wife believes that they shot him in the forehead to ensure his death.

After tossing his sandals, Pablo ran upstairs to a small window that faced a neighbour's roof. Not wanting to end up like Limón, he stayed against a wall, which blocked clear shots at him even though gunmen were everywhere. Aiming to escape down a back street, he hastened along the wall.

Shots erupted.

The gunfire was so intense from all sides of the house that it tore up the bricks and the roof, and some members of Los Pepes thought they were under attack by Pablo's bodyguards and radioed for help. As he ran across the roof, Seed fired at him. A bullet entered Pablo's thigh above the knee and emerged below his kneecap. Another went in below his right shoulder and got stuck between two teeth in his lower jaw.

Pablo fell.

Having pledged to never be captured or killed, he most likely shot himself in the head to deprive the government of being able to claim that they had killed him. The bullet went into the right ear at the centre and came out in front of his left ear, slicing through his brain, killing him instantly. To this day, Roberto and Juan Pablo believe the wound above the ear was a suicide shot.

The shooting stopped.

"It's Pablo! It's Pablo!"

Los Pepes members approached the blood-soaked corpse and flipped it over. One used his foot to remove Pablo's gun and lifted his hair. Stood at a window, Don Berna felt no emotion gazing at the obese, shoeless corpse leaking blood.

"Viva Colombia! We've just killed Pablo Escobar!"

"We won! We won!"

Amid men shooting in the air and yelling, "Viva Colombia!" Aguilar arrived and hugged Don Berna, Seed and Frequency. "You and your men need to leave immediately," he told Don Berna, "because the media are coming."

The police shaved a Hitler moustache onto Pablo's face and posed for pictures with him.

After leaving the death scene, Don Berna called Fidel Castaño: "Commander, Pablo is dead."

"Are you sure?"

"Yes, Commander, I saw it myself."

"Meet us at Montecasino as soon as possible."

With Los Pepes gone, the police told the media, "We advanced rapidly up the stairs and we saw two subjects throw themselves from the window at the back of the house, falling onto the roof of the house next door, where they were neutralised by the personnel located in this part of the house, who fired back after coming under attack."

It was the birth of the official version of Pablo's death, which still existed on Wikipedia as of April 7, 2020: "The two fugitives attempted to escape by running across the roofs of adjoining houses to reach a back street, but both were shot and killed by Colombian National Police. Escobar suffered gunshots to the leg and torso, and a fatal gunshot through the ear."

Years later, the chief of intelligence for the Colombian National

Police claimed that Pablo had been killed at close range because nobody had wanted to risk the disaster that would have arisen if he had been captured alive. He compared Pablo to a trophy at the end of a long hunt. According to the official reports, a sergeant who died two years after Pablo's death, along with a police chief and another officer, were the only three who shot Pablo.

After Don Berna wrote his book, *Killing the Boss*, describing his brother, Seed, as one of the main shooters, Colonel Martínez denied the role of Los Pepes: "It's not true what he says. I was constantly communicating by radio with Colonel Aguilar and Lieutenant Hugo Martínez Bolívar, my son, and the operation was carried out entirely by policemen."

In 2014, Juan Pablo wrote in *Pablo Escobar: My Father* that he had overheard Pablo on a radiophone to a bodyguard stating that he would never allow the authorities to take him alive. He had told his son that when the inevitable showdown came, he would fire fourteen rounds from his Sig Sauer pistol, leaving one to shoot himself in the right ear. The photo of Pablo on the roof shows him next to his Sig Sauer pistol, which had been fired. His Glock was still holstered. Even *Narcos* showed Pablo's blood-soaked right hand, which would have arisen from the spray if he had shot himself in the ear. Juan Pablo is convinced that his father honoured the suicide pledge.

Shortly after Pablo's death, his mother and two sisters arrived. At first, they thought that only Limón was dead. "It's Pablo," one of his sisters said, identifying the second corpse.

Hermilda later described what happened when she found his corpse: "I felt something I have never felt in my life. It was terrible. Since then, my soul has been destroyed because there will never be anyone like Pablo again."

Manuela was singing in the shower and Victoria was on the phone with her sister when Juan Pablo yelled that his father had been killed. Pablo's wife told her sister to find out what had happened. The return call confirmed his death and added that helicopters were circling his hideout.

At Montecasino, Don Berna described what had happened to Carlos and Fidel. "Now that Pablo is dead," Carlo said, "we must start a new fight against the guerrillas. With all the weapons, contacts and resources we've obtained from the war against Pablo, we'll build a political military organisation. From this moment on, Don Berna and Seed, you belong to this new anti-subversive organisation as members of the general staff."

From his personal wine cellar, Fidel brought a 1948 French vintage. After the celebration, Don Berna asked for permission to rest because he was exhausted. Back in his apartment, he reminisced about the friends he had lost. Feeling alone, he wondered if it had all been worth it and finally fell into a deep sleep.

The American president wrote a letter:

"December 2, 1993

Dear Mr President:

I just learned of the success of your long struggle to bring Pablo Escobar to justice. I want to offer my congratulations to you and the Colombian security forces for your courageous and effective work in this case. Hundreds of Colombians, brave police officers and innocent people, lost their lives as a result of Escobar's terrorism. Your work honors the memory of all of these victims. We are proud of the firm stand you have taken, and I pledge to you our continued cooperation in our joint efforts to combat drug trafficking.

Sincerely,
BILL CLINTON"

At 6 AM on December 4, 1993, in Bogotá, at a military airport, a plane scheduled to collect the president stopped by the VIP lounge. Inside, Gaviria was on a natural high, celebrating and toasting glasses of orange juice with Rafael Pardo, his advisers and the police and military commanders. A dozen journalists accompanied them on the flight to Medellín. After Gaviria removed his coat, grey suit and shirt to put on a bulletproof vest, a cameraman started recording, but was quickly instructed to stop. The festivities continued for the duration of the short flight.

In Rionegro, officials at the airport expanded Gaviria's entourage, some of whom yelled, "Hurray!" and congratulated the Search Bloc. At an army facility, the policemen whom the government had credited for eliminating Pablo were paraded to the media. The journalists were instructed to turn the men into heroes. A presidential adviser coached the journalists on what to report: the bravery of the Search Bloc and the security forces, the historical importance of Pablo's demise … "This is the beginning of the end of narco-trafficking in Colombia," the adviser boasted.

CHAPTER 18
JUAN PABLO'S DEADLY MISTAKE

In a statement to a reporter in the aftermath of Pablo's death, Juan Pablo exploded on his father's enemies. He was going to murder the fuckers who had killed his father. He would kill the bastards himself. After refusing to comment any further, he hung up and sobbed. With the whole family crying hysterically, he imagined how he would destroy his enemies: he would become even more dangerous than El Patrón.

As his reaction subsided, he saw the error of the gangster lifestyle. He remembered the stress that Pablo had caused his family, and all the people who had died, including so many family and friends. He could not go down the same road as his father. He regretted vowing revenge. His father's incensed enemies would have heard his statement to the reporter and would now be plotting to kill him. Hoping to undo the damage, he contacted a TV station and announced that he would not seek revenge. His only care was his family's safety. They had all suffered. He wanted to work hard to promote peace.

Having heard Juan Pablo vow to kill his father's enemies, the Cali godfathers sentenced him to death. Before killing him, they wanted all of Pablo's assets transferred over from his family members. If the family refused, the cartel would wipe out every generation of Pablo's family and have corrupt officials give them everything. To make their intentions clear, they sent a bomb to Pablo's brother in prison …

To be continued in Pablo Escobar's Story Part 4

GET A FREE BOOK:
JOIN SHAUN'S NEWSLETTER
SIGN UP PAGE

REFERENCES

Bowden, Mark. *Killing Pablo*. Atlantic Books, 2001.

Bowen, Russell. *The Immaculate Deception*. America West Publishers, 1991.

Castaño, Carlos. *My Confession*. Oveja Negra, 2001.

Caycedo, Germán Castro. *In Secret*. Planeta, 1996.

Chepesiuk, Ron. *Crazy Charlie*. Strategic Media Books, 2016.

Chepesiuk, Ron. *Drug Lords: The Rise and Fall of the Cali Cartel*. Milo Books, 2003.

Chepesiuk, Ron. *Escobar vs Cali: The War of the Cartels*. Strategic Media, 2013.

Cockburn, Leslie. *Out of Control*. Bloomsbury, 1988.

Cockburn and Clair. *Whiteout*. Verso, 1998.

Don Berna. *Killing the Boss*. ICONO, 2013.

Escobar, Juan Pablo. *Pablo Escobar: My Father*. Ebury Press, 2014.

Escobar, Roberto. *Escobar*. Hodder & Stoughton, 2009.

Grillo, Joan. *El Narco*. Bloomsbury, 2012.

Gugliotta and Leen. *Kings of Cocaine*. Harper and Row, 1989.

Hari, Johann. *Chasing the Scream*. Bloomsbury, 2015.

Henao, Victoria Eugenia. *Mrs Escobar: My Life with Pablo*. Ebury Press, 2019.

Hopsicker, Daniel. *Barry and the Boys*. MadCow Press, 2001.

Leveritt, Mara. *The Boys on the Tracks*. Bird Call Press, 2007.

Levine, Michael. *The Big White Lie*. Thunder's Mouth Press, 1993.

MacQuarrie, Kim. *Life and Death in the Andes*. Simon & Schuster, 2016.

Márquez, Gabriel García. *News of a Kidnapping*. Penguin, 1996.

Martínez, Astrid María Legarda. *The True Life of Pablo Escobar*. Ediciones y Distribuciones Dipon Ltda, 2017.

Massing, Michael. *The Fix*. Simon & Schuster, 1998.

McAleese, Peter. *No Mean Soldier*. Cassell Military Paperbacks, 2000.

McCoy, Alfred. *The Politics of Heroin in Southeast Asia*. Harper and Row, 1972.

Mollison, James. *The Memory of Pablo Escobar*. Chris Boot, 2009.

Morris, Roger. *Partners in Power*. Henry Holt, 1996.

Noriega, Manuel. *The Memoirs of Manuel Noriega*. Random House, 1997.

North, Oliver. *Under Fire*. Harper Collins, 1991.

Paley, Dawn. *Drug War Capitalism*. AK Press, 2014.

Porter, Bruce. *Blow*. St Martin's Press, 1993.

Reed, Terry. *Compromised*. Clandestine Publishing, 1995.

Rempel, William. *At the Devil's Table: Inside the Fall of the Cali Cartel, the World's Biggest Crime Syndicate*. Random House, 2011.

Ross, Rick. *Freeway Rick Ross*. Freeway Studios, 2014.

Ruppert, Michael. *Crossing the Rubicon*. New Society Publishers, 2004.

Salazar, Alonso. *The Words of Pablo*. Planeta, 2001.

Salazar, Alonso. *Born to Die in Medellín*. Latin America Bureau, 1992.

Saviano, Roberto. *Zero Zero Zero*. Penguin Random House UK, 2013.

Schou, Nick. *Kill the Messenger*. Nation Books, 2006.

Shannon, Elaine. *Desperados*. Penguin, 1988.

Stich, Rodney. *Defrauding America* 3rd Ed. Diablo Western Press, 1998.

Stich, Rodney. *Drugging America* 2nd Ed. Silverpeak, 2006.

Stokes, Doug. *America's Other War: Terrorizing Colombia*. Zed Books, 2005.

Stone, Roger. *The Clintons' War on Women*. Skyhorse, 2015.

Stone, Roger. *Jeb and the Bush Crime Family*. Skyhorse, 2016.

Streatfield, Dominic. *Cocaine*. Virgin Publishing, 2001.

Tarpley and Chaitkin. *George Bush*. Progressive Press, 2004.

Tomkins, David. *Dirty Combat*. Mainstream Publishing, 2008.

Valentine, Douglas. *The Strength of the Pack*. Trine Day LLC, 2009.

Vallejo, Virginia. *Loving Pablo, Hating Escobar*. Vintage, 2018.

Velásquez Vásquez, Jhon Jairo. *Surviving Pablo Escobar*. Ediciones y Distribuciones Dipon Ltda, 2017.

Woods, Neil. *Good Cop Bad War*. Ebury Press, 2016.

SHAUN'S BOOKS

English Shaun Trilogy
Party Time
Hard Time
Prison Time

War on Drugs Series
Pablo Escobar: Beyond Narcos
American Made: Who Killed Barry Seal? Pablo Escobar or George HW Bush
The Cali Cartel: Beyond Narcos
Clinton Bush and CIA Conspiracies:
From the Boys on the Tracks to Jeffrey Epstein

Un-Making a Murderer:
The Framing of Steven Avery and Brendan Dassey
The Mafia Philosopher: Two Tonys
Life Lessons

Pablo Escobar's Story (4-book series)

SOCIAL-MEDIA LINKS

Email: attwood.shaun@hotmail.co.uk
YouTube: Shaun Attwood
Blog: Jon's Jail Journal
Website: shaunattwood.com
Instagram: @shaunattwood
Twitter: @shaunattwood
LinkedIn: Shaun Attwood
Goodreads: Shaun Attwood
Facebook: Shaun Attwood, Jon's Jail Journal,
T-Bone Appreciation Society

Shaun welcomes feedback on any of
his books and YouTube videos.
Thank you for the Amazon and Goodreads reviews and to all of
the people who have subscribed to Shaun's YouTube channel!

SHAUN'S JAIL JOURNEY STARTS IN HARD TIME NEW EDITION

CHAPTER 1

Sleep deprived and scanning for danger, I enter a dark cell on the second floor of the maximum-security Madison Street jail in Phoenix, Arizona, where guards and gang members are murdering prisoners. Behind me, the metal door slams heavily. Light slants into the cell through oblong gaps in the door, illuminating a prisoner cocooned in a white sheet, snoring lightly on the top bunk about two thirds of the way up the back wall. Relieved there is no immediate threat, I place my mattress on the grimy floor. Desperate to rest, I notice movement on the cement-block walls. *Am I hallucinating?* I blink several times. The walls appear to ripple. Stepping closer, I see the walls are alive with insects. I flinch. So many are swarming, I wonder if they're a colony of ants on the move. To get a better look, I put my eyes right up to them. They are mostly the size of almonds and have antennae. American cockroaches. I've seen them in the holding cells downstairs in smaller numbers, but nothing like this. A chill spread over my body. I back away.

Something alive falls from the ceiling and bounces off the base of my neck. I jump. With my night vision improving, I spot cockroaches weaving in and out of the base of the fluorescent strip light. Every so often one drops onto the concrete and resumes crawling. Examining the bottom bunk, I realise why my cellmate is sleeping at a higher elevation: cockroaches are pouring from gaps in the decrepit wall at the level of my bunk. The area is thick with them. Placing my mattress on the bottom bunk scatters them. I walk towards the toilet, crunching a few under my shower sandals. I urinate and grab the toilet roll. A cockroach darts from the centre of the roll onto my hand, tickling my fingers. My arm jerks as if it has a mind of its own, losing the cockroach and the toilet roll. Using a towel, I wipe the bulk of them off the bottom bunk, stopping only to shake the odd one off my hand. I unroll my mattress. They begin to regroup and inhabit my mattress. My adrenaline is pumping so much, I lose my fatigue.

Nauseated, I sit on a tiny metal stool bolted to the wall. *How will I sleep? How's my cellmate sleeping through the infestation and my arrival?* Copying his technique, I cocoon myself in a sheet and lie down, crushing more cockroaches. The only way they can access me now is through the breathing hole I've left in the sheet by the lower half of my face. Inhaling their strange musty odour, I close my eyes. I can't sleep. I feel them crawling on the sheet around my feet. *Am I imagining things?* Frightened of them infiltrating my breathing hole, I keep opening my eyes. Cramps cause me to rotate onto my other side. Facing the wall, I'm repulsed by so many of them just inches away. I return to my original side.

The sheet traps the heat of the Sonoran Desert to my body, soaking me in sweat. Sweat tickles my body, tricking my mind into thinking the cockroaches are infiltrating and crawling on me. The trapped heat aggravates my bleeding skin infections and bedsores. I want to scratch myself, but I know better. The outer layers of my skin have turned soggy from sweating constantly in this concrete oven. Squirming on the bunk fails to stop the relentless itchiness of my skin. Eventually, I scratch myself. Clumps of moist skin detach under my nails. Every now and then I become so uncomfortable, I must open my cocoon to waft the heat out, which allows the cockroaches in. It takes hours to drift to sleep. I only manage a few hours. I awake stuck to the soaked sheet, disgusted by the cockroach carcasses compressed against the mattress.

The cockroaches plague my new home until dawn appears at the dots in the metal grid over a begrimed strip of four-inch-thick bullet-proof glass at the top of the back wall – the cell's only source of outdoor light. They disappear into the cracks in the walls, like vampire mist retreating from sunlight. But not all of them. There were so many on the night shift that even their vastly reduced number is too many to dispose of. And they act like they know it. They roam around my feet with attitude, as if to make it clear that I'm trespassing on their turf.

My next set of challenges will arise not from the insect world, but from my neighbours. I'm the new arrival, subject to scrutiny about my charges just like when I'd run into the Aryan Brotherhood prison gang on my first day at the medium-security Towers jail a year ago. I wish my cellmate would wake up, brief me on the mood of the locals and introduce me to the head of the white gang. No such luck. Chow is announced over a speaker system in a crackly robotic voice, but he doesn't stir.

I emerge into the day room for breakfast. Prisoners in black-and-white bee-striped uniforms gather under the metal-grid stairs and tip dead cockroaches into a trash bin from plastic peanut-butter containers they'd set as traps during the night. All eyes are on me in the chow line. Watching who sits where, I hold my head up, put on a solid stare and pretend to be as at home in this environment as the cockroaches. It's all an act. I'm lonely and afraid. I loathe having to explain myself to the head of the white race, who I assume is the toughest murderer. I've been in jail long enough to know that taking my breakfast to my cell will imply that I have something to hide.

The gang punishes criminals with certain charges. The most serious are sex offenders, who are KOS: Kill On Sight. Other charges are punishable by SOS – Smash On Sight – such as drive-by shootings because women and kids sometimes get killed. It's called convict justice. Gang members are constantly looking for people to beat up because that's how they earn their reputations and tattoos. The most serious acts of violence earn the highest-ranking tattoos. To be a full gang member requires murder. I've observed the body language and techniques inmates trying to integrate employ. An inmate with a spring in his step and an air of confidence is likely to be accepted. A person who avoids eye contact and fails to introduce himself to the gang is likely to be preyed on. Some of the failed attempts I saw ended up with heads getting cracked against toilets, a sound I've grown familiar with. I've seen prisoners being extracted on stretchers who looked dead – one had yellow fluid leaking from his head. The constant violence gives me nightmares, but the reality is that I put myself in here, so I force myself to accept it as a part of my punishment.

It's time to apply my knowledge. With a self-assured stride, I take my breakfast bag to the table of white inmates covered in neo-Nazi tattoos, allowing them to question me.

"Mind if I sit with you guys?" I ask, glad exhaustion has deepened my voice.

"These seats are taken. But you can stand at the corner of the table."

The man who answered is probably the head of the gang. I size him up. Cropped brown hair. A dangerous glint in Nordic-blue eyes. Tiny pupils that suggest he's on heroin. Weightlifter-type veins bulging from a sturdy neck. Political ink on arms crisscrossed with scars. About the same age as me, thirty-three.

"Thanks. I'm Shaun from England." I volunteer my origin to show I'm different from them but not in a way that might get me smashed.

"I'm Bullet, the head of the whites." He offers me his fist to bump. "Where you roll in from, wood?"

Addressing me as wood is a good sign. It's what white gang members on a friendly basis call each other.

"Towers jail. They increased my bond and re-classified me to maximum security."

"What's your bond at?"

"I've got two $750,000 bonds," I say in a monotone. This is no place to brag about bonds.

"How many people you kill, brother?" His eyes drill into mine, checking whether my body language supports my story. My body language so far is spot on.

"None. I threw rave parties. They got us talking about drugs on wiretaps." Discussing drugs on the phone does not warrant a $1.5 million bond. I know and beat him to his next question. "Here's my charges." I show him my charge sheet, which includes conspiracy and leading a crime syndicate – both from running an Ecstasy ring.

Bullet snatches the paper and scrutinises it. Attempting to pre-empt his verdict, the other whites study his face. On edge, I wait for him to respond. Whatever he says next will determine whether I'll be accepted or victimised.

"Are you some kind of jailhouse attorney?" Bullet asks. "I want someone to read through my case paperwork." During our few minutes of conversation, Bullet has seen through my act and concluded that I'm educated – a possible resource to him.

I appreciate that he'll accept me if I take the time to read his case. "I'm no jailhouse attorney, but I'll look through it and help you however I can."

"Good. I'll stop by your cell later on, wood."

After breakfast, I seal as many of the cracks in the walls as I can with toothpaste. The cell smells minty, but the cockroaches still find their way in. Their day shift appears to be collecting information on the brown paper bags under my bunk, containing a few items of food that I purchased from the commissary; bags that I tied off with rubber bands in the hope of keeping the cockroaches out. Relentlessly, the cockroaches explore the bags for entry points, pausing over and probing the most worn and vulnerable regions. *Will the nightly swarm eat right through the paper?* I read all morning, wondering whether my cellmate has died in his cocoon, his occasional breathing sounds reassuring me.

Bullet stops by late afternoon and drops his case paperwork off. He's been charged with Class 3 felonies and less, not serious crimes, but is facing a double-digit sentence because of his prior convictions and Security Threat Group status in the prison system. The proposed sentencing range seems disproportionate. I'll advise him to reject the plea bargain – on the assumption he already knows to do so, but is just seeking the comfort of a second opinion, like many un-sentenced inmates. When he returns for his paperwork, our conversation disturbs my cellmate – the cocoon shuffles – so we go upstairs to his cell. I tell Bullet what I think. He is excitable, a different man from earlier, his pupils almost non-existent.

"This case ain't shit. But my prosecutor knows I done other shit, all kinds of heavy shit, but can't prove it. I'd do anything to get that sorry bitch off my fucking ass. She's asking for something bad to happen to her. Man, if I ever get bonded out, I'm gonna chop that bitch into pieces. Kill her slowly though. Like to work her over with a blowtorch."

Such talk can get us both charged with conspiring to murder a prosecutor, so I try to steer him elsewhere. "It's crazy how they can catch you doing one thing, yet try to sentence you for all of the things they think you've ever done."

"Done plenty. Shot some dude in the stomach once. Rolled him up in a blanket and threw him in a dumpster."

Discussing past murders is as unsettling as future ones. "So, what's all your tattoos mean, Bullet? Like that eagle on your chest?"

"Why you wanna know?" Bullet's eyes probe mine.

My eyes hold their ground. "Just curious."

"It's a war bird. The AB patch."

"AB patch?"

"What the Aryan Brotherhood gives you when you've put enough work in."

"How long does it take to earn a patch?"

"Depends how quickly you put your work in. You have to earn your lightning bolts first."

"Why you got red and black lightning bolts?"

"You get SS bolts for beating someone down or for being an

enforcer for the family. Red lightning bolts for killing someone. I was sent down as a youngster. They gave me steel and told me who to handle and I handled it. You don't ask questions. You just get blood on your steel. Dudes who get these tats without putting work in are told to cover them up or leave the yard."

"What if they refuse?"

"They're held down and we carve the ink off them."

Imagining them carving a chunk of flesh to remove a tattoo, I cringe. He's really enjoying telling me this now. His volatile nature is clear and frightening. *He's accepted me too much. He's trying to impress me before making demands.*

At night, I'm unable to sleep. Cocooned in heat, surrounded by cockroaches, I hear the swamp-cooler vent – a metal grid at the top of a wall – hissing out tepid air. Giving up on sleep, I put my earphones on and tune into National Public Radio. Listening to a Vivaldi violin concerto, I close my eyes and press my tailbone down to straighten my back as if I'm doing a yogic relaxation. The playful allegro thrills me, lifting my spirits, but the wistful adagio provokes sad emotions and tears. I open my eyes and gaze into the gloom. Due to lack of sleep, I start hallucinating and hearing voices over the music whispering threats. I'm at breaking point. Although I have accepted that I committed crimes and deserve to be punished, no one should have to live like this. I'm furious at myself for making the series of reckless decisions that put me in here and for losing absolutely everything. As violins crescendo in my ears, I remember what my life used to be like.

SHAUN'S INCARCERATION CONCLUDES IN PRISON TIME

CHAPTER 1

"I've got a padlock in a sock. I can smash your brains in while you're asleep. I can kill you whenever I want." My new cellmate sizes me up with no trace of human feeling in his eyes. Muscular and pot-bellied, he's caked in prison ink, including six snakes on his skull, slithering side by side. The top of his right ear is missing in a semi-circle.

The waves of fear are overwhelming. After being in transportation all day, I can feel my bladder hurting. "I'm not looking to cause any trouble. I'm the quietest cellmate you'll ever have. All I do is read and write."

Scowling, he shakes his head. "Why've they put a fish in with me?" He swaggers close enough for me to smell his cigarette breath. "Us convicts don't get along with fresh fish."

"Should I ask to move then?" I say, hoping he'll agree if he hates new prisoners so much.

"No! They'll think I threatened you!"

In the eight by twelve feet slab of space, I swerve around him and place my property box on the top bunk.

He pushes me aside and grabs the box. "You just put that on my artwork! I ought to fucking smash you, fish!"

"Sorry, I didn't see it."

"You need to be more aware of your fucking surroundings! What you in for anyway, fish?"

I explain my charges, Ecstasy dealing and how I spent twenty-six months fighting my case.

"How come the cops were so hard-core after you?" he asks, squinting.

"It was a big case, a multi-million-dollar investigation. They raided over a hundred people and didn't find any drugs. They were pretty pissed off. I'd stopped dealing by the time they caught up with me, but I'd done plenty over the years, so I accept my punishment."

"Throwing raves," he says, staring at the ceiling as if remembering something. "Were you partying with underage girls?" he asks, his voice slow, coaxing.

Being called a sex offender is the worst insult in prison. Into my third year of incarceration, I'm conditioned to react. "What you trying to say?" I yell angrily, brow clenched.

"Were you fucking underage girls?" Flexing his body, he shakes both fists as if about to punch me.

"Hey, I'm no child molester, and I'd prefer you didn't say shit like that!"

"My buddy next door is doing twenty-five to life for murdering a child molester. How do I know Ecstasy dealing ain't your cover story?" He inhales loudly, nostrils flaring.

"You want to see my fucking paperwork?"

A stocky prisoner walks in. Short hair. Dark eyes. Powerful neck. On one arm: a tattoo of a man in handcuffs above the word OMERTA – the Mafia code of silence towards law enforcement. "What the fuck's going on in here, Bud?" asks Junior Bull – the son of "Sammy the Bull" Gravano, the Mafia mass murderer who was my biggest competitor in the Ecstasy market.

Relieved to see a familiar face, I say, "How're you doing?"

Shaking my hand, he says in a New York Italian accent, "I'm doing alright. I read that shit in the newspaper about you starting a blog in Sheriff Joe Arpaio's jail."

"The blog's been bringing media heat on the conditions."

"You know him?" Bud asks.

"Yeah, from Towers jail. He's a good dude. He's in for dealing Ecstasy like me."

"It's a good job you said that 'cause I was about to smash his ass," Bud says.

"It's a good job Wild Man ain't here 'cause you'd a got your ass thrown off the balcony," Junior Bull says.

I laugh. The presence of my best friend, Wild Man, was partly the reason I never took a beating at the county jail, but with Wild Man in a different prison, I feel vulnerable. When Bud casts a death stare on me, my smile fades.

"What the fuck you guys on about?" Bud asks.

"Let's go talk downstairs." Junior Bull leads Bud out.

I rush to a stainless-steel sink/toilet bolted to a cement-block wall by the front of the cell, unbutton my orange jumpsuit and crane my neck to watch the upper-tier walkway in case Bud returns. I bask in relief as my bladder deflates. After flushing, I take stock of my new home, grateful for the slight improvement in the conditions versus what I'd grown accustomed to in Sheriff Joe Arpaio's jail. No cockroaches. No blood stains. A working swamp cooler. Something I've never seen in a cell before: shelves. The steel table bolted to the wall is slightly larger, too. *But how will I concentrate on writing with Bud around?* There's a mixture of smells in the room. Cleaning chemicals. Aftershave. Tobacco. A vinegar-like odour. The slit of a window at the back overlooks gravel in a no-man's-land before the next building with gleaming curls of razor wire around its roof.

From the doorway upstairs, I'm facing two storeys of cells overlooking a day room with shower cubicles at the end of both tiers. At two white plastic circular tables, prisoners are playing dominoes, cards, chess and Scrabble, some concentrating, others yelling obscenities, contributing to a brain-scraping din that I hope to block out by purchasing a Walkman. In a raised box-shaped Plexiglas control tower, two guards are monitoring the prisoners.

Bud returns. My pulse jumps. Not wanting to feel like I'm stuck in a kennel with a rabid dog, I grab a notepad and pen and head for the day room.

Focussed on my body language, not wanting to signal any weakness, I'm striding along the upper tier, head and chest elevated, when two hands appear from a doorway and grab me. I drop the pad. The pen clinks against grid-metal and tumbles to the day room as I'm pulled into a cell reeking of backside sweat and masturbation, a cheese-tinted funk.

"I'm Booga. Let's fuck," says a squat man in urine-stained boxers, with WHITE TRASH tattooed on his torso below a mobile home, and an arm sleeved with the Virgin Mary.

Shocked, I brace to flee or fight to preserve my anal virginity. I can't believe my eyes when he drops his boxers and waggles his penis.

Dancing to music playing through a speaker he has rigged up, Booga smiles in a sexy way. "Come on," he says in a husky voice. "Drop your pants. Let's fuck." He pulls pornography faces. I question his sanity. He moves closer. "If I let you fart in my mouth, can I fart in yours?"

"You can fuck off," I say, springing towards the doorway.

He grabs me. We scuffle. Every time I make progress towards the doorway, he clings to my clothes, dragging me back in. When I feel his penis rub against my leg, my adrenalin kicks in so forcefully I experience a burst of strength and wriggle free. I bolt out as fast as my shower sandals will allow and snatch my pad. Looking over my shoulder, I see him stood calmly in the doorway, smiling. He points at me. "You have to walk past my door every day. We're gonna get together. I'll lick your ass and you can fart in my mouth." Booga blows a kiss and disappears.

I rush downstairs. With my back to a wall, I pause to steady my thoughts and breathing. In survival mode, I think, *What's going to come at me next?* In the hope of reducing my tension, I borrow a pen to do what helps me stay sane: writing. With the details fresh in my mind, I document my journey to the prison for my blog readers, keeping an eye out in case anyone else wants to test the new prisoner. The more I write, the more I fill with a sense of purpose. Jon's Jail Journal is a connection to the outside world that I cherish.

Someone yells, "One time!" The din lowers. A door rumbles open. A guard does a security walk, his every move scrutinised by dozens of scornful eyes staring from cells. When he exits, the din resumes, and the prisoners return to injecting drugs to escape from reality, including the length of their sentences. This continues all day with "Two times!" signifying two approaching guards, and "Three times!" three and so on. Every now and then an announcement by a guard over the speakers briefly lowers the din.

Before lockdown, I join the line for a shower, holding bars of soap in a towel that I aim to swing at the head of the next person to try me. With boisterous inmates a few feet away, yelling at the men in the showers to "Stop jerking off," and "Hurry the fuck up," I get in a cubicle that reeks of bleach and mildew. With every nerve strained, I undress and rinse fast.

At night, despite the desert heat, I cocoon myself in a blanket from head to toe and turn towards the wall, making my face more difficult to strike. I leave a hole for air, but the warm cement block inches from my mouth returns each exhalation to my face as if it's breathing on me, creating a feeling of suffocation. For hours, my heart drums so hard against the thin mattress I feel as if I'm moving even though I'm still. I try to sleep, but my eyes keep springing open and my head turning towards the cell as I try to penetrate the darkness, searching for Bud swinging a padlock in a sock at my head.

OTHER BOOKS BY SHAUN ATTWOOD

Pablo Escobar: Beyond Narcos
War on Drugs Series Book 1

The mind-blowing true story of Pablo Escobar and the Medellín Cartel beyond their portrayal on Netflix.

Colombian drug lord Pablo Escobar was a devoted family man and a psychopathic killer; a terrible enemy, yet a wonderful friend. While donating millions to the poor, he bombed and tortured his enemies – some had their eyeballs removed with hot spoons. Through ruthless cunning and America's insatiable appetite for cocaine, he became a multi-billionaire, who lived in a $100-million house with its own zoo.

Pablo Escobar: Beyond Narcos demolishes the standard good versus evil telling of his story. The authorities were not hunting Pablo down to stop his cocaine business. They were taking over it.

American Made: Who Killed Barry Seal?
Pablo Escobar or George HW Bush
War on Drugs Series Book 2

Set in a world where crime and government coexist, *American Made* is the jaw-dropping true story of CIA pilot Barry Seal that the Hollywood movie starring Tom Cruise is afraid to tell.

Barry Seal flew cocaine and weapons worth billions of dollars into and out of America in the 1980s. After he became a government informant, Pablo Escobar's Medellin Cartel offered a million for him alive and half a million dead. But his real trouble began after he threatened to expose the dirty dealings of George HW Bush.

American Made rips the roof off Bush and Clinton's complicity in cocaine trafficking in Mena, Arkansas.

"A conspiracy of the grandest magnitude." Congressman Bill Alexander on the Mena affair.

The Cali Cartel: Beyond Narcos
War on Drugs Series Book 3

An electrifying account of the Cali Cartel beyond its portrayal on Netflix.

From the ashes of Pablo Escobar's empire rose an even bigger and more malevolent cartel. A new breed of sophisticated mobsters became the kings of cocaine. Their leader was Gilberto Rodríguez Orejuela – known as the Chess Player due to his foresight and calculated cunning.

Gilberto and his terrifying brother, Miguel, ran a multi-billion-dollar drug empire like a corporation. They employed a politically astute brand of thuggery and spent $10 million to put a president in power. Although the godfathers from Cali preferred bribery over violence, their many loyal torturers and hit men were never idle.

Clinton Bush and CIA Conspiracies:
From the Boys on the Tracks to Jeffrey Epstein
War on Drugs Series Book 4

In the 1980s, George HW Bush imported cocaine to finance an illegal war in Nicaragua. Governor Bill Clinton's Arkansas state police provided security for the drug drops. For assisting the CIA, the Clinton Crime Family was awarded the White House.

The #clintonbodycount continues to this day, with the deceased including Jeffrey Epstein.

This book features harrowing true stories that reveal the insanity of the drug war. A mother receives the worst news about her son. A journalist gets a tip that endangers his life. An unemployed man becomes California's biggest crack dealer. A DEA agent in Mexico is sacrificed for going after the big players.

The lives of Linda Ives, Gary Webb, Freeway Rick Ross and Kiki Camarena are shattered by brutal experiences. Not all of them will survive.

Pablo Escobar's Story (4-book series)

"Finally, the definitive book about Escobar, original and up-to-date" – UNILAD

"The most comprehensive account ever written" – True Geordie

Pablo Escobar was a mama's boy who cherished his family and sang in the shower, yet he bombed a passenger plane and formed a death squad that used genital electrocution.

Most Escobar biographies only provide a few pieces of the puzzle, but this action-packed 1000-page book reveals everything about the king of cocaine.

Mostly translated from Spanish, Part 1 contains stories untold in the English-speaking world, including:

The tragic death of his youngest brother Fernando.

The fate of his pregnant mistress.

The shocking details of his affair with a TV celebrity.

The presidential candidate who encouraged him to eliminate their rivals.

The Mafia Philosopher

"A fast-paced true-crime memoir with all of the action of Good-fellas" – UNILAD

"Sopranos v Sons of Anarchy with an Alaskan-snow backdrop" – True Geordie Podcast

Breaking bones, burying bodies and planting bombs became second nature to Two Tonys while working for the Bonanno Crime Family, whose exploits inspired The Godfather.

After a dispute with an outlaw motorcycle club, Two Tonys left a trail of corpses from Arizona to Alaska. On the run, he was pursued by bikers and a neo-Nazi gang blood-thirsty for revenge, while a homicide detective launched a nationwide manhunt.

As the mist from his smoking gun fades, readers are left with an unexpected portrait of a stoic philosopher with a wealth of charm, a glorious turn of phrase and a fanatical devotion to his daughter.

Party Time

An action-packed roller-coaster account of a life spiralling out of control, featuring wild women, gangsters and a mountain of drugs.

Shaun Attwood arrived in Phoenix, Arizona, a penniless business graduate from a small industrial town in England. Within a decade, he became a stock-market millionaire. But he was leading a double life.

After taking his first Ecstasy pill at a rave in Manchester as a shy student, Shaun became intoxicated by the party lifestyle that would change his fortune. Years later, in the Arizona desert, he became submerged in a criminal underworld, throwing parties for thousands of ravers and running an Ecstasy ring in competition with the Mafia mass murderer Sammy 'The Bull' Gravano.

As greed and excess tore through his life, Shaun had

eye-watering encounters with Mafia hit men and crystal-meth addicts, enjoyed extravagant debauchery with superstar DJs and glitter girls, and ingested enough drugs to kill a herd of elephants. This is his story.

Hard Time

"Makes the Shawshank Redemption look like a holiday camp" – NOTW

After a SWAT team smashed down stock-market millionaire Shaun Attwood's door, he found himself inside of Arizona's deadliest jail and locked into a brutal struggle for survival.

Shaun's hope of living the American Dream turned into a nightmare of violence and chaos, when he had a run-in with Sammy the Bull Gravano, an Italian Mafia mass murderer.

In jail, Shaun was forced to endure cockroaches crawling in his ears at night, dead rats in the food and the sound of skulls getting cracked against toilets. He meticulously documented the conditions and smuggled out his message.

Join Shaun on a harrowing voyage into the darkest recesses of human existence.

Hard Time provides a revealing glimpse into the tragedy, brutality, dark comedy and eccentricity of prison life.

Featured worldwide on Nat Geo Channel's Locked-Up/Banged-Up Abroad Raving Arizona.

Prison Time

Sentenced to 9½ years in Arizona's state prison for distributing Ecstasy, Shaun finds himself living among gang members, sexual predators and drug-crazed psychopaths. After being attacked by a Californian biker in for stabbing a girlfriend, Shaun writes about the prisoners who befriend, protect and inspire him. They include T-Bone, a massive African American ex-Marine who risks his life saving vulnerable inmates from rape, and Two Tonys, an old-school Mafia murderer who left the corpses of his rivals from Arizona to Alaska. They teach Shaun how to turn incarceration to his advantage, and to learn from his mistakes.

Shaun is no stranger to love and lust in the heterosexual world, but the tables are turned on him inside. Sexual advances come at him from all directions, some cleverly disguised, others more sinister – making Shaun question his sexual identity.

Resigned to living alongside violent, mentally-ill and drug-addicted inmates, Shaun immerses himself in psychology and philosophy to try to make sense of his past behaviour, and begins applying what he learns as he adapts to prison life. Encouraged by Two Tonys to explore fiction as well, Shaun reads over 1000 books which, with support from a brilliant psychotherapist, Dr Owen, speed along his personal development. As his ability to deflect daily threats improves, Shaun begins to look forward to his release with optimism and a new love waiting for him. Yet the words of Aristotle from one of Shaun's books will prove prophetic: "We cannot learn without pain."

Un-Making a Murderer:
The Framing of Steven Avery and Brendan Dassey

Innocent people do go to jail. Sometimes mistakes are made. But even more terrifying is when the authorities conspire to frame them. That's what happened to Steven Avery and Brendan Dassey, who were convicted of murder and are serving life sentences.

Un-Making a Murderer is an explosive book which uncovers the illegal, devious and covert tactics used by Wisconsin officials, including:

– Concealing Other Suspects

– Paying Expert Witnesses to Lie

– Planting Evidence

– Jury Tampering

The art of framing innocent people has been in practice for centuries and will continue until the perpetrators are held accountable. Turning conventional assumptions and beliefs in the justice system upside down, *Un-Making a Murderer* takes you on that journey.

ABOUT SHAUN ATTWOOD

Shaun Attwood is a former stock-market millionaire and Ecstasy trafficker turned YouTuber, public speaker, author and activist, who is banned from America for life. His story was featured worldwide on National Geographic Channel as an episode of Locked Up/Banged Up Abroad called Raving Arizona.

Shaun's writing – smuggled out of the jail with the highest death rate in America run by Sheriff Joe Arpaio – attracted international media attention to the human rights violations: murders by guards and gang members, dead rats in the food, cockroach infestations…

While incarcerated, Shaun was forced to reappraise his life. He read over 1,000 books in just under six years. By studying original texts in psychology and philosophy, he sought to better understand himself and his past behaviour. He credits books as being the lifeblood of his rehabilitation.

Shaun tells his story to schools to dissuade young people from drugs and crime. He campaigns against injustice via his books and blog, Jon's Jail Journal. He has appeared on the BBC, Sky News and TV worldwide to talk about issues affecting prisoners' rights.

As a best-selling true-crime author, Shaun is presently writing a series of action-packed books exposing the War on Drugs, which feature the CIA, Pablo Escobar and the cocaine Mafia. He is also writing the longest ever Escobar biography: *Pablo Escobar's Story*, a 4-book series with over 1,000 pages. On his weekly true-crime podcast on YouTube, Shaun interviews people with hard-hitting crime stories and harrowing prison experiences.